399 games, puzzles & trivia challenges specially designed to keep your brain young.

NANCY LINDE

Foreword by Daniel G. Amen, M.D.

Introduction by Philip D. Harvey, Ph.D.

WORKMAN PUBLISHING, NEW YORK

Library of Congress Cataloging-in-Publication Data

Linde, Nancy.
  399 games, puzzles & trivia challenges specially designed to keep your brain young /
Nancy Linde ; foreword by Daniel G. Amen, M.D.
      p. cm.
  ISBN 978-0-7611-6825-6 (alk. paper)
  1. Word games. 2. Puzzles. I. Title.
  GV1507.W8L56 2012
  793.734--dc23
                      2012021099

Cover design by Raquel Jaramillo
Cover art © Carlos Gardel/ Shutterstock
Design by Janet Vicario and Orlando Adiao

Workman books are available at special discounts when purchased in bulk for
premiums and sales promotions as well as for fund-raising or educational use.
Special editions or book excerpts also can be created to specification. For details,
contact the Special Sales Director at the address below, or send an email to
specialmarkets@workman.com.

Workman Publishing Company, Inc.
225 Varick Street
New York, NY 10014-4381
workman.com

WORKMAN is a registered trademark of Workman Publishing Co., Inc.

Printed in the United States

First printing October 2012

10 9 8 7 6

dedication

This book is dedicated to my mother, Ellen, my friend and cheerleader, who taught me about the power of play at the beginning of my life and about the importance of grace and dignity at the end of hers. I miss you Mom, every day.

acknowledgments

Gertrude Stein once noted that "silent gratitude isn't much use to anyone." So I'd like to shout out my profound thanks to the following people: Faith Hamlin, agent extraordinaire, who believed in this project from the very start. It was also my good fortune to work with the wonderful editor Bruce Tracy—if only all authors could be so lucky. I am grateful to the entire Workman Publishing team for their tireless efforts to make this book better: Suzie Bolotin, Ruth Sullivan, Janet Vicario, Anne Kerman, Jessica Rozler, Justin Krasner, Orlando Adiao, and Peter Workman. My grateful thanks are extended to the many seniors in the Greater Boston area who tested my games and provided helpful feedback, with a special thanks to the residents of Sunrise Senior Living in Arlington, MA. Also, Sue Bowdridge and the staff at Neville Place in Cambridge, MA, have my endless gratitude for their many kindnesses to my mother. And because it's impossible to thank all the many friends over the years who have put up with my penchant to make a game out of almost anything, I will single out only these few: Anne Damon, George Harrar, Linda Harrar, Michael Coyne, Leo Abbett, Josh Clark, and of course the best gift my parents ever gave me, my brother, Michael.

contents

foreword

Daniel G. Amen, M.D.

"While getting older is not optional, having a brain that feels older is."
— from *Use Your Brain to Change Your Age*

It is never too late to improve your brain. That's so important it bears repeating: It's never too late to improve your brain. Whether you're forty-five or ninety-five, you can slow, and in many cases, reverse the aging process if you start making some brain-smart choices now.

You just need to see it to believe it. Look at the first SPECT image below. Picture A is a scan of the brain of a fifty-seven-year-old former NFL player who was beginning to feel some cognitive decline, especially with his memory.

Although it looks like a picture of his physical brain, SPECT scans are actually a visual representation of brain function. The holes and indentations on this former footballer's brain show areas of decreased blood flow and activity.

But damaged brains can be repaired as the scan on the right proves! Picture B is the same individual's brain function after one year of a brain healthy program that included targeted supplements and playing games. His brain is smooth, the spots and indentations have disappeared, and his memory improved one thousand percent.

If you're thinking about improving your brain's health, the best advice I have can be summed up in three simple strategies:

1. Brain envy. You have to want to have a better brain.

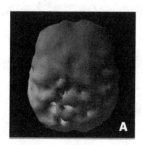
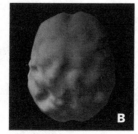

2. Avoid anything that hurts your brain, such as drugs, alcohol, brain injuries, obesity, hypertension, diabetes, sleep apnea, depression, and excessive stress.

3. Engage in regular brain healthy habits.

Regular brain healthy habits, of course, means making good decisions including healthy food choices, getting seven or eight hours of quality sleep each night, daily physical exercise, and taking simple supplements, such as a multiple vitamin, fish oil, and optimizing your vitamin D level. It also means to have fun, learn new things, and engage your brain every day. Mental workouts (like the games in this book) and other lifelong learning strategies are essential to keep your brain young, agile, and adaptable.

Scientific research has shown that the biggest mental declines occur after we complete our formal schooling and after retirement. Why?

Because we are no longer exercising our brains and pushing ourselves to continue to learn and grow. No matter your age, income, IQ, or education, there are dozens of ways to help your neurons grow, stretch, and branch into a younger, more beautiful brain.

399 Games, Puzzles, and Trivia Challenges Specially Designed to Keep Your Brain Young is one of those strategies. Adding these games on a daily basis to your healthy brain habits will pay you back many times over with increased feelings of calm, happiness, and focus.

The wide variety of games included in this book will help improve your memory, reasoning skills, and what we brain scientists call *executive functioning,* or the capacity to control and apply your mental skills.

New research even suggests that regular brain engagement and training in the form of games can enhance and strengthen your brain. So make time in your schedule, at least ten or fifteen minutes a day, for a fun brain workout—and see if you don't find a new confidence in your cognitive abilities and your brain working better and faster.

introduction

Philip D. Harvey, Ph.D.
Professor of Psychiatry and Behavioral Sciences
and Director of the Division of Psychology,
University of Miami Miller School of Medicine

This book is, first and foremost, a book of games—fun and engaging trivia quizzes, brainteasers, puzzles, and word games. If you bought this book because you love high-quality games, feel free to just skip this introduction, turn over to page 1, and start playing. But if you are also a person who wants to improve your memory and sharpen your mind, then read on. Because this is not just a book of games, it is also a rigorous exercise workout to keep your brain in tip-top shape.

Games are beneficial to us in lots of ways. They can be a fun way to spend time with the people we love. They promote social interaction. They're also (as the games in this book are) an absorbing way to spend our solitary time. They challenge us intellectually, and they are rich in new learning opportunities. But what science has also shown us over the last decade or so is that games can actually improve the health of your brain. In the same way that regular physical exercise makes your heart stronger and your body more limber, a daily dose of games can make your brain function better.

How is this possible? The very act of thinking in new and novel ways triggers a physical reaction in the brain—a cascade of events, called *neurogenesis,* in which proteins and enzymes and stem cells all combine to grow new brain cells that rejuvenate your brain and help it to work better and more efficiently. You will find that playing these games will not only make you a better game player, but you'll feel more cognitively "with it" in general.

Our ideas about exercise, for the brain and the body, have evolved a lot since the days when the brain was viewed as fixed and unchangeable. Back in the 1950s, people over the age of forty were discouraged from exercising because it might cause a heart attack. As recently as the mid-1970s, most scientists believed that the number of brain cells was set early in your life—around age twelve—and only decreased after that point. This belief led to the conclusion that the mental functions of the brain were also fixed, and destined to change only for the worse as aging occurred and "brain cells were lost." Today we know this is not the case. The brain is arguably the most flexible organ in the body, able to constantly adapt, repair, and improve throughout our lifespan. If the brain is injured, by a stroke or tumor, for example, it can generate new cells and repair itself. But it doesn't require injury for new cells to form. The brain can also generate new cells and new interconnections in response to its environment. Unlike your height or hat size, you can make your brain change in volume and increase in efficiency by engaging in certain activities—especially games and puzzles.

Of course, the opposite can also happen. The concept of "use it or lose it" has been applied for years to physical fitness, but it applies to cognitive fitness as well. People who are mentally active in their later years (playing games, doing crossword puzzles, etc.) are known from clinical research to be more mentally sharp, cognitively agile, and to have better memory functions. The good news is that if you've let your brain "go flabby," you can reverse the damage. In the same way that physical exercise postpones and reduces loss of muscle mass and increases physical flexibility, mental exercise sharpens memory, concentration, and mental flexibility.

A word of caution is necessary here. Games are just one part of a healthy lifestyle for a healthy brain. Nothing beats the basics that include eating properly, getting enough sleep, getting some physical exercise every day . . . you know the drill. But with the possible exception of good food, playing games will be the most fun healthy thing you can do.

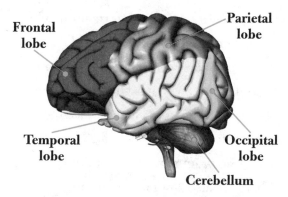

Frontal
lobe

Parietal
lobe

Temporal
lobe

Occipital
lobe

Cerebellum

A Brief Tour of the Human Brain

In the same way that it's important to understand the abdominal muscles if you want to trim your midriff, it's helpful to understand the brain lobes and the functions they control if you want to improve your cognitive abilities.

For an overview of how it works, let's take a very abbreviated tour of the brain, the most complicated part of any living organism on earth, which is organized for conceptual convenience into several large regions called *lobes.* There is clear evidence from evolutionary biology that the regions of the human brain have developed in response to evolution. The earliest animal brains in, for example, worms or snails, are not much more than brain stems, where the most basic functions of the body are located: pain, temperature, crude touch, sleep, etc. Throughout the process of evolution, the brain has grown larger, added mass and more complex functions. The parts of the human brain that are higher and located toward the front and sides of the cerebral cortex are generally more advanced, more recent in their origin, and define more "human" qualities.

The **frontal lobes** (one on the right, one on the left) are home to all that is intrinsically human including problem solving, the regulation of emotion, and the ability to develop plans and strategies. The frontal lobes are also critical to the most human of all abilities—language and abstraction, including the capacity to create symbolic representations such as words, letters, and numbers. These functions are more highly developed in humans than in any other species.

The **temporal lobes** are the home of multiple forms of memory, as well as auditory processing—and the functions are a bit different on each side of the brain. On the left side, the temporal lobes code and store verbal information for later recall; on the right side they store similar spatial memories.

The **parietal lobes** are primarily responsible for spatial information, including cognitive skill such as figuring out routes, organizing complex visual materials, or putting together a puzzle.

The **occipital lobes,** located at the back of the brain, process visual information. They perform basic perceptual processes such as stimulus detection and maintenance of visual perceptual processing.

The **cerebellum** is responsible largely for motor coordination including functions such as gait and balance, although it is becoming increasingly understood that cognitive activities require an intact cerebellum.

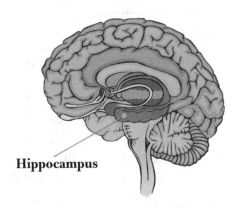

Hippocampus

The **limbic** region is the oldest area of the brain. It generates emotional responses, originates and controls attentional functions, such as maintaining focus on information until it can be processed and transitioning information that has been processed recently into memory storage so that it can be used later. The classic memory region of the limbic system is the **hippocampus,** which is critical to

being able to learn new information. The hippocampus is also the region of the brain most likely to change and respond to stimulation, which is good news for all of us who are getting older and feeling like our memory is not aging gracefully.

But no brain region works alone. There are also a number of important connections between regions that need exercise to perform at top level. Consider this scenario (a good example of the importance of communication among brain regions and the circuits that facilitate it): Let's say you go to a five-star restaurant with a group of good friends and order the chef's best dish. It's a feast for the senses. It smells wonderful, looks perfect, tastes delicious, and the dinner conversation with your companions is delightful. To fully appreciate the whole dinner experience your brain is working overtime, making important connections. The sensory cortex has the job of detecting information from the five senses (taste, touch, sight, smell, and hearing). But it doesn't interpret that information. Instead, it transfers the information along to the "association cortex" that in turn combines the input from multiple sensation systems and integrates it into a single event that can be experienced in real time, in a multifaceted way, and recalled later upon demand. The association cortex is not located in a single lobe: It is spread among regions of several lobes, including frontal, temporal, and parietal regions. These regions are "multimodal," meaning that they integrate information from all five senses.

Without the association among those different sensations, the restaurant dinner would not be a coherent event. If your brain only perceived the taste of the meal, the smell of the food, or the sound of the restaurant, the experience would not be complete. But that's not all the association systems of the brain do. In addition to integrating the sensory information into a coherent whole, they also have the job of retrieving memories ("The last time I had paella was in New York"), making comparisons with those older memories ("I like this paella because it has more saffron"), preparing the information for later recall ("I won't forget this meal"), and making plans for the future ("When I go to Barcelona next year, I have to see what paella is like there").

All of the brain regions above function best when they are interconnected and operating in synchrony. One of the biggest benefits from regular, challenging

> # The good news is that if you've let your brain "go flabby," you can reverse the damage.

cognitive activity is to enhance this synchrony, which will then lead to improvements in everyday cognitive functioning.

Brains and Games

Of course, like many other parts of the body, the brain does change as we get older. Around the age of fifty, people often start noticing small memory lapses ("Where did I put those keys?" or "Where did I park the car?"). We might notice that we don't concentrate as well as we used to or process information as speedily. While it might be embarrassing to momentarily forget the name of a coworker, it's really a minor problem that happens to all of us. Many cognitive functions are unaffected by the aging process—creativity, wisdom, reasoning, and the rules of language appear to be age resistant. But learning, memory, problem solving, speed, and efficiency can be vulnerable to aging, and these cognitive functions are the ones we concentrate on in this book.

> # The idea of exercise, both physical and mental, is to select an optimum level of difficulty and gradually increase it.

Let's just think about this from a simple, nonscientific perspective. If you wanted to build up a muscle group by weight lifting, and you know that you can lift ten pounds already, would you lift five pounds for building exercises? Of course not. By the same token, if you want to improve mentally, in any way, and had two hours a day to do it, would you spend those hours reading a book that you've already read or studying a map of your own neighborhood? No. The idea of exercise, both physical and mental, is to select an optimum level of difficulty and gradually increase it. Supported by research from both the physical and cognitive domains, we make these suggestions on how to use this book most effectively:

• You should play the games in this book for at least fifteen minutes every day.

• For optimal impact, you should start at the beginning of the book. Each chapter is carefully organized to increase just slightly in difficulty from chapter to chapter (and within each chapter), so starting at the first page and working toward the end will be most beneficial. If the initial games are easy for you, make them more difficult by putting a time limit on them. You can remove the timer as the games become more challenging.

The games you play should exercise a broad set of cognitive skills. In the same way that we cross-train (i.e., do a mix of exercises) to work more than just one muscle and build physical fitness, playing the same type of game over and over will not build cognitive skills as broadly. Playing an assortment of different games each day is the best strategy for diversified brain improvement. So again, as you work through the book from page one toward the end, the games are strategically placed to provide a healthy mix of games that exercise the key cognitive skills that are vulnerable in normal aging (more on this in the next section).

Critical Mental Functions for Healthy Brain Aging

Living normally and independently in the world requires many different cognitive abilities. Some, such as basic perception and sensory processes, usually don't change much in normal aging. In this book, we have chosen to focus on the key mental functions that can change with age including: long-term memory, working memory, executive functioning, attention to detail, multitasking, and processing speed. Even among that group, some seem more vulnerable to the aging process than others, but all of them share several critical features.

• They are complex.

• They are not performed by a single region of the brain, but by multiple regions linked by circuits.

• They are critically important for functioning well and independently in the world. If *any one* of these mental functions was suddenly wiped out by an injury or an illness, living independently would be a real challenge.

• They can improve with regular brain exercise.

So let's take an in-depth look at each of the cognitive functions, the symptoms that frequently occur when age-related deterioration has taken place, and some of the games to look for that work specifically on that mental skill. You'll note that throughout the book the editors have labeled each game with the cognitive skill (or skills) that it primarily exercises.

1. LONG-TERM MEMORY—If you have noticed occasional memory lapses, such as forgetting the names of people, objects, or events that occurred in the distant past, you should play games that exercise your long-term memory skills. **Run the Alphabet** (on page 3) and **Endings and Beginnings** (on page 43) are both good examples.

2. WORKING MEMORY—Sometimes called functional short-term memory, working memory is the ability to actively hold information in your mind to accomplish a task at hand. This includes remembering verbal information like a phone number (without needing to have it repeated over and over), a short list of grocery items, or a sequence of directions to complete a task. Games that boost your working memory skills include: **Put the List in Order** (on page 48) and vocabulary quizzes such as **Rhyme Time** (on page 6).

3. EXECUTIVE FUNCTIONING—Simply put, executive functioning involves solving problems by using information you already have to work out novel solutions. If, for example, you are finding it more challenging to get organized and to accomplish routine tasks, such as running your weekend errands; or if you find it hard to get out the door with everything you need (keys, phone, glasses), you need to shape up your executive functioning skills. A couple of examples of fun ways to do that include the **Odd Man Out** games (see page 92) and **Stinky Pinky** (on page 10).

> Playing an assortment of different games each day is the best strategy for diversified brain improvement.

4. ATTENTION TO DETAIL—The process of absorbing small details when learning new information requires the ability to concentrate and stay focused. If you're finding it hard to follow instructions when setting up or using new appliances (such as a microwave oven or a DVD player); or if you have to study a subway map again and again to figure out which stop you want; or if you are having problems navigating a website to purchase an item or fill a prescription, you may need to play games that exercise your concentration skills. The visual games in this book, including **Picture Themes** (see pages 34–35) and **The Shape of the States** (page 5), are all good examples of games that improve your attention to detail.

5. MULTITASKING—Multitasking is a modern word that basically means doing more than one thing at a time. Do you find yourself interrupting a conversation on the phone because you can't take notes at the same time? Do you have trouble operating multiple controls in the car (radio, wipers, lights) while you are driving? Or do you need complete silence around you in order to read a book or work on your computer? If so, you will benefit from games, such as **Follow the Rules** (page 38) and **Trimble** (page 89), that focus on multitasking skills.

6. **Processing speed**—This is the speed at which your brain processes information, which includes being mentally fast enough to keep up with conversations, following the plot of television programs or movies, and completing tasks efficiently. If you have noticed that it takes longer for you to get simple tasks done, or if you need people to repeat things because you could not keep up, you may need to upgrade your processing skills. Try any game that imposes a time limit, such as the **One-Minute Madness** games (page 23) and **Alma's Shopping List** (page 9).

Much of what I've said here is known intuitively by just about anyone over the age of forty. In my work with senior citizens, I often hear how much better they feel when they use their brain—when they play a word game, complete a crossword puzzle, take a trivia quiz, or play bridge. What's great about this book is that it is filled with hundreds of fun and engaging games that just happen to also be superb cognitive exercises. There are no boring neurological tests here. No repetitive rehabilitation exercises. Just good games with real cognitive benefits.

a word from the author

Oddly enough, the seeds for this book were planted way back in the 1960s. I confess that as a child, I would occasionally fake an illness so I could stay home from school. Then around lunchtime, I would have a miraculous recovery, and my mother would stop what she was doing and play games with me for hours. I still believe she liked those "sick" days as much as I did.

Fast forward about forty years, during which time I finished school (despite the occasional absences), went to college, and embarked on my career as a documentary filmmaker, working mostly for the PBS series *NOVA*. Even *NOVA* recognized my passion for games and tapped me to work on two science quiz shows, one for the series' fifteenth broadcast anniversary season and another for the twentieth.

In 2005, my work life was interrupted when my now elderly mother began needing more help and attention. We decided it was time for her to move into an assisted living residence. It was a traumatic change that she faced with all the bravery she could muster. Little did I know then that my two-year journey into the world of the elderly would be the inspiration for my own second act.

Watching my mother navigate through her ninth decade, I came to understand how important it is to remain engaged in life, to be intellectually challenged, and to laugh and have fun as often as possible. I also saw how many of the activities designed for seniors did not truly respect their life experience and intellectual capabilities. Those thoughts all coalesced in a new direction for my life—one that combined my love of games and my deep affection for seniors.

Because I believe passionately in the power of play to enhance health and happiness at all life stages, I decided to start a website that provided high-quality games for activities professionals who work with seniors in assisted living and independent-living residences, senior centers, and other senior-serving organizations. I launched Never2Old4Games.com in 2009 and today many seniors around the country are enjoying my games. Sadly, my own mother never got to see this new phase of my life. She died at age ninety-one in late 2007. But every time I visit a senior facility to test out game formats, I think of her. And I see how games can enhance confidence, stimulate conversation, and

be a fun learning experience. And it's especially gratifying to know that my games are not simply a fun pastime, but also a pathway to improve memory and overall cognitive function.

Now, through this book, I'm delighted that my games can reach many more seniors (and aspiring seniors) who want to keep their brains in tip-top shape. This book has been strategically organized to provide a rigorous program that will exercise the key cognitive functions that are vulnerable to the normal aging process. Just start on page 1 and work toward the end of the book for the best overall results. But most of all, have fun. Learn a little. Share the games with friends and family. Start a weekly game playing group with your peers. And be well—both in body and brain!

—*Nancy Linde*

Chapter One

WARM-UP

it's *play*time

All the answers in this word definition game contain either the word *play* or the word *time*.

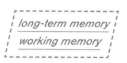
long-term memory
working memory

1. Where kids go to swing and seesaw.

PLAY Ground

2. Punch this, if you want to get paid.

time clock

3. Scott Joplin's musical milieu.

Ragtime

4. A promiscuous, often wealthy, male.

PLAY Boy

5. A break taken by basketball players ... and by naughty children who need a little cooling off.

time out

6. A type of glass case, often found in jewelry stores.

DISPLAY CASE

7. An enclosure for babies so they don't crawl off and get into trouble.

PLAYPEN

8. As Gershwin wrote, this is when "the livin' is easy."

Summertime

9. Additional time worked . . . and the pay earned for additional time worked.

OVERTIME

10. A script written for the movies.

PLAY

11. Charts with train or bus schedules.

time chart

12. Printed program handed to theatergoers before a performance.

PLAYBILL

13. Sporting term for a series of games that decides a championship.

PLAY OFF

14. To treat something as less important than it really is.

DOWNPLAY

Federal Holidays

How many of the ten official U.S. federal holidays
can you name in thirty seconds?

_____   _____

_____   _____

_____   _____

_____   _____

---

letter speller

All the answers in this game sound as if they're just one letter long.
Sample clue: The plural of "is." Answer: R ("are").

1. The Caribbean or
Mediterranean. _____

2. Seeing orb. _____

3. Late comedian/
actor Danny. _____

4. Be indebted. _____

5. Pod legume. _PEA____

6. Honey-maker. _BEE__

7. Pool or
billiards tool. _Que__

8. Earl Grey. _TEA__

9. Female sheep. _EWE_

ANIMALS

Can you come up with at least one animal for every letter of the alphabet?
For an extra brain boost, see how many you can name in two minutes.

A _____   N _____

B _____   O _____

C _____   P _____

D _____   Q _____

E _____   R _____

F _____   S _____

G _____   T _____

H _____   U _____

I _____   V _____

J _____   W _____

K _____   X _____

L _____   Y _____

M _____   Z _____

Famous Movie Lines

How many of these memorable movie lines can you identify? Four stars if you can name the character, the actor who said the line, and the name of the film.

1. "Frankly, my dear, I don't give a damn."

_____

2. "You don't understand! I coulda had class. I coulda been a contender."

_____

3. "Here's looking at you, kid."

_____

4. "Go ahead, make my day."

_____

5. "All right, Mr. DeMille, I'm ready for my close-up."

_____

6. "Fasten your seatbelts. It's going to be a bumpy night."

_____

7. "You talkin' to me?"

_____

8. "What we've got here is [a] failure to communicate."

_____

9. "I love the smell of napalm in the morning!"

_____

10. "Love means never having to say you're sorry."

_____

11. "They call me _Mister_ Tibbs!"

_____

12. "Made it, Ma! Top of the world!"

_____

13. "Tell 'em to go out there with all they got and win just one for the Gipper."

_____

14. "A census taker once tried to test me. I ate his liver with some fava beans and a nice Chianti."

_____

15. "There's no place like home."

_____

16. "There's no crying in baseball!"

_____

The Shape of the States

How many of these U.S. states can you identify by their shape? (*Note: The states are not drawn to scale.*)

A _____

B _____

C _____

D _____

E _____

F _____

G _____

H _____

I _____

rhyme ◆ time ◆

Each question in this game includes two definitions for two different words. The twist is, they will rhyme.

1. Not used; and the moisture that forms on plants at night.

_____

2. Humorous; and cash.

_____

3. An estimation or conjecture; and, to iron.

_____

4. A gentle wind; and to store food below 32° Fahrenheit.

_____

5. A percussion instrument; and how your jaw feels after Novocain.

_____

6. To look for someone or something; and a place of worship.

_____

7. Watermelon shell; and sightless.

_____

8. Large gathering of people; and tilled the soil.

_____

9. To break or divide into two or more parts; and to leave a job.

_____

10. Land alongside a river; and to give corporal punishment to a child.

_____

11. The cowardly color; and the wiggly dessert.

_____

12. You need this to play Double Dutch; and he entertained the troops for decades.

_____

13. Courageous, heroic; and to remove a beard or mustache.

_____

14. A dam-building mammal; and elevated body temperature.

_____

trivia

"I" COUNTRIES

long-term memory

executive functioning

Nine countries begin with the letter I. Can you name four of them in this quiz?

● Vatican City, a sovereign state with a population of nine hundred people, lies entirely within this country.

● With almost fourteen million people, Mumbai, which used to be called Bombay, is this country's largest city.

● This nation's airline is called Aer Lingus, which means "air fleet" in Gaelic.

● This ancient country, known as Persia until 1935, was led by a succession of Shahs until the Islamic Revolution in 1979.

Finish the Jingle

The most successful advertising jingles are the ones you can't get out of your head. If these were successful, you should be able to finish the jingles given the first few words.

1. "The incredible, edible _____."

2. "The best part of waking up _____
_____."

3. "I'd like to teach the world to sing _____
_____."

4. "I am stuck on a Band-Aid, _____
_____."

5. "My bologna has a first name, _____
_____."

6. "N-E-S-T-L-E-S, _____
_____."

7. "I'm a Pepper, he's a Pepper, _____
_____."

8. "Two all-beef patties, special sauce, _____
_____
_____."

9. "Call Roto-Rooter, that's the name, _____
_____."

10. "Nothin' says lovin' _____
_____."

11. "Like a good neighbor, _____
_____."

12. "See the USA _____."

13. "Plop plop, fizz fizz, _____."

14. "Winston tastes good _____
_____."

15. "Double your pleasure, _____
_____."

16. "Rice-A-Roni, _____
_____."

17. "Ace is the place _____
_____."

★ JANUARY IN HISTORY ★

This trivia quiz will stretch your long-term memory muscles.

1820 Two Russian explorers discovered this unpopulated continent.

1848 This was discovered at Sutter's Mill in Northern California.

1870 Political cartoonist Thomas Nast first used this animal symbol for the Democratic Party in a *Harper's Weekly* cartoon.

1892 An immigrant-processing gateway opened on this small island between New York and New Jersey.

1922 Leonard Thompson, a 14-year-old diabetic who lay dying in a Canadian hospital, was given the first injection of this drug to treat his diabetes.

1942 The wife of Clark Gable and star of *My Man Godfrey* and *To Be or Not to Be* died in a plane crash near Las Vegas.

1945 Officials added this chemical to the drinking water in Grand Rapids, Michigan, in an experiment to improve dental health.

1952 *Today* (also known as *The Today Show*) made its debut with this host, who shared the stage with a chimp named J. Fred Muggs.

1953 Sixty-eight percent of all televisions in the U.S. were tuned to watch the episode in which this sitcom star give birth to her onscreen baby.

1954 A famous center fielder for the New York Yankees married an even more famous actress. Can you name the couple?

1959 President Eisenhower signed a proclamation admitting the forty-ninth state to the Union. What state was it?

1959 The western series *Rawhide*, starring this young actor, premiered on CBS.

1962 This innovative, cigar-smoking comedian, and husband of singer/actress Edie Adams, was killed when he lost control of his Chevrolet Corvair on a Los Angeles roadway and crashed into a power pole.

1973 The Supreme Court delivered its decision to legalize elective abortion in all fifty states, sparking a politically turbulent debate that continues today. What was the name given to that case?

1974 In response to an energy crisis, President Nixon signed an emergency bill that changed these signs on highways across America.

1976 Supersonic travel began with the introduction of this jet into commercial service. It reduced a nearly eight-hour London to New York flight to three-and-a-half hours.

1981 Fifty-two hostages were released after being held for 444 days in this country.

1991 Operation Desert Storm began with the expressed purpose of expelling Iraqi forces from this oil-rich country, which Iraq had invaded a few months earlier.

1994 This Olympic hopeful was clubbed on the leg by the ex-husband of a skating rival.

2009 US Airways pilot Captain Chesley Sullenberger made a miracle emergency landing on this river after his plane flew into a flock of birds that disabled both engines.

Alma's Shopping List

working memory
executive function
speed processing

Alma is a great shopper, but a bad speller. Every item on her shopping list is misspelled by one letter. Can you fix it? (*Note: All of the items on the list are common brand names or generic names for foods and other items that are found in a grocery store.*) For an extra brain boost, see how many answers you can get in one minute.

1. Scrimp

2. Winded

3. Snackers

4. Porn

5. Crib

6. Paupers

7. Parrots

8. Skimpy

9. Silk

10. Rookies

11. Raffles

12. Butler

13. Paste

14. Hello

Stinky Pinky

We have twentieth-century humorist George S. Kaufman to thank for this game (and for its unusual title). Each Stinky Pinky answer contains two words that rhyme—but you have to figure out what that answer is from an offbeat definition.

1. Mrs. Onassis's tan pants.

2. An introverted insect.

3. Parsimonious wool producers.

4. Inebriated animal that emits a bad smell.

5. Former President Clinton's medicine.

6. Blouse made of soil.

7. Stupid Wrigley's or Beechnut.

8. A peculiar-looking goatee.

9. An adorable orange or banana.

10. Mr. Crosby's jewelry.

11. An ailing baby bird.

12. A flounder's hope.

13. An intelligent painting.

14. Square container for smoked salmon.

BIG BANG

All of the two-word answers in this game begin with the initials B and B.

1. An insect . . . or a brand of tuna fish.

_____ _____

2. Style of pants very popular in the 1960s.

_____ _____

3. London's famous timekeeper.

_____ _____

4. Nickname for anyone born between 1946 and 1964.

_____ _____

5. Halitosis.

_____ _____

6. Gymnastic apparatus that looks like a two-by-four on legs.

_____ _____

7. Wispy white plant often used as filler in flower bouquets.

_____ _____

8. Where an angel of God appeared and told Moses to lead the Israelites out of Egypt.

_____ _____

9. Informal term for the U.S. region in which conservative evangelical Protestantism is prominent.

_____ _____

10. This pest has resurged in the last decade, disturbing the sleep of many city-dwellers.

_____ _____

---

 trivia

WHERE WERE THEY BORN?

long-term memory

executive functioning

The only clue we'll give you is that none of these famous people were born in the United States.

● Henry Kissinger and Albert Einstein

● Bob Hope, Elizabeth Taylor, and Cary Grant

● Dag Hammarskjöld, Ann-Margret, and Alfred Nobel

● Lorne Green, Alex Trebek, Peter Jennings, and Michael J. Fox

rhyming words and phrases

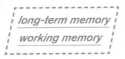
All the answers in this word definition game have two-syllable or two-word answers that rhyme.

1. A magician's phrase.

2. 8:00 P.M. to 10:00 P.M. on television.

3. A compendium of recipes.

4. A bag often used by students to carry books.

5. A portable two-way radio device used for communication.

6. A VIP.

7. A minor car accident.

8. The exodus of an intellectual elite.

9. To retrace one's steps.

10. Name for a Native American tent.

11. A casino game also called Twenty-One.

12. A Chinese dumpling often found in soup.

13. A distress call traditionally used by seamen and aviators.

14. A city center or shopping area.

15. A small bedroom illumination often required by children.

Who the What?

In this game we supply the who, and you must supply the what. For example: *Felix the _____*

Answer: *Cat*

1. Bozo the _____

2. Attila the _____

3. Dennis the _____

4. Kermit the _____

5. Frosty the _____

6. Popeye the _____

7. Billy the _____

8. Mack the _____

9. Blackbeard the _____

10. Stan the _____

11. Alexander the _____

WORD PARTS

The word *menace* is defined as "a threat." In this game, however, we don't supply the definition of a word, but of its parts. For example, given the first clue "male adults," plus the second clue "the highest card in the deck," the answer is *menace (men + ace).*

1. The opposite of pro + the opposite of back

2. The opposite of on + frozen water

3. Mr. Rickles + locking device

4. Chum + highest/lowest card

5. A summer complexion color + a corner Monopoly space

6. A bovine used for pulling carts + Nixon's successor

7. A narrow canvas bed + two thousand pounds

8. For each + a male descendant

9. Sprinted + Mr. DeLuise

10. In favor of + in shape

it's *charming*

All of the answers in this word definition game begin with the letters CH.

1. A fowl meal.

_____

2. George Washington's favorite pie.

_____

3. This begins at home.

_____

4. Offspring.

_____

5. Miserly.

_____

6. Swiss or Jack.

_____

7. It's open every Sunday.

_____

8. The fastest mammal on earth.

_____

9. Ben-Hur's wheels.

_____

10. King me!

_____

11. A dog—*muy pequeño*.

_____

12. Miss Daisy employed one of these.

_____

13. Bobby Fischer's *forte*.

_____

14. Treasure or tool.

_____

CLASSIC RIDDLE
EMERGENCY

As with many classic riddles, the answer lies in a detail that is omitted from the story.

On a rainy autumn night, Robert Johnson went to pick up his son James from college. On the way back, Robert was driving, and James was sitting in the passenger seat. Suddenly, a large truck appeared and crashed head-on into the Johnson car. Robert was killed instantly. James was seriously injured and taken to the hospital by ambulance. Rushing into the operating room, James's would-be surgeon took one look at him and exclaimed, "I can't operate on this patient. He's my son!"

How is that possible?

FASHION FORWARD

Can you find all twenty clothing-related items in the grid—spelled forward, backward, and diagonally? For an extra-challenging brain workout, put a two-minute timer on this game and don't use the word list unless you get stuck.

```
W  P  R  O  M  D  R  E  S  S  X  I
Q  E  S  O  H  Y  T  N  A  P  N  C
M  A  D  S  W  I  M  S  U  I  T  T
F  C  Z  D  X  E  R  J  K  W  R  J
J  O  S  H  I  E  I  I  H  I  I  E
A  A  K  S  S  N  B  T  K  F  H  A
C  T  C  U  Z  G  S  K  A  S  N
K  B  O  I  Q  S  V  G  W  C  R  S
E  R  S  T  U  X  E  D  O  Z  E  B
T  S  C  A  R  F  F  V  X  W  D  N
Y  K  N  W  O  G  T  H  G  I  N  H
H  I  G  H  H  E  E  L  S  J  U  Y
```

Word List

- Bra
- Vest
- Suit
- Jeans
- Socks
- Skirt
- Scarf
- Jacket
- Bikini
- Tuxedo
- Pantyhose
- Peacoat
- Necktie
- Trousers
- Swimsuit
- High Heels
- Prom Dress
- Nightgown
- Undershirt
- Wedding Gown

Compound Word

Each picture represents one half of a compound word. For example, if you combine *key* and *hole,* you get *keyhole.* How many of the twelve possible compound words can you find? For an extra brain boost, see how many compound words you can find in two minutes. (*Note: Each picture is used only once.*)

working memory
executive functioning
attention to detail
multitasking
processing speed

Search

1 _____

2 _____

3 _____

4 _____

5 _____

6 _____

7 _____

8 _____

9 _____

10 _____

11 _____

12 _____

REPLACE THE
SWAMP

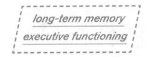

There's something wrong with these titles. Can you fix them by replacing the word SWAMP with the correct geographical feature?

1. *The Bridge Over the SWAMP Kwai* by Pierre Boulle

_____

2. Go *Tell It on the SWAMP* by James Baldwin

_____

3. *Treasure SWAMP* by Robert Louis Stevenson

_____

4. *20,000 Leagues Under the SWAMP* by Jules Verne

_____

5. *Little House on the SWAMP* by Laura Ingalls Wilder

6. *On Golden SWAMP* by Ernest Thompson

_____

7. *Brighton SWAMP Memoirs* by Neil Simon

_____

8. *Swan SWAMP* (ballet) by Pyotr Ilyich Tchaikovsky

_____

9. *How Green Was My SWAMP* by Richard Llewellyn

_____

10. *The Old Man and the SWAMP* by Ernest Hemingway

---

what's the missing number?

Fill in the missing number from this list of sayings and titles.

1. _____ *Angry Men*

2. _____ original colonies

3. _____ bean salad

4. The _____ Commandments

5. The _____ *Musketeers*

6. _____ states in the U.S.

7. "_____ bottles of beer on the wall . . ."

8. "_____ Ways to Leave Your Lover"

9. _____ days in a year

10. _____ deadly sins

11. _____ gun salute

just *J*'s

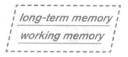

All the answers in this word definition game begin with the letter J.

1. You need this to change a tire.

2. A carpenter's tool . . . or a kind of puzzle.

3. An old, barely operable, car; a clunker.

4. If you were a native, you'd call this country *Nippon*.

5. The ultimate win at a casino or in the lottery.

6. Olympic event that involves throwing a spear.

7. Duke Ellington, Count Basie, and Louis Armstrong were all early innovators of this twentieth-century type of music.

8. The green-eyed monster.

9. A hard stone, usually green, that's often used in Chinese jewelry.

10. Another name for a hospital gown.

11. On a sailboat, this is the smaller triangular sail in the front of the mast.

12. A person or thing that brings back luck.

13. A large meeting or rally; this term is commonly used for a gathering of Boy Scouts or Girl Scouts.

14. The name of this rugged vehicle probably came from its military designation as a "General Purpose" automobile.

What Do They Have in Common?

Each question contains a list of several items. Can you figure out what they have in common?

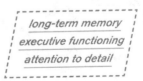

1. Paper, rag, and kewpie

2. A pair of jeans, a pool table, and a catcher's mitt

3. Barney, Socks, Millie, and Checkers

4. An airplane, a tuxedo, a comet, and a horse

5. Jig, Twist, and Tango

6. A monarch, Miss America, and a broken tooth

7. Bowling alleys, seamstresses, and hand grenades

8. Pike, ray, chub, and tang

9. A pen, a newspaper, and a squid

10. Clams, cabbage, bread, and dough

11. Hardy, Cromwell, and Twist

12. Rodham, Welch, and Robinson

13. Malibu, Bel Air, and Corvette

14. An artist, a dental hygienist, and a hairdresser

Finish the Food Idiom

Can you identify the foods that complete the following common idioms?

1. Couch _____

2. Flat as a _____

3. Bring home the _____

4. The proof is in the _____

5. Sour _____

6. Spill the _____

7. Packed in like _____

8. Nutty as a _____

9. The big _____

10. The best thing since _____
_____

11. Cut the _____

12. Slower than _____

13. Walk on _____

14. Selling like _____

15. Tough _____

WOOD YOU KNOW?

long-term memory

executive functioning

You don't have to be a carpenter to answer these wood-related questions.

● This strongly scented, weather-resistant wood is used for house shingles and closet linings.

● Most wines are aged in barrels made of wood from this tree.

● Native Americans prized the bark of this tree for use in lightweight and waterproof canoes, bowls, and wigwams.

● The bark of this species of oak tree is stripped every nine years and provides material for bulletin boards and bottle stoppers.

*p*atchwork

long-term memory
working memory

All of the answers in this word definition game begin with the letters PAT.

1. An hors d'oeuvre that's often made from duck or goose liver.

_____

2. A paved area in the backyard.

_____

3. A small, round, flat cake of hamburger meat.

_____

4. Legal proof that you invented something.

_____

5. Official name of the kneecap.

_____

6. "Customers" for a hospital.

_____

7. Tom Brady is one; Nathan Hale was another.

_____

8. If you want to sew a dress, you may need to buy one of these.

_____

9. You buy croissants here; it's the French word for "bakery."

_____

10. You're guilty of this crime if you murder your father.

_____

11. To keep watch over a neighborhood by walking or driving around it.

_____

12. Pitiful, or miserably inadequate.

_____

13. This is a virtue.

_____

Famous Critters

Can you identify what type of animal each of these famous critters is?

1. Bambi

2. Black Beauty

3. Daffy

4. Dino (Flintstone)

5. Flipper

6. Garfield

7. Harvey

8. Moby Dick

9. Mr. Ed

10. Rin Tin Tin

11. Rudolph

12. Snoopy

ONE > MINUTE > MADNESS
The Ten Commandments

How many of the Ten Commandments can you name in one minute?

the wedding party

In this scene, there are forty-six
words **that begin with the letter P.**
How many can you find?

working memory
executive functioning
attention to detail
multitasking
processing speed

brrrr!

All the answers in this word definition game begin with the letters BR.

1. The largest country in South America.

_____

2. A contusion.

_____

3. The person who makes the money to support a family.

_____

4. To make coffee or beer.

_____

5. The organ of thought and feeling.

_____

6. System of reading and writing for the blind.

_____

7. An adornment for the wrist.

_____

8. An old-fashioned word for trousers.

_____

9. A mixture of copper and tin, this metal is often used for sculpture.

_____

10. The extreme edge . . . or the very point at which a disastrous turn of events will occur.

_____

11. An archaic term for sulfur, it's also one of a pair of words used to describe a style of preaching that creates vivid pictures of eternal damnation to encourage repentance.

_____

12. Fragile, easily broken . . . and a candy made of caramel and nuts.

_____

13. One of the largest animals that ever lived, this herbivorous dinosaur had a very long neck and an equally long tail. Today it's known as an apatosaurus.

_____

14. An illegal gift, usually money, to persuade an official or to influence an action.

_____

15. Your mother's son.

_____

Anagrams

The letters of each word in this list can be arranged in multiple ways to form other words. We provide the word and the number of anagrams that are possible to make.

1. Inks (2) _____ _____

2. Evil (3) _____ _____ _____

3. Gnus (3) _____ _____ _____

4. Leap (3) _____ _____ _____

5. Acres (3) _____ _____ _____

6. Caret (3) _____ _____ _____

7. Emits (4) _____ _____ _____ _____

8. Teaks (4) _____ _____ _____ _____

Three-Way Order the List

Given the following list of six states, can you put them in three different orders? First, order them by size, largest state to smallest. Second, order them by population, largest number of residents to fewest. Third, order them by median income per household, highest income to lowest.

	Size	Population	Median Income
New York			
California	❶ _____	❶ _____	❶ _____
Texas	❷ _____	❷ _____	❷ _____
Alaska	❸ _____	❸ _____	❸ _____
New Jersey	❹ _____	❹ _____	❹ _____
	❺ _____	❺ _____	❺ _____
Virginia	❻ _____	❻ _____	❻ _____

e c h o
echo

All the answers in this quiz have repeating sounds, such as Papa, Bye-Bye, and Bora Bora.

1. Yogi Bear's companion . . . or a little cut or bruise to a child.

2. Popular nickname for President Kennedy's son.

3. Toy gun that shoots round projectiles.

4. Perfect vision.

5. Slang for a train, especially in Chattanooga.

6. He killed Robert Kennedy.

7. High-kicking dance performed by a chorus line.

8. It's likely that this flightless bird became extinct around 1700.

9. Average, mediocre, passable.

10. Made up of a string and two discs, this toy has been around for a couple of thousand years.

11. The title and chorus of a Yale football fight song written in 1901.

12. More British than American, it means "good-bye."

GOLLY GEE

All of the two-word answers in this game begin with the initials G and G.

1. This San Francisco bridge is actually red.

2. Charlie Brown's favorite saying.

3. Her most famous movie line mirrored her reclusive lifestyle: "I vant to be alone!"

4. Term for a very fuel-inefficient car.

5. From the 1890s to the 1920s, these illustrated beauties, depicted with thin waists and hair piled high on their heads, personified the feminine ideal.

6. *Rhapsody in Blue* composer.

7. Your daughter's daughter's daughter.

8. You don't want this to get too near "E" when you're on a long drive.

9. In the 1960s and 1970s this phrase described the strained relationship between young people and their parents brought about by differences in values, tastes, and outlooks.

10. A young Japanese female who is trained as a professional singer, dancer, and companion for men.

---

 trivia

ON A FIRST NAME BASIS

long-term memory

executive functioning

All of the answers in this quiz share a common first name.

● A nineteenth-century English author; the creator of *Peanuts*; and a river in Boston.

● Jimmy Carter's vice president; an actor who played Oscar Madison; and a former news anchorman.

● An astronaut; an actress who played Gidget and Norma Rae; and the actress who played Archie Bunker's daughter Gloria.

● The capital of British Columbia, Canada; the largest lake in Africa; and a nineteenth-century British queen.

just one letter, please

We're looking for one-letter answers in this game.

1. Kellogg's "special" cereal. _____

2. A kind of turn... or German submarine. ____

3. Movie rating which requires anyone under age seventeen to be accompanied by a parent or guardian. _____

4. The acceleration force astronauts experience during blastoff. _____

5. A very casual shirt. _____

6. A hand gesture for winning or peace. _____

7. How an egotist often starts a sentence. _____

8. The flip side of a hit record. _____

9. This *A-Team* actor "pities fools." _____

10. The street in Washington, DC, where lobbyists work. _____

11. The letter inside a circle in e-mail addresses. _____

12. The mark on a pirate's map showing where to find the treasure. _____

CHARTREUSE TITLES

Something is wrong with these titles. You can correct them by replacing the word CHARTREUSE with the right color.

1. "Snow CHARTREUSE and the Seven Dwarfs"

2. *Anne of CHARTREUSE Gables*

3. *CHARTREUSE Christmas*

4. *The CHARTREUSE Panther*

5. *On CHARTREUSE Pond*

6. *Hill Street CHARTREUSES*

7. *"The CHARTREUSE Rose of Texas"*

8. *The Man in the CHARTREUSE Flannel Suit*

9. *The CHARTREUSE Letter*

10. *How CHARTREUSE Was My Valley*

11. *The Hunt for CHARTREUSE October*

12. *A Clockwork CHARTREUSE*

Don't Be an Idiom

Complete the following sentences with the correct idiom. Each idiom will begin with the word *on*.

long-term memory
executive functioning

1. If your TV stops working, it's
on the _____.

2. If you're having success after success,
you are on a _____.

3. If the assistant you hired is well-informed
and capable, she is on the _____.

4. If you've stopped drinking alcohol,
you're on the _____.

5. If you're very worried about the results of
your blood test, you're on _____
and _____ until the doctor calls.

6. If your company is laying off workers and
you know you're on the list, then you're
on the _____
_____. (two words)

7. If you're receiving federal assistance
such as welfare or food stamps, you're
on the _____.

8. If you want your guests to arrive on time,
you tell them to come at seven o'clock on
the _____.

9. If a waiter brings you an appetizer that
you don't have to pay for, you're getting it
on the _____.

10. If you're running away from the police
or have just escaped from jail, you're
on the _____.

11. If you know the word for something, but
can't quite remember it, the word is on the
_____
_____. (four words)

12. If you're on the campaign trail making
speeches and asking for votes, you're
on the _____.

13. If you meet someone with whom you
share the same ideas and opinions, the two
of you are on the _____
_____. (two words)

What a Pair

Harvard and Yale, Thunder and Lightning, Coke and Pepsi are all common pairs . . . but what about *Wonder and Perrier?* If you redefine *Wonder and Perrier* correctly, you'll come up with the more familiar pairing *Bread and Water.* How many familiar pairs can you make from the clues below?

1. Scarlet hosiery . . . and Union soldiers

2. Steak or chicken . . . and Yukon golds

3. Sleeping furniture . . . and the morning meal

4. Flounder . . . and Fritos

5. Macintoshes . . . and navels

6. Garfield . . . and Mickey

7. Ivory . . . and Poland Spring

8. Cow juice . . . and bee juice

9. Upper limb . . . and nail-driving tool

10. Movie actors . . . and zebra pattern

11. Oscar Mayer strips . . . and free-range jumbo hen fruit

12. 6:00 P.M. to 6:00 A.M. . . . and . . . 6:00 A.M. to 6:00 P.M.

---

 trivia

FOWL FACTS
long-term memory
executive functioning

Test your bird IQ with these clues.

● This is the most common bird in the world.

● The plumage of this bird is so stunning that NBC chose it as its symbol when color TV was first introduced.

● The finest—and most expensive—down comes from this feathered fowl.

● This ancient Mexican culture is credited with the domestication of the turkey.

whoozy

How many clues do you need to guess who the WHOOZY is? One to three clues—Outstanding; three to seven clues—Very Good; seven to ten clues—Time to study up on your WHOOZYs.

1. Born in 1925 to a poor Irish American family in San Mateo, California, WHOOZY earned extra money for his family as a church organist when he was a teenager.

2. At age nineteen, WHOOZY began singing on a radio station in San Francisco, then with the Freddy Martin orchestra.

3. Classified as 4-F because of a heart murmur, WHOOZY never served in World War II.

4. WHOOZY appeared in several movies but became more interested in the new medium of television. Starting in 1958, WHOOZY hosted a series of television game shows.

5. In the early 1960s, WHOOZY met Jack Paar and parlayed that meeting into a guest host spot on *The Tonight Show*.

6. For the next twenty years, WHOOZY hosted his own talk show, often tackling controversial subjects such as the Vietnam War.

7. In 1963 WHOOZY's wife gave him an idea for a new game show, in which the questions and answers were reversed.

8. When that game show was canceled after eleven years, WHOOZY produced its successor, a game show based on the classic word game Hangman.

9. The profits from his game shows made WHOOZY one of the world's wealthiest entertainers. At the time of his death in 2007, WHOOZY was worth an estimated $1.2 billion.

10. If you haven't guessed WHOOZY by now, it may help to know that WHOOZY's talk show sidekick was Arthur Treacher, and that the game shows he developed and produced were *Jeopardy!* and *Wheel of Fortune*.

PICTURE THEMES

The pictures in each column may seem like they have nothing in common. But if you look carefully, you'll see a theme emerge. Can you figure out the unique theme for each column of three pictures?

Column A

Column B

A _____

B _____

Column C

C _____

Column D

D _____

whatzit

How many clues do you need to guess what the WHATZIT is? One to three clues—Outstanding; three to seven clues—Very Good; seven to ten clues—Time to study up on your WHATZITs.

1. WHATZITs are native to South America, most likely originating in Peru, and were probably introduced into central Mexico by the Aztecs around A.D. 700.

2. Some experts believe that Christopher Columbus may have introduced WHATZITs to Europe. At that time, WHATZITs were probably small and yellow.

3. The earliest known writing about WHATZITs appeared in a book by an Italian botanist in 1544. And the earliest known cookbook using WHATZITs was published in Naples in 1692.

4. WHATZITs grew easily in the Mediterranean climate and spread quickly throughout the region.

5. England was slower to adopt WHATZITs because herbalist John Gerard thought they were poisonous. (The leaves and stems do contain some poisons, but the fruit does not.)

6. Today WHATZITs are grown worldwide, and many different types have been cultivated.

7. The heaviest recorded WHATZIT weighed almost eight pounds.

8. Most WHATZIT cultivars produce red fruit, but they can also be found in yellow, orange, pink, purple, green, black, white, and even stripes.

9. Some WHATZIT cultivars include: Beefsteak, Better Boy, Early Girl, Brandywine, Cherry, and Plum.

10. It's hard to imagine Italian food without WHATZITs, but the ancient Romans never used them because WHATZITs hadn't yet been introduced to Europe.

Palindromes

Palindromes are words or phrases that read the same backward and forward. *Madam, I'm Adam* is a well-known palindrome. In this game, all of the answers are one-word palindromes.

1. Restaurants offer this with boiled lobster to protect your clothes.

_____

2. A mature female sheep.

_____

3. Type of small tent for one or two people.

_____

4. A polite, formal term of address for a woman.

_____

5. Adam's gal.

_____

6. Mr. Barker of *The Price Is Right*.

_____

7. A failed firecracker.

_____

8. A one-night job for a rock band.

_____

9. Nickname of the Egyptian pharaoh whose tomb of riches was discovered virtually intact in 1922.

_____

10. To choke . . . or a kind of joke.

_____

11. A lightweight, one-person canoe of Eskimo origin.

_____

12. Inhabitant of a convent.

_____

down to the wire

Fill in the blank space with the word or words that complete each expression.

1. _____ to the wise

2. _____ to the bar

3. _____ to the chase

4. _____ to the nines

5. _____ to the finish

6. _____ to the brim

7. "_____ to the Chief"

8. _____ to the center of the earth

9. _____ to the grindstone

10. _____ to the races

11. _____ to the choir

12. _____ to the gills

Follow the Rules

It seems like a simple game: the beginning of a proverb or saying is provided, and you need to follow each instruction to uncover the ending. We've filled in the answers to the first two lines to get you started. Caution! This game is harder than you think.

1. With no spaces between words, write down the phrase: TELL THE TRUTH

2. Place an N after every fourth letter.

3. Place an A in the third position.

4. If the University of Notre Dame is in Wisconsin, place a D before the first N. If not, place a D after the first N.

5. Remove the sixteenth letter.

6. Remove the first E.

7. Remove all L's.

8. Remove the first, third, and last T's.

T	E	L	L	T	H	E	T	R	U	T	H
T	E	L	L	N	T	H	E	T	N	R	U	T	H	N

Did you get the right answer?

Chapter Two

FANCY FOOTWORK

IT'S A KICK

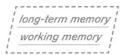

All of the answers in this quiz begin with the letter K.

1. To abduct a person for ransom.

Kidnap

2. Six-foot-tall Australian marsupial.

Kangaroo

3. A musical toy that produces a buzzing sound when a player hums into it.

Kazoo

4. A smack or a peck.

Kiss

5. Menswear, Scottish style.

KILT

6. A barrel for doling out beer.

KEG

7. A type of long brown seaweed.

Kelp

8. One seed of corn.

Kernel

9. He lost his bid for the U.S. presidency in 2004 by just over two percent of the popular vote.

10. Jewish dietary laws.

Kosher

11. World War II Japanese suicide pilots.

Kamakazee

12. A dry dog food.

Kibble

13. Spicy Polish sausage.

Kielbasa

14. An oven for firing pottery.

Kiln

15. Start of a football game.

KICK OFF

16. Yiddish term for a clumsy person.

KLUTZ

HOMONYMS

Homonyms are two or more words that are pronounced the same way but have different meanings and/or spellings. In this game, we supply the definitions, and you must not only provide the homonyms, but SPELL them correctly as well!

1. Consumed; or, seven plus one.

_____ _____

2. A fragrance; or, a penny.

_____ _____

3. A blossom; or, a basic baking ingredient.

_____ _____

4. Plant seeds; or, to use a needle and thread.

_____ _____

5. The top of a mountain; or, a quick, furtive glance.

_____ _____

6. A mortgage or cash advance; or, solitary.

_____ _____

7. A part in a play or movie; or, dinner bread.

_____ _____

8. Having a husky or weak voice; or, a stallion or mustang.

_____ _____

9. Temporary stop in action or speech; or, an animal's feet.

_____ _____

10. Spooky, creepy; or, one of the Great Lakes.

_____ _____

11. A man who served the king in the Middle Ages; or, the period from sunset to sunrise.

_____ _____

12. The basic structural unit of all living organisms; or, to offer something for purchase.

_____ _____

13. Bread, before it's baked; or, a female deer.

_____ _____

HIDDEN ANIMALS

Can you identify the animals that complete the words in this list? For example, the animal that completes "s_ _ _ ter" is *cat* (s*cat*ter). For a more strenuous brain exercise, try covering up the definitions and solving the incomplete word without any hints.

1. Wh __ __ __ barrow — *A single wheeled cart for moving loads.*

2. Videot __ __ __ — *Medium for recording visual images.*

3. __ __ __ __ radish — *Pungent root used as a condiment.*

4. Kn __ __ __ edge — *The facts, information, and skills a person possesses.*

5. __ __ __ astrophe — *A disaster.*

6. __ __ __ htub — *Place for a relaxing soak.*

7. Gi __ __ __ — *A being of superhuman size.*

8. S __ __ __ __ ble — *Popular word game.*

9. Fris __ __ __ — *Plastic toy that is thrown back and forth.*

Presidential Nicknames

Can you identify these U.S. presidents by their nicknames?

1. Bubba

2. Dubya

3. The Teflon President

4. Give 'Em Hell Harry

5. The Rail Splitter

6. Ike

7. Silent Cal

8. Barry

9. Tricky Dick

it starts with a letter

All of the answers in this game start with a letter, as in *X-Ray*, *I Beam,* or *V Chip*.

1. Discount store chain formerly known as S. S. Kresge Company.

_____

2. A brand of cotton swab.

_____

3. Surgical baby delivery.

_____

4. Cut of steak also called Porterhouse.

_____

5. June 6, 1944.

_____

6. U.S. clothing retailer with a popular catalog.

_____

7. Well-known joint or gasket that caused the space shuttle *Challenger* disaster.

_____

8. Do-it-yourself moving equipment company.

_____

9. Some strains of this bacterium can cause serious food poisoning.

_____

10. The group of Hollywood actors who get the best parts, the most money, and often the most attention.

_____

11. Nuclear weapon that gets its explosive energy from hydrogen fusion.

_____

12. Genetically, this separates the men from the women.

_____

trivia

FINISH THE SONG LINE

long-term memory

executive functioning

It might help to sing the answers to this quiz.

● "That old black magic has me . . ."

● "I'm gonna love you like nobody's loved you . . ."

● "A, You're adorable. . . ."

● "Look at me. I'm as helpless as . . ."

Rhymin' Geography

Each question has clues to two different geographical places that rhyme, such as *Bali and Mali* or *Taos and Laos.*

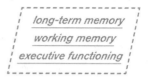

1. U.S. state that is home to Portland and Kennebunk; and the country where you'll find Madrid and Barcelona.

2. U.S. state that is home to Lincoln and Omaha; and the U.S. state that is home to Juneau and Fairbanks.

3. The capital of Texas; and the capital of Massachusetts.

4. Largest city in New Mexico; and the country where you'll find the cities of Ankara and Istanbul.

5. Battlefield where Napoleon was defeated; and the Michigan city where Glenn Miller "had a girl."

6. The "Tac" in Washington's Sea-Tac Airport; and the U.S. state that is home to the cities of Enid and Tulsa.

7. Windswept island resort near the coast of Venezuela; and the only country in the Western Hemisphere with a Communist government.

8. A huge, frigid, sparsely populated region of Russia; and the African country settled by American slaves.

9. The capital of Italy; and the Alaskan city that marks the end of the Iditarod sled dog race.

10. "The Land of 10,000 Lakes"; and a Florida city on the Gulf of Mexico located between Venice and Bradenton.

11. A major tourist center and leading resort on the French Riviera; and, the nation that gave birth to democracy and the Olympics.

THE S HAVE IT: ANIMALS

Can you identify these animals just by looking at their eyes?

long-term memory
executive functioning
attention to detail

1 _____

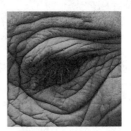

2 _____

3 _____

4 _____

5 _____

6 _____

7 _____

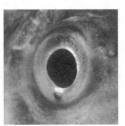

8 _____

Finish the Saying

Can you finish these familiar proverbs and sayings? (The number in parentheses indicates how many words are in the correct answer.)

1. Beauty is only

_____ (2)

2. Birds of a feather

_____ (2)

3. Actions speak

_____ (3)

4. Opportunity seldom

_____ (2)

5. Blood is

_____ (3)

6. Dead men

_____ (3)

7. Two heads are

_____ (3)

8. Good fences

_____ (3)

9. It takes two

_____ (2)

10. A man's home

_____ (3)

11. Give credit where

_____ (3)

12. Honesty is

_____ (3)

13. Money is

_____

_____ (5)

14. All is fair

_____

_____ (4)

---

 trivia

TWO OUT OF THREE

long-term memory
executive functioning

Two answers are required for each question in this quiz.

● Who are two of the Three Stooges?

● What are two of the three things that "little girls are made of"?

● What are two of the three branches of the U.S. government?

● What are two of the three races that make up the famous Triple Crown of Thoroughbred horse racing?

PUT **THE LIST** IN ORDER

Put each list of four or five items in the order called for in the question.

① Put this list of dog breeds in order, starting with the largest (based on an average-sized adult dog for each breed):

___ **a.** German Shepherd

___ **b.** Great Dane

___ **c.** Cocker spaniel

___ **d.** Chihuahua

② Put this list of continents in order of their total size (in area), starting with the largest:

___ **a.** Antarctica

___ **b.** South America

___ **c.** Africa

___ **d.** North America

___ **e.** Europe

③ Put this list of television series in order of when they were first broadcast, starting with the earliest broadcast date:

___ **a.** *Bonanza*

___ **b.** *Dr. Kildare*

___ **c.** *Jeopardy!*

___ **d.** *What's My Line?*

___ **e.** *Perry Mason*

④ Put this list of letters in order of their value in Scrabble, starting with the highest value:

___ **a.** L

___ **b.** K

___ **c.** F

___ **d.** J

___ **e.** G

⑤ Put this list of famous women in order of their age, starting with the youngest:

___ **a.** Mary Tyler Moore

___ **b.** Meryl Streep

___ **c.** Katie Couric

___ **d.** Barbra Streisand

___ **e.** Goldie Hawn

⑥ Put this list of newspapers in order, starting with the one with the largest daily circulation:

___ **a.** *The New York Times*

___ **b.** *The Wall Street Journal*

___ **c.** *USA Today*

___ **d.** *The Washington Post*

⑦ Put this list of states in the alphabetical order of their capital cities, going from A to Z:

___ **a.** New York

___ **b.** New Jersey

___ **c.** Michigan

___ **d.** Louisiana

⑧ Put this list of events in order, starting with the earliest:

___ **a.** The U.S. celebrates its bicentennial

___ **b.** The Iran hostage crisis

___ **c.** The Woodstock music festival

___ **d.** Gerald Ford becomes the thirty-eighth president

long-term memory
working memory
executive functioning
multitasking

9. Put this list of national parks in order from east to west:

____ **a.** Mt. Rainier

____ **b.** Everglades

____ **c.** Yellowstone

____ **d.** Great Smoky Mountains

10. Put these books in order of how many copies have been sold (in all languages), starting with the most copies sold (according to Wikipedia):

____ **a.** *The Diary of a Young Girl* (1947) by Anne Frank

____ **b.** *The Cat in the Hat* (1957) by Dr. Seuss

____ **c.** *The Da Vinci Code* (2003) by Dan Brown

____ **d.** *The Lord of the Rings* (1954) by J.R.R. Tolkien

____ **e.** *The Godfather* (1969) by Mario Puzo

GUESS THE GAS

long-term memory
executive functioning

The title of this game says it all.

● Being lighter than air, this gas is widely used in airships and balloons.

● This gas produces the bubbles in soda. It's also so prevalent in the atmosphere that it's a major contributor to global warming.

● When placed in a glass tube, this noble gas produces an unmistakable bright red-orange glow.

● Used in surgery and dentistry, this is also called "laughing gas," due to the euphoric effects of inhaling it.

ONE › MINUTE › MADNESS

South America

How many of the thirteen countries (plus one dependency) in South America can you name in one minute?

long-term memory
working memory
processing speed

_____

_____

_____

_____

_____

_____

_____

_____

_____

_____

_____

_____

_____

_____

*mar*k my words

All the answers in this word definition game begin with the letters MAR.

1. It's 26 miles and 385 yards long, precisely.

_____

2. The Taj Mahal is made mostly of this.

_____

3. Hemp, ganja, Maryjane, or weed.

_____

4. A bitter jam made from citrus.

_____

5. These mammals, such as kangaroos, koalas, and possums, have pouches.

_____

6. The interior portion of large bones; it's where new red blood cells are produced.

_____

7. This candy is made from sugar and almond paste and is often colored and shaped into the form of fruits and vegetables.

_____

8. A traditional Mexican musical ensemble. Originally these bands were street musicians from the state of Jalisco. Today they play the emblematic music of Mexico.

_____

9. A puppet controlled by strings.

_____

10. Gin, vermouth, and an olive.

_____

11. Someone who suffers persecution and death for refusing to renounce a belief, usually religious.

_____

12. The sign above the entrance to a movie theater.

_____

13. Unlike its cousin the swordfish, this large marine fish with a spear-like snout is rarely eaten. Most sport fishermen unhook and release them.

_____

FRUITS AND VEGGIES

Can you come up with the name of at least one fruit or vegetable for every letter of the alphabet? For an extra brain boost, see how many you can name in two minutes.

long-term memory
working memory
executive functioning
processing speed

A _____

B _____

C _____

D _____

E _____

F _____

G _____

H _____

I _____

J _____

K _____

L _____

M _____

N _____

O _____

P _____

Q _____

R _____

S _____

T _____

U _____

V _____

W _____

X _____

Y _____

Z _____

★ FEBRUARY IN HISTORY ★

This trivia quiz will stretch your long-term memory muscles.

1692 Dr. William Griggs diagnosed two girls as "bewitched," eventually leading to a series of witch trials in this Massachusetts village.

1848 *The Communist Manifesto,* one of the world's most influential political manuscripts, was published. Who wrote it?

1886 This holiday was first observed in Punxsutawney, PA.

1896 Candy inventor Leo Hirshfeld introduced this chewy treat: a chocolate-like candy that would not spoil nor melt in the heat. By World War II, it had become a standard part of American soldiers' field rations.

1909 This association was founded by W.E.B. Du Bois, Ida Wells-Barnett, and others to battle against lynching and other forms of racial oppression.

1935 Dr. Wallace Carothers discovered this synthetic silk-like material, which was first used commercially in toothbrush bristles.

1954 This physician led the first test of his newly developed polio vaccine in Pittsburgh, PA. It was the most elaborate mass inoculation in history.

1959 This thirty-three-year-old revolutionary was sworn in as prime minister of the Caribbean country he would control for more than half a century.

1960 Four African American college students began a sit-in protest at a lunch counter inside this store in Greensboro, NC.

1964 More than 40 percent of the U.S. population tuned in to *The Ed Sullivan Show* to watch this new rock and roll band.

1964 A twenty-two-year-old boxer knocked out Sonny Liston to win the heavyweight title for the first time. By what two names is that boxer known?

1965 Canada replaced the Union Jack with a new flag that featured this prominent design in its center.

1972 President Richard Nixon became the first U.S. president in history to set foot in this country.

1974 The first issue of this magazine, now ubiquitous in doctors' offices, hair salons, and airports, went on sale. On the cover was a photo of Mia Farrow, then starring in *The Great Gatsby*.

1983 A record-breaking 106 million Americans gathered in front of their television sets to watch the two-and-a-half-hour final episode of this much beloved series.

1990 Nelson Mandela was freed after twenty-seven years in prison in this country.

1992 This businessman appeared on CNN's *Larry King Live* to announce his intention to run for president as an Independent if his supporters could get his name on the ballot in all fifty states.

1993 This tennis player died of AIDS, a disease he contracted from contaminated blood received during heart surgery.

1998 President Bill Clinton signed a bill changing the name of Washington's National Airport to this.

2000 The last original *Peanuts* comic strip appeared in newspapers—one day after the death of this cartoonist.

---

letter speller

long-term memory

The twist in this game is that all the answers sound as if they're just one or two letters long. For example: *The plural of "is."* Answer: *R* ("are"). *A disreputable hotel.* Answer: *C, D* ("seedy").

1. Actress Ruby. _____

2. For what reason? _____

3. It's not a bluebird, but it is a blue bird. _____

4. Television's top award. _____

5. Not filled or occupied. _____

6. To be jealous of someone's luck or possessions. _____

7. Sheriff Andy Taylor's TV son. _____

8. Exxon's previous name. _____

9. To perform exceptionally well. _____

10. Pasta in the form of tubes. _____

M & M'S

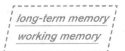
All of the two-word answers in this game begin with the initials M and M.

1. Term for a small amount of cash carried by a young woman to pay for cab fare home should her date not work out.

_____

2. Felt-tip pens.

_____

3. A famous French mime.

_____

4. Mixture of chopped dried fruit, distilled spirits, and spices. (Sometimes beef suet, beef, or venison is included.)

_____

5. Evangelical political lobbying organization founded by Jerry Falwell in 1979 (and later dissolved in the late 1980s).

_____

6. Term used to describe a Native American healer and spiritual leader.

_____

7. She wrote *Gone with the Wind.*

_____

8. If you let the time run over, she will surely give you a parking ticket.

_____

9. This devoted follower of Jesus, traditionally depicted as a repentant prostitute, is now viewed by some scholars as the first female minister.

_____

10. A seaman dedicated to commercial rather than military activity.

_____

11. The phrase used to describe Superman's alter ego Clark Kent.

_____

12. The highest mountain peak in North America, it's better known in Alaska as Denali.

_____

---

 trivia

FICTIONAL DOCTORS

long-term memory

executive functioning

Can you name these fictional healers?

● This British doctor shuns his human patients for animals with whom he can speak in their own languages.

● This fictional surgeon hailed from Crabapple Cove, Maine and served in a M*A*S*H unit during the Korean War.

● This evil psychiatrist was also a serial killer who dabbled in cannibalism.

● This idealistic physician-poet lost Lara, the love of his life, and suffered the horrors of World War I and the Russian Revolution.

GEOGRAPHICAL DOUBLE ENTENDRES

This is a word game combined with a trivia game in which you name the geographical place—which is also a word for something entirely different.

1. An Asian country or . . . ceramic tableware.

2. A city on Lake Erie or . . . a bison.

3. A New York City borough or . . . a group of royal ladies.

4. A South American country or . . . a large nut.

5. A city in Florida or . . . the largest planet in the solar system.

6. An ancient English city or . . . a nice, long soak.

7. A city in Germany or . . . ground beef.

8. A group of islands off Morocco or . . . a small bird.

9. A river in China or . . . a primary color.

10. A river in South America or . . . an online retailer.

11. A county in southern California or . . . a citrus fruit.

long-term memory
working memory
executive functioning

x, y, or z

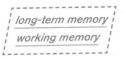
All of the answers in this word definition game begin with an X, Y, or Z.

1. Striped equine animal.

_____

2. This is often a child's first musical instrument.

_____

3. A large pleasure boat.

_____

4. It promotes fermentation and makes bread rise.

_____

5. Photocopy brand.

_____

6. The greatest height; or a former television set manufacturer.

_____

7. Domesticated ox of Tibet.

_____

8. Absolutely nothing.

_____

9. An oversized "rebellious" man's suit from the 1930s and '40s.

_____

10. Thirty-six-inch ruler.

_____

11. The largest city in Switzerland.

_____

12. Japanese currency.

_____

13. Crazy, ludicrous.

_____

14. Afraid of anything foreign.

_____

15. It smooths the ice in a skating rink.

_____

---

trivia

1939

long-term memory

executive functioning

1939 was quite a year in the U.S.—and around the rest of the world as well.

● Missing for eighteen months, this aviation pioneer was declared dead on January 5, 1939.

● This motion picture debuted on December 15, 1939, with a three-day premiere festival in Atlanta, GA.

● He wrote _The Grapes of Wrath_, which was published in 1939 and chronicled the Great Depression and Dust Bowl years.

● On September 1, 1939, the Nazi invasion of this country signaled the start of World War II in Europe.

what's your movie song IQ?

Some of the music world's greatest hits come from songs written for or used in movies. Given a sampling of the lyrics, can you identify the movie from its famous song?

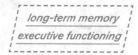

long-term memory
executive functioning

1. "You must remember this, a kiss is just a kiss . . ."

2. "And here's to you, Mrs. Robinson . . ."

3. "Memories light the corners of my mind . . ."

4. "The hills are alive . . ."

5. "What good is sitting alone in your room?"

6. "Everybody's talkin' at me. . . ."

7. "Raindrops keep fallin' on my head . . ."

8. "I like to be in America . . ."

9. "When the moon is in the seventh house and Jupiter aligns with Mars . . ."

10. "Supercalifragilisticexpialidocious!"

11. "Oh, one last kiss, oh, give me one last kiss . . ."

12. "I don't know how to love him . . ."

13. "Don't tell me not to live, just sit and putter."

DOUBLE TROUBLE

Compound words are made up of two smaller words, such as *hayloft* or *watchtower*. In this game, we give the second half of some compound words. You must identify the one word that precedes each of them to make a compound word. For example, given the words *weed, coast,* and *sick,* the one word that makes each a compound word is *sea* (*seaweed, seacoast,* and *seasick*).

1. Hound, thirsty, stream

_____ (hint: b)

2. Catcher, fight, wood, house

_____ (hint: d)

3. Mother, father, parent, stand

_____ (hint: g)

4. Sick, work, land, room

_____ (hint: h)

5. Land, berg, box, breaker

_____ (hint: i)

6. Hammer, ass, knife, pot

_____ (hint: j)

7. Beam, shine, walk, light

_____ (hint: m)

8. Bow, coat, drop, forest

_____ (hint: r)

9. Proof, melon, fall, color

_____ (hint: w)

10. Back, house, land, grocer

_____ (hint: g)

11. Quake, shaking, worm

_____ (hint: e)

12. Maker, stick, box, book

_____ (hint: m)

13. Study, wear, privileged

_____ (hint: u)

14. Cushion, stripe, wheel, point, ball

_____ (hint: p)

UNDER THE WEATHER

You've got one minute to come up with as many one-word answers as possible to complete the phrase *Under the _____*. We came up with sixteen of them, including *Under the weather*.

Under the ___*weather*___

Under the _____

Under the _____

Under the _____

Under the _____

Under the _____

Under the _____

Under the _____

Under the _____

Under the _____

Under the _____

Under the _____

Under the _____

Under the _____

Under the _____

Under the _____

OVER THE HILL

How many one-word answers can you come up with in one minute that complete the phrase *Over the _____*? We found thirteen of them, including *Over the hill*.

Over the ___*hill*___

Over the _____

Over the _____

Over the _____

Over the _____

Over the _____

Over the _____

Over the _____

Over the _____

Over the _____

Over the _____

Over the _____

Over the _____

Add It Up

This game involves simple addition—but you have to figure out which numbers to add up.

1. Add the number of dimes in a dollar to the age when a child becomes a teenager.

_____

2. Add the number of innings in a standard baseball game to the number of sides in a triangle.

_____

3. Add the year that John F. Kennedy was assassinated to the number of years in two decades.

_____

4. Add the traditional "unlucky" number to the traditional "lucky" number.

_____

5. Add the number of the month that Valentine's Day is in to the number of the month that Labor Day is in.

_____

6. Add the number of hours in a day to the number of points scored in a grand slam home run.

_____

7. Add the street address of the White House to the number of goals in a "hat trick" in hockey.

_____

8. Add the Spanish numbers *cinco* plus *cinco* plus *ocho* and give the answer in English.

_____

STEVE, STEPHEN, OR STEVEN

long-term memory

executive functioning

Can you identify these famous Steves?

● He wrote his first published novel *Carrie* while he was teaching in a high school near Bangor, Maine.

● He says his career began in 1958 when he made a nine-minute film to earn a Boy Scout merit badge. One of his first professional jobs was directing an episode of *Marcus Welby, M.D.*

● In 1974, after a string of hits including *Bullitt*, *Papillon*, and *The Towering Inferno*, he became the highest paid movie star in the world.

● He is the "other" Steve, five years older than Steve Jobs, who cofounded Apple Computer, Inc. in 1976.

HIDDEN ANATOMY

Can you identify the body parts that complete the words in this list? For example, the body part that completes "te _ _ _ raph" is *leg* (te*leg*raph). For a more strenuous brain exercise, try covering up the definitions and solving the incomplete words without any hints.

1. H __ __ __ony — *Notes sung together in a pleasing combination of sounds.*

2. Ob __ __ __d — *Did as you were told.*

3. Ghet __ __ __s — *City areas inhabited by minorities.*

4. Th __ __ __ __ __ss — *Unappreciative; ungrateful.*

5. C__ __ __munk — *Small rodent with stripes on its back.*

6. P__ __ __l — *An oyster's offering.*

7. Diag __ __ __ __d — *Identified an illness.*

8. Zuc__ __ __ __i — *Green summer squash.*

9. Hor __ __ __le — *Awful.*

10. Pan__ __ __ __le — *To beg money from strangers.*

11. P__ __ __ __er — *A plumber's helper.*

12. Paper__ __ __ __ — *Book with a flexible cover.*

13. Or__ __ __ __ __ra — *A large group of musicians.*

14. Paci__ __ __ __ — *One who believes that war is never justified.*

15. De __ __ __ __ __ y — *Items brought to someone.*

16. __ __ __ __ __ial — *America before independence from Britain.*

17. __ __ __ __ny — *Thin.*

18. __ __ __ __age — *A length of film.*

BACK WORDS

All the answers in this game are *semordnilaps*—words that spell a different word forward and backward, such as *faced* and *decaf*. (Give yourself a gold star if you noticed something special about the word *semordnilap!*)

1. Forward it's a state of armed conflict; backward it's uncooked.

_____

2. Forward they're spinning toys; backward it's a small stain on a shirt or tie.

_____

3. Forward they are tasty seeds such as almonds or cashews; backward it means to astonish or shock.

_____

4. Forward it's a collective term for Fidos and Fluffys; backward it means to put one foot in front of the other.

_____

5. Forward it's Arnold Palmer's game; backward it means to beat someone with a whip or stick as a punishment.

6. Forward it's the movement of the ocean; backward it means to correct or improve written material.

_____

7. Forward it's an auger or chisel; backward it means to steal things during a riot or war.

_____

8. Forward it means intelligent; backward it's another word for trolleys.

_____

9. Forward it's a civil wrongdoing; backward it's a medium-slow gait for a horse.

_____

(trivia)

FICTIONAL LAST WORDS

long-term memory
executive functioning

Can you name the book or movie these "famous last words" came from?

● "I have been wicked in my day, but I never thought a little girl like you would ever be able to melt me and end my wicked deeds. Look out, here I go!"

● "The croc! The croc! The croc! Pan, no words of mine can express me utter contempt for ye!"

● "Rosebud!"

● ". . . let me then tow to pieces, while still chasing thee, though tied to thee, thou damned whale! Thus, I give up the spear!"

NAME MERGE

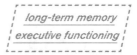

long-term memory
executive functioning

Given a clue for each of two famous people, can you figure out what name they share? For example: *Clarence Thomas Jefferson* or *Jesse James Cagney.*

1. Star of TV's *Make Room for Daddy;* and the inventor of the lightbulb.

2. Comic who insisted that he was thirty-nine years old for about forty years; and the bandleader dubbed "The King of Swing."

3. Colonial captain whose name is synonymous with the word traitor; and the actor and former governor of California.

4. Rugged actor nicknamed "The Duke"; and legendary hockey player nicknamed "The Great One."

5. British star of *My Fair Lady* and *Dr. Dolittle*; and the American actor who played Indiana Jones.

6. Singer-songwriter famous for "Blowin' in the Wind" and "The Times They Are A-Changin'"; and Welsh author of *A Child's Christmas in Wales.*

7. Star of *Rebel Without a Cause* who died in a car accident at age twenty-four; and the hard-drinking partner of Jerry Lewis.

8. Popular singer of "You Give Me Fever" and "Is That All There Is?"; and the assassin of John F. Kennedy.

9. Blind singer of "Hit the Road, Jack" and "Georgia on My Mind"; and the nineteenth-century English naturalist who proposed the theory of evolution.

10. The Brooklyn Dodgers player who broke the color barrier in baseball; and Daniel Defoe's fictional castaway who spent twenty-eight years on a remote island.

11. She prosecuted O. J. Simpson; and Superman's more human alter ego.

wacky wordies

TheTheCatcherRye

candles   candles   candles   candles
candles   candles   candles   candles
candles   candles   candles   candles
candles   candles   candles   candles

1 _____

2 _____

SEA
diver

gniklaW

3 _____

4 _____

To solve these fun puzzles, look carefully at each frame, because the arrangement of the letters is a key clue to the familiar phrase contained within. For example, if the word *school* were placed high up in the frame, the answer would be *high school.* Or if the phrase "easy pieces" occurred five times in the frame, the answer would be *Five Easy Pieces.*

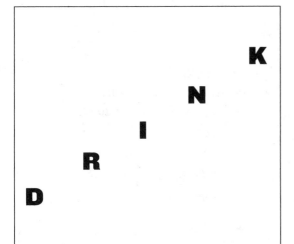

the weather

feeling

⑤ _____

⑥ _____

Apeapeapod

⑦ _____

⑧ _____

sheesh

All of the answers in this word definition game either begin or end with the letters SH.

1. This tool helps you put your loafers on.

2. A delicious crustacean.

3. You might play this game on the deck of a cruise ship.

4. A meat and vegetable stew, Hungarian style.

5. A county is called this in Louisiana.

6. Pilfering small items from a store.

7. In many states, this elected official is in charge of the prisons.

8. A mixture of corn and lima beans.

9. You can cast this on the sidewalk, but only on a sunny day.

10. According to Shakespeare, this bad-tempered woman is not easy to tame.

11. A small, round pungent root, mostly used in salads.

12. A word that's often used to describe a nervous or shy cat.

13. The national plant (and emblem) of Ireland.

14. A computer . . . or a crisp fall fruit.

Roman Numerals

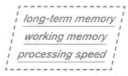

How many of the seven Roman numerals can you name in thirty seconds? And for an extra brain boost, provide the number value of each Roman numeral.

REPLACE THE
ELBOW

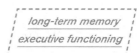

There's something wrong with these book, story, and movie titles. Can you fix them by replacing the word ELBOW with the correct body part?

1. *A Farewell to ELBOWS* by Ernest Hemingway

2. *Adam's ELBOW* (Movie)

3. *ELBOW of the Needle* by Ken Follett

4. *GoldELBOW* by Ian Fleming

5. *ScarELBOW* (Movie)

6. "Tom ELBOW" by The Brothers Grimm

7. "The Telltale ELBOW" by Edgar Allan Poe

8. *The Three ELBOWS* of Eve (Movie)

★ MARCH IN HISTORY ★

This trivia quiz will stretch your long-term memory muscles.

1457 This became the first book ever printed, thanks to the Gutenberg printing press.

1857 This new-fangled technology, invented by Elisha Otis, was first installed in a five-story building at 488 Broadway in New York City.

1876 "Mr. Watson, come here. I want to see you" were the first words ever transmitted by telephone. Who said them?

1887 Anne Sullivan moved from Massachusetts to Tuscumbia, Alabama, to teach this seven-year-old deaf and blind child.

1889 The French flag was raised atop this newly completed structure, which served as the dramatic entrance to the 1889 World's Fair.

1894 The first championship series for this highest award in hockey was played in Montreal, Canada.

1905 This new type of physical evidence was used for the first time to help convict an accused murderer in London.

1911 One hundred forty-six garment workers—mostly young immigrants—died at the Triangle Shirtwaist dress factory in this city. This tragedy galvanized the labor union movement in the U.S. and changed fire codes across the country.

1916 This scientist published his general theory of relativity.

1931 In an attempt to lift the state from the hard times of the Great Depression, the Nevada state legislature voted to legalize this.

1935 This country's name was changed to Iran.

1938 The world would be forever changed when oil was discovered in this country of nomadic peasants and subsistence merchants.

1943 As the final "liquidation" of this Jewish ghetto in Poland began, this German businessman worked furiously to save as many Jews as possible by taking them in as workers in his enamelware factory.

1946 Winston Churchill popularized the phrase to describe all the capitals of the ancient states of Central and Eastern Europe: Warsaw, Berlin, Prague, Vienna, Budapest, etc., that were falling under Soviet influence.

1947 The Truman Doctrine was proclaimed to help contain the spread of communism. Its main tenet was that if one country in a region fell under the influence of communism, then the surrounding countries would follow. By what less formal name did this foreign policy theory come to be known?

1961 The twenty-third amendment to the Constitution was ratified, giving these U.S. citizens the right to vote in presidential elections.

1964 A jury in Dallas, Texas, convicted this local nightclub owner for the "murder with malice" of Lee Harvey Oswald.

1968 President Lyndon Johnson made this startling announcement on national television.

1969 Beatle John Lennon married this Japanese-born avant-garde artist in Gibraltar.

1981 He replaced the recently retired Walter Cronkite as anchorman for *The CBS Evening News,* a post he then held for the next twenty-four years.

Smallest U.S. States

How many of the ten smallest (in square miles) U.S. states can you name in one minute?

_____

_____

_____

_____

_____

_____

_____

_____

long-term memory
working memory
processing speed

kangaroo words

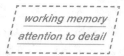

working memory
attention to detail

A Kangaroo Word is a word that contains letters of another word, in the correct order (though not necessarily contiguous), that has the same meaning. For example, the word *acrid* contains the word *acid,* and both words have similar meanings. The word *expurgate* contains its synonym *purge.* In this game, we provide the longer word. Can you find the shorter one? (*Note: The longer word is called the "kangaroo," and the shorter word is called the "joey," which is the name for a baby kangaroo that lives in its mother's pouch.*)

1. Myself

2. Banish

3. Burst

4. Stocking

5. Arch

6. Enjoyment

7. Cooled

8. Lighted

9. Blossom

10. History

11. Latest

12. Alone

13. Rampage

14. Masculine

15. Salvage

What a Pair

Harvard and Yale, Thunder and Lightning, Coke and Pepsi are all common pairs . . . but what about *Wonder and Perrier?* If you redefine *Wonder* and *Perrier* correctly, you'll come up with the more familiar pairing *Bread and Water.* How many familiar pairs can you make from the clues below?

1. Enclosure for a pig . . . and the liquid released by a squid.

2. A state or county festival . . . and a shape with four equal sides.

3. A smooch . . . and the legendary William who shot an apple on his son's head.

4. A pebble, stone, or boulder . . . and sandwich bread in the shape of a bun.

5. Lockable container for money and valuables . . . and any type of noise.

6. Siamese and Manx . . . and boxers and beagles.

7. Penny loafers . . . and Chelsea Clinton's White House cat.

8. Donald or Daffy . . . and to put a lid on something.

9. Captain in *Peter Pan* . . . and the seeing organ.

10. The staff of life . . . and Land O' Lakes product.

11. Smoked pork shoulder . . . and mozzarella.

12. Torso or carcass . . . and the spiritual part of a human.

13. Court proceeding . . . and a mistake or miscalculation.

14. Fine goose feathers . . . and three strikes.

What Do They Have in Common?

long-term memory
executive functioning
attention to detail

Each question contains a list of several items. Can you figure out what they have in common?

1. The U.S. flag, Hollywood, and the night sky

_____

2. Cliff, Norm, Woody, and Sam

_____

3. Chipper, driver, and wood

_____

4. Blouses, elevators, and your belly

_____

5. Eggplants, Barney, bruises, and amethysts

_____

6. A car, a bull, a shoe salesman, and a brass band

_____

7. Irving Berlin, Rose Kennedy, and Bob Hope

_____

8. A mailbox, the alphabet, and a high school sports sweater

_____

9. An engaged woman, a telephone, a school bell, and Saturn

_____

10. Penny Lane, Lovely Rita, and Michelle

_____

11. A hurricane, a needle, and a potato

_____

12. Kidney, Orson, garbanzo, and jelly

_____

13. Corn, cane, beet, and maple

_____

 trivia

ENGLAND

long-term memory

executive functioning

If you've spent any time "across the pond," you should ace this quiz.

● This airport, twelve miles west of central London, handles the most international passenger traffic in the world.

● England is one of four countries that make up Great Britain. What are the other three?

● Bangers and mash, a traditional English dish, consists of what two ingredients?

● Everyone knows London; but can you name the *second* largest city in England (in terms of population)?

red, white, or blue

All of the answers in this word definition game contain the words *red, white,* or *blue.*

1. What British soldiers were called in colonial America.

_____

2. Automobile tires considered stylish in the 1920s and '30s.

_____

3. An architect's design plan or technical drawing.

_____

4. Nickname for a late-night cross-country flight.

_____

5. This fruit is great in muffins.

_____

6. An ocean wave with a foamy top.

_____

7. A gourmet type of tuna.

_____

8. A blizzard with zero visibility.

_____

9. The tallest known trees on earth native to California and Oregon.

_____

10. It's a flower . . . and a margarine.

_____

11. A common backyard North American bird, it is often noisy and aggressive.

_____

12. A person of noble birth.

_____

13. A deliberate concealment of a person's mistakes or faults to make him look better or to clear his name.

_____

14. A despicable storybook character who killed his first seven wives.

_____

HOMO**NYMS**

Homonyms are two or more words that are pronounced the same way but have different meanings and/or spellings. In this game, we supply the definitions, and you must not only provide the homonyms, but SPELL them correctly as well!

1. A large coffee dispenser; or, to make money.

_____ _____

2. Not working, lazy; or, a person who is greatly admired.

_____ _____

3. Tasty mollusks; or, biceps and gluteus maximus.

_____ _____

4. Word that follows *press* or *peace;* or, the inedible part of an apple.

_____ _____

5. A requirement or necessary thing; or, the act of folding and stretching bread dough.

_____ _____

6. To bide one's time; or, measurement of heaviness.

_____ _____

7. The period in which a king or queen rules; or, precipitation.

_____ _____

8. A lodger; or, the line that separates one country from another.

_____ _____

9. To interfere in something that is not your business; or, a military or athletic award.

_____ _____

10. Fixed gazes; or, a flight of steps.

_____ _____

11. A long slender rod; or, a survey of opinions or votes.

_____ _____

12. True or correct as a fact; or, to pen a letter.

_____ _____

13. To select something from a group of alternatives; or, masticates.

_____ _____

14. Greater in altitude; or, to employ someone.

_____ _____

where's grandma?

Grandma is quite the world traveler. Can you tell which U.S. states she went to last year by the places she visited?

long-term memory
executive functioning

1. Grandma did some surfing at Big Sur, bought some sourdough bread at Fisherman's Wharf, and saw the ancient Greek and Roman art at the Getty Museum.

2. Grandma took a wine tasting tour in the Finger Lakes, went for a boat ride on the Erie Canal, and bet on a couple of horses at the race track in Saratoga.

3. Grandma went to the beach at South Padre Island, visited the School Book Depository in Dealey Plaza, and saw a Cowboys football game.

4. Grandma went to a music festival on Beale Street, watched whiskey being made at the Jack Daniels distillery, and took a guided tour of Graceland.

5. Grandma toured the historic sailing ships at Mystic Seaport, played a little blackjack at Foxwoods, and saw a production of *Hamlet* at the Yale University Theatre.

6. Grandma played some tennis at Mar-a-Lago, saw the auto races at Daytona, and swam with the manatees.

7. Grandma went to her grandson's graduation at Rutgers University, visited the Thomas Edison Museum in Menlo Park, and won a poker tournament at the Trump Taj Mahal.

8. Grandma visited Warm Springs (where FDR recuperated from polio), took a boat tour of the Okefenokee Swamp, and watched a Braves game at Turner Field.

9. Grandma went to a film festival in Telluride, visited her niece at the Air Force Academy, and went skiing in Aspen.

10. Grandma enjoyed three walks back in history at the Jamestown settlement, at Colonial Williamsburg, and at the Civil War battlefield in Manassas.

endings and beginnings

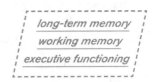
A compound word is made up of two smaller words, such as *stopwatch* or *panhandle*. In this game, we provide the first half of one compound word and the second half of another. Can you figure out the one word that completes them both? (If you get stuck, the first letter of the answer is provided in a hint.)

1. Gun_____cracker (hint: f)

2. Snake_____bull (hint: p)

3. Wheel_____man (hint: c)

4. Blood_____punch (hint: s)

5. Flower_____belly (hint: p)

6. Short_____shake (hint: h)

7. Pan_____bars (hint: h)

8. Home_____fill (hint: l)

9. Dead_____backer (hint: l)

10. Boy_____ship (hint: f)

11. Sheep_____head (hint: s)

12. Play_____hog (hint: g)

13. Side_____stand (hint: k)

14. Flash_____bulb (hint: l)

Monopoly Streets

long-term memory
working memory
processing speed

How many of the twenty-two streets in a
standard Monopoly game can you name in one minute?

_____   _____

_____   _____

_____   _____

_____   _____

_____   _____

_____   _____

_____   _____

_____   _____

---

trivia

FAMOUS FREDS

long-term memory
executive functioning

This quiz is all about people named Fred.

● Modeled after Ralph Kramden, this fictional Fred lived in prehistoric times.

● Perhaps best remembered for his mock feuds with Jack Benny, this Fred was one of radio's most admired—and censored—comics during the Golden Age of Radio.

● This actor and effortless dancer was actually born Frederick Austerlitz in Omaha in 1899.

● This famous Fred began every television show by changing his shoes and putting on a red cardigan sweater.

OUT OF BOUNDS

You've got one minute to come up with as many one-word answers as possible to complete the phrase *Out of _____*. We came up with thirty, including *Out of bounds*.

Out of ___*bounds*___   Out of _____   Out of _____

Out of _____   Out of _____   Out of _____

Out of _____   Out of _____   Out of _____

Out of _____   Out of _____   Out of _____

Out of _____   Out of _____   Out of _____

Out of _____   Out of _____   Out of _____

Out of _____   Out of _____   Out of _____

Out of _____   Out of _____   Out of _____

Out of _____   Out of _____   Out of _____

Out of _____   Out of _____   Out of _____

FOOD HISTORY

long-term memory

executive functioning

Most foods have fascinating histories; here's just a taste.

● This ancient treat is simply boiled sugar and water, with flavoring and color added, which is then molded into shapes. The sticks weren't included until the twentieth century.

● In 1912 Nabisco filed a patent for this product, described as "two beautifully embossed chocolate flavored wafers with a rich cream filling."

● In the 1890s this company slashed the shipping price of a can of soup by condensing it (removing the water).

● Most historians agree that this sweet ending to a Chinese meal was invented in California in the 1930s.

up and *down*

Add "up" to a word or phrase and it has one meaning. Add "down" to the same word or phrase and the meaning is entirely different.

1. With "up" it means to make a small improvement. With "down" it's a way to score points in football.

2. With "up" it means to stop talking. With "down" it means to close a factory . . . or turn off a computer.

3. With "up" it means to end a relationship. With "down" it's the sudden collapse of a person's mental health.

4. With "up" it means to drive a short distance in reverse. With "down" it means to give up in an argument.

5. With "up" it means to burst into unrestrained laughter. With "down" it means to take severe measures to limit crime or bad behavior.

6. With "up" it's a person who likes to tell jokes or play pranks. With "down" it means to insult or belittle a person.

7. With "up" it means to slow down or stop, as with rain or snow. With "down" it means to disappoint or fail to keep a promise.

8. With "up" it means to make radical changes in an organization or routine. With "down" it means to extort or cheat money from someone.

9. With "up" it's what a pitcher does just before throwing the ball. With "down" it means to slowly come to an end.

10. With "up" it means to appear suddenly or at the appointed time. With "down" it's what a chambermaid does to prepare the bed linens at night.

Follow the Rules

How well do you follow rules? If you follow each instruction carefully, you will find out the answer to the proverbial question: "What do women want?" We've filled in the first line; you have to do the rest. Beware! This game is harder than you think.

1. With no spaces between words, write down the phrase: W H A T D O W O M E N W A N T

2. Remove the E and place it at the end.

3. If F is a Roman numeral, put an F in the eleventh position. If F is not a Roman numeral, put an L in the eleventh position.

4. Replace the second W with two C's.

5. Swap the first and the eighth letters.

6. If Maryland was one of the original U.S. colonies, remove the letters MD. If not, remove the first N and the first O.

7. Remove the third and fourth letters.

8. Remove all N's and W's.

W H A T D O W O M E N W A N T

Did you get the right answer?

WHO, WHAT, AND WHERE

long-term memory

executive functioning

Just the facts, ma'am (or sir)— we're looking for who, what, or where.

● **Who** hosted *You Bet Your Life* on NBC from 1950 to 1961?

● **Who** was known as "The Wizard of Menlo Park?"

● **Who** are the two Beatles that are still alive?

● **Whom** did the British newspapers label "Bush's poodle" in 2002?

● **What** do the children listen for in the song "White Christmas"?

● **What** weeklong holiday, created in 1966 and held from December 26 to January 1, celebrates African American heritage, unity, and culture?

● **What** is the name of the multibranched candelabrum that is used on Hanukkah?

● **What,** according to Western tradition, are the names of the three wise men who brought gifts to the baby Jesus?

● **Where** is the Baseball Hall of Fame?

● **Where** would you find Three Mile Island, the site of a 1979 nuclear power plant accident?

● **Where** would you find the summer residence of George H. W. and Barbara Bush?

● **In** what hilly city would you find Lombard Street, the so-called crookedest street in the world?

BACK WORDS

All the answers in this game are *semordnilaps*—words that spell a different word forward and backward, such as *faced* and *decaf*.

1. Forward it describes the movement of water, like a river; backward it's the largest member of the dog family.

_____

2. Forward they're cartographical charts; backward it's unwanted e-mail.

_____

3. Forward it's a slightly naughty term for buttocks; backward it means to rebuff or ignore another person.

_____

4. Forward it's the dried grass used in primitive roofs or for animal feed; backward it means small benign growths on the skin caused by a virus (not by toads!).

_____

5. Forward it's a main feature of a bureau; backward it's a sum of money offered for information that helps solve a crime.

_____

6. Forward it's the absorbent sheet a baby wears; backward it means to have settled a loan.

_____

7. Forward it's the collective term for cakes, pies, and ice cream; backward it's how you feel if you're in a state of mental or emotional strain or tension.

_____

8. Forward it means to bring a letter or package to the proper recipient; backward it means hated or despised.

_____

WORD PARTS

The word *menace* is defined as "a threat." In this game, however, we don't supply the definition of a word, but of its parts. For example, given the first clue "male adults," plus the second clue "the highest card in the deck," the answer is *menace (men + ace)*.

1. The opposite of out + verdict deciders

2. Take a breather + Mr. Linkletter

3. "The Raven" author + to make an effort or attempt

4. Wally and the Beaver's dad + attire for a judge

5. Sunday church service + how old you are

6. Water barrier + writing instrument

7. Deface + alcoholic beverage often mixed with tonic

8. Nearest star + devoid of moisture

9. Male + bowler or pillbox + darkened skin

10. The final part + organ of hearing

---

 trivia

THE GOLDEN AGE OF RADIO

long-term memory

executive functioning

Here are a few questions on the history of the radio.

● Known as "The Schnozz," this radio comedian later accused young singer-comedian Danny Thomas of stealing his nose.

● This Indiana-born comedian is remembered for characters such as Clem Kadiddlehopper and Freddie the Freeloader.

● Their real names were Jim and Marion Jordan. What character names did they use on the radio from 1935 to 1959?

● Lucille Ball was the producers' first choice to play the lead in *Our Miss Brooks,* but this actress got the part, first on radio and then on television in 1952.

hurrah!

All the answers in this word definition game begin and end with the letter H.

1. Popular children's game that usually involves a chalk outline drawn on the sidewalk.

_____

2. With chopped potatoes, a good way to use leftover roast beef or corned beef.

_____

3. An ancient Middle Eastern candy usually made of sesame flour and honey.

_____

4. To fasten . . . or to marry.

_____

5. Nonsense! Bunk! Hooey!

_____

6. An exclamation in praise of God; it's also the chorus from Handel's _Messiah_.

_____

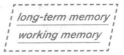

7. A feeling, a sixth sense, a premonition.

_____

8. A type of pipe that has a well of water to cool the smoke.

_____

9. As a noun, it's a small opening; as a verb, it means to emerge from an egg.

_____

10. Severe, cruel, unkind, or strict.

_____

11. A cage for rabbits . . . or a cupboard that usually has open shelves.

_____

☡ CLASSIC RIDDLE
JUST ONE ANSWER

If this riddle stumps you, think of each question individually.

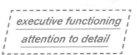

What is greater than God and more evil than the devil? The rich need it and the poor have it. And if you eat it you will die.

COLORS

long-term memory
working memory
executive functioning
processing speed

Can you come up with the name of at least one color for every letter of the alphabet? For an extra brain boost, see how many you can name in two minutes.

A _____

B _____

C _____

D _____

E _____

F _____

G _____

H _____

I _____

J _____

K _____

L _____

M _____

N _____

O _____

P _____

Q _____

R _____

S _____

T _____

U _____

V _____

W _____

X _____

Y _____

Z _____

concert time

working memory
executive functioning
attention to detail
multitasking
processing speed

In this scene, there are sixty-seven words **that begin with the letter C.** How many can you find?

rhyme ◆ time ◆

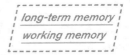
Each question in this game includes two definitions for two different words. The twist is, they will rhyme.

1. Tire changing tool; and the darkest color.

2. Fish enticer; and one less than nine.

3. Mini, midi, or dirndl; and actor Mr. Reynolds's first name.

4. Distracted and uninterested; and maker of the Mustang.

5. Strike with a fist, hit; and the midday meal.

6. A coquette or tease; and garment for the upper body,

7. The skin and fur of an animal; and to liquefy a solid by heat.

8. To despise or detest; and word that follows *roller* or *ice*.

9. A royal chair; and a piece of a skeleton.

10. Chubby Checker's dance; and the joint that connects the hand and the arm.

11. Domestic fowls; and the author of *Oliver Twist*.

12. Office supplies store; and a city in Italy or Florida.

13. An involuntary tremble as a result of being cold or frightened; and the Rhône or the Rhine.

14. Ten-pin or candlepin; and walking casually.

THIRTY › SECOND › MADNESS
The Seven Deadly Sins

How many of the seven deadly sins can you name in thirty seconds?

TRIMBLE

Trimble is a trivia game and a word jumble combined. First, answer the trivia questions and cross out the letters of each answer in the letter grid. Then rearrange the remaining letters (those that have not been crossed out) to reveal another word or phrase related to the same theme.

Questions: The theme is *beverages*, and the jumble consists of two words.

1. It takes twenty-one pounds of this to make a pound of butter.

2. Tart summer refresher.

3. The type of fruit juice recommended by the U.S. Kidney Foundation.

4. Two forms of this beverage are latté and espresso.

5. This is the only beverage necessary for life.

6. Made from the root or bark of the sassafras tree, this carbonated beverage was Dennis the Menace's favorite.

7. This sports drink was originally developed at the University of Florida to help athletes replace lost fluids.

A	A	A	A	A	A	B	B	C	C	C
D	D	D	E	E	E	E	E	E	E	E
E	E	E	F	F	G	I	I	K	L	L
M	M	N	N	O	O	O	O	O	R	R
R	R	R	R	R	T	T	T	T	W	Y

REPLACE THE
ARMADILLO

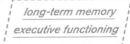

There's something wrong with these book, story, and movie titles. Can you fix them by replacing the word ARMADILLO with the correct animal?

1. *The Maltese ARMADILLO* by Dashiell Hammett

2. *One Flew Over the ARMADILLO'S Nest* by Ken Kesey

3. *Dances with ARMADILLOS* by Michael Blake

4. *The Velveteen ARMADILLO* by Margery Williams

5. *ARMADILLO Soup for the Soul* by Jack Canfield and Mark Victor Hansen

6. *The Silence of the ARMADILLOS* by Thomas Harris

7. *To Kill a ARMADILLO* by Harper Lee

8. *Lonesome ARMADILLO* by Larry McMurtry

9. *Raging ARMADILLO: My Story* by Jake LaMotta

10. *ARMADILLOS in the Mist* by Dian Fossey

11. *Of ARMADILLOS and Men* by John Steinbeck

12. *The ARMADILLO of the Baskervilles* by Sir Arthur Conan Doyle

13. *They Shoot ARMADILLOS, Don't They?* by Horace McCoy

14. *Six Days of the ARMADILLO* by James Grady

15. *ARMADILLO, Run* by John Updike

16. *The ARMADILLO That Roared* by Leonard Wibberley

portmanteaus

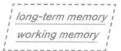

long-term memory
working memory

The word *portmanteau,* meaning suitcase, was given a new definition by Lewis Carroll (of *Alice in Wonderland* fame) to mean words that are made up of elements of two or more other words. Carroll was a prodigious coiner of portmanteaus, including *slithy* (from slimy and lithe) and *mimsy* (from miserable and flimsy). Portmanteaus can refer to most anything: geographical places (*Texarkana*), people (*Brangelina,* combining the names of Brad Pitt and Angelina Jolie), or things (*Blog,* from web log). Can you guess the two (or more) word origins of the following portmanteaus?

1. Alphabet

2. Motown

3. Brunch

4. Glitz

5. Interpol

6. Palimony

7. Monicagate

8. Beefalo

9. Biopic

10. Spanglish

11. Bollywood

12. Motel

13. Chortle

14. Intercom

15. Cockapoo

ODD MAN OUT

All of the items in each list have something in common except one thing. Your job is to figure out which item is the "Odd Man Out"—and why.

1. Iraq; France; Fiji; Peru

2. Cronkite; Winchell; Rather; Mondale; Matthau

3. Coffee; postcard; tattoo; balloon

4. Rita Hayworth; Lucille Ball; Audrey Hepburn; Maureen O'Hara

5. Melbourne; Milan; Munich; Marseille

6. Cherry; grapefruit; peach; plum; nectarine

7. Davis; Ellington; Armstrong; Haydn

8. Welsh rarebit; nachos; tempura; fondue

9. "Don't Be Cruel"; "All Shook Up"; "Please, Please Me"; "Hound Dog"

10. Advil; Motrin; Aleve; Zyrtec

11. Fusilli; Wapiti; Tagliatelle; Vermicelli

eponyms

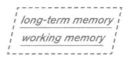

An eponym is a noun that is associated with a person's name. For example, calling someone a "Benedict Arnold" means that he's a traitor. Some eponyms are a little less obvious. The Barbie doll takes its name from Barbara Handler, the daughter of the doll's inventor. It's also common for a disease, such as Alzheimer's, to take the name of the researcher who first identified it. How many eponyms do you know?

1. A reading and writing system for the blind, named after its French inventor.

2. An epithet that means miserly or cheap, derived from a character in a Charles Dickens's story.

3. A salad with Romaine lettuce, croutons, Parmesan cheese, anchovies, and a raw egg, named after the Italian American restaurateur who created it.

4. An ornamental mat often placed on side tables or under lamps, named after a seventeenth-century drape maker.

5. A common small aquarium fish, named after the nineteenth-century British naturalist who discovered it near Trinidad.

6. A one-piece, tight-fitting garment worn by gymnasts and dancers, named after a nineteenth-century French acrobat.

7. An addictive substance, named after the sixteenth-century French diplomat who introduced tobacco to France.

8. Usually the tallest ride at a fair or amusement park, named after the American engineer who invented it for the 1893 Chicago World's Columbian Exposition.

9. The process of sterilizing milk and other dairy products, named after the pioneering French chemist and microbiologist who invented it.

10. A hide-away bed named after its American inventor who was granted a patent in 1916.

PUT **THE LIST** IN ORDER

Put each list of four or five items in the order called for in the instruction.

① Put this list of famous men in order of their age, starting with the youngest:

___ **a.** Harrison Ford

___ **b.** Woody Allen

___ **c.** Donald Trump

___ **d.** Warren Beatty

② Put these animals in order by how much they weigh, starting with the heaviest:

___ **a.** Gorilla

___ **b.** Polar bear

___ **c.** Hippopotamus

___ **d.** African elephant

___ **e.** Giraffe

③ Put this list of lakes in order, going from east to west:

___ **a.** Lake Erie

___ **b.** Lake Champlain

___ **c.** Lake Tahoe

___ **d.** Great Salt Lake

④ Put this list of recent U.S. presidents in order of their birthplace, going from north to south:

___ **a.** Ronald Reagan

___ **b.** Bill Clinton

___ **c.** Barack Obama

___ **d.** George W. Bush

⑤ Put these countries in order by population, starting with the largest:

___ **a.** Germany

___ **b.** Russia

___ **c.** Brazil

___ **d.** United Kingdom

___ **e.** Mexico

⑥ Put this list of the four longest rivers in the world in order, starting with the longest:

___ **a.** Yangtze

___ **b.** Mississippi

___ **c.** Amazon

___ **d.** Nile

⑦ Put these inventions in order of when they were invented, starting with the earliest:

___ **a.** Scissors

___ **b.** Helicopter

___ **c.** Bicycle

___ **d.** Cash register

___ **e.** Sewing Machine

⑧ Put this list of the five most-spoken languages in the world (by native speakers) in order, starting with the most native speakers:

___ **a.** Russian

___ **b.** English

___ **c.** Hindi

___ **d.** Mandarin Chinese

___ **e.** Spanish

⑨ Put this list of the longest-running television shows (that are still on the air) in order, starting with the longest running:

___ **a.** *General Hospital*

___ **b.** *Masterpiece Theater*

___ **c.** *The Tonight Show*

___ **d.** *Meet the Press*

⑩ Put this list of presidents' children in order of when they were born, starting with the earliest born:

___ **a.** John F. Kennedy Jr.

___ **b.** Ron Reagan

___ **c.** Caroline Kennedy

___ **d.** Amy Carter

Stinky Pinky

We have twentieth-century humorist George S. Kaufman to thank for this game (and its unusual title). Each Stinky Pinky answer contains two words that rhyme—but you have to figure out what that answer is from an offbeat definition.

1. A juvenile breathing organ

2. Manolo Blahniks for a female sheep

3. A "how-to" volume for felons

4. An unkind place of learning

5. A boring pituitary

6. A plumber's tool from Marseilles

7. A bankrupt part of an egg

8. The center violin

9. A dreadful breakfast cake

10. A frosty precious metal

11. A scary Indian tent

12. A steak burglar

13. Evil man of the cloth

14. Faux snow

ELEMENTARY SCIENCE

long-term memory
executive functioning

A little geology and chemistry in this quiz.

● This is the hardest mineral on earth . . . and a "girl's best friend."

● Even babies know that this is the softest mineral on earth.

● This addictive substance, which is a powerful stimulant, is consumed by 90 percent of Americans daily in their food and drink.

● All non-alloy (unmixed) metals —such as platinum, aluminum, zinc, and tin—are grayish-white, except for these two common ones.

What a Pair

Harvard and Yale, Thunder and Lightning, Coke and Pepsi are all common pairs . . . but what about *Wonder and Perrier?* If you redefine *Wonder and Perrier* correctly, you'll come up with the more familiar pairing *Bread and Water.* How many familiar pairs can you make from the clues below?

1. Mr. Brokaw . . . and Mr. Springer

2. A mixed fruit juice drink . . . and Ms. Garland

3. Mr. Flintstone . . . and a root spice that makes delicious cookies

4. Comic actress Ms. White . . . and 1940s femme fatal Ms. Lake

5. Mr. Franklin, for short . . . and Mr. Lewis, Dean's former partner

6. Mongrel dog . . . and Mr. Foxworthy

7. Mr. Cavett . . . and Ms. Fonda

8. Mr. Kerouac . . . and Ms. St. John

9. William _____, founder of the Keystone State . . . and the person who serves customers in a bank

10. Mr. Gibson or Kuralt . . . and Ms. Ross of the Supremes.

11. Where cows and sheep sleep . . . and belonging to the aristocratic class or showing high moral principles

---

 trivia

ISLANDS

long-term memory

executive functioning

How well do you know the world's islands?

● Although this state is the nation's fourth smallest, it is composed of 132 islands, reefs, and shoals that extend for 1,500 miles in the Pacific Ocean.

● Scientists aren't entirely sure whether this land mass is the largest island or the smallest continent in the world.

● This Italian city, famous for the gondolas that glide through its canals, is made up of 118 small islands.

● This small South Carolina island sports more than two dozen golf courses.

DOUBLE TROUBLE

Compound words are made up of two smaller words, such as *hayloft* or *watchtower*. In this game, we give the second half of some compound words. You must identify the one word that precedes each of them to make a compound word. For example, given the words *weed, coast,* and *sick,* the one word that makes each a compound word is *sea* (*seaweed, seacoast,* and *seasick*).

1. House, robe, water, tub

_____ (hint: b)

2. Dream, break, light, time

_____ (hint: d)

3. Cut, brush, dresser, spray

_____ (hint: h)

4. Lord, mark, slide, locked

_____ (hint: l)

5. Mail, smith, berries, jack

_____ (hint: b)

6. Beam, shine, walk, light

_____ (hint: m)

7. Holder, luck, belly, hole

_____ (hint: p)

8. Shield, fall, pipe, swept

_____ (hint: w)

9. Bell, knob, mat, way

_____ (hint: d)

10. Bee, comb, dew, moon

_____ (hint: h)

11. Back, boy, hanger, weight

_____ (hint: p)

12. Sty, pen, tail, skin

_____ (hint: p)

*oop*s!

All the answers in this word definition game contain the consecutive letters OOP.

1. A brief film or television outtake that has a humorous error.

2. A group of soldiers or boy scouts.

3. A small porch with stairs in front of an apartment building. (It's a great place to sit and talk to the neighbors!)

4. Where the chickens go home to roost.

5. A quantity of ice cream.

6. To hang down, like a hound dog's ears.

7. An informal name for the game of basketball.

8. To nose around into someone's private affairs.

9. To collaborate or work jointly together toward the same end.

10. An ambiguity or omission in a law or contract that a person can use to avoid a penalty or responsibility.

11. A sailboat with a single mast, a mainsail, and a jib.

12. A barrel maker . . . or CNN's nighttime anchorman Anderson.

Finish the Saying

Can you finish these familiar proverbs and sayings? (The number in parentheses indicates how many words are in the correct answer.)

1. Experience is the

_____ (2)

2. Discretion is the

_____

_____ (4)

3. Bad news

_____ (2)

4. Jack of all trades,

_____ (3)

5. Necessity is the

_____ (3)

6. Nothing is certain but

_____ (3)

7. Nothing ventured,

_____ (2)

8. Once bitten,

_____ (2)

9. Still waters

_____ (2)

10. Practice

_____ (2)

11. Home is where

_____ (3)

Body Expressions

Fill in the blank space with the body part that completes the two-word adjectival phrase.

1. _____ -tingling

2. _____ -opening

3. _____ -curdling

4. _____ -tapping

5. _____ -crushing

6. _____ -raising

7. _____ -rending

8. _____ -dropping

9. _____ -boggling

10. _____ -watering

wacky wordies

Shot

THE KNIFE
go

① _____

② _____

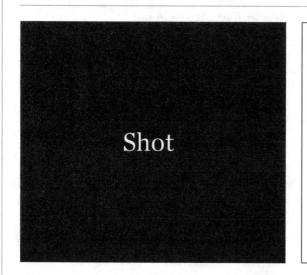

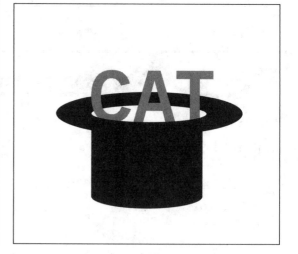

③ _____

④ _____

To solve these fun puzzles, look carefully at each frame, because the arrangement of the letters is a key clue to the familiar phrase contained within. For example, if the word *school* were placed high up in the frame, the answer would be *high school.* Or if the phrase "easy pieces" occurred five times in the frame, the answer would be *Five Easy Pieces.*

Benny & Kennedy

The UtahIowaMaineIdaho

5 _____

6 _____

|||Read|||

year year year year year year year *ITCH*

7 _____

8 _____

Finish the Quote

Can you finish these well-known quotations?

1. John F. Kennedy: "Ask not what your country can do for you, . . ." (8 words)

_____

2. Ronald Reagan: "Mr. Gorbachev, open this gate! Mr. Gorbachev, . . ." (4 words)

_____

3. George H. W. Bush: "And [Congress will] push, and I'll say no, and they'll push again, and I'll say to them, 'Read my lips, . . .'" (3 words)

_____

4. Franklin D. Roosevelt: "First of all, let me assert my firm belief that the only thing we have to fear . . ." (3 words)

_____

5. Henry Ford: "People can have a Model T in any color, so long as . . ." (2 words)

_____

6. Muhammad Ali: "I'm gonna float like a butterfly and . . ." (4 words)

_____

7. Harry Truman: "If you can't stand the heat . . ." (5 words)

_____

8. Nathan Hale: "I only regret that I have but one life . . ." (5 words)

_____

9. Lou Gehrig: "Today I consider myself the luckiest man . . ." (6 words)

_____

10. Theodore Roosevelt: "I have always been fond of the West African proverb: 'Speak softly and . . .'" (4 words)

_____

world of music

All of the geographical locations in these song lyrics are missing. Can you supply them?

1. There'll be bluebirds over the white cliffs of _____.

2. How're you gonna keep 'em down on the farm after they've seen _____ ?

3. He's leavin' (leavin') on a midnight train to _____.

4. Do you know the way to _____ ?

5. Meet me in _____.

6. O, little town of _____, how still we see thee lie . . .

7. And the _____ lineman is still on the line.

8. If you're going to _____, be sure to wear some flowers in your hair.

9. The sun shines bright on my old _____ home.

10. I was dancin' with my darlin' to the _____ waltz.

Famous Critters

Can you identify what type of animal each of these famous critters is?

1. Cheeta

2. Chuck E. Cheese

3. Curious George

4. Flicka

5. Gentle Ben

6. Kermit

7. Pegasus

8. Pepe Le Pew

9. Punxsutawney Phil

10. Rocky and Bullwinkle

11. Sea Biscuit

12. Topo Gigio

13. Winnie-the-Pooh

Anagrams

The letters of each word in this list can be arranged in multiple ways to form other words. We provide the word and the number of anagrams that are possible to make.

1. Loop (2) _____ _____

2. Mesa (2) _____ _____

3. Abets (4) _____ _____ _____ _____

4. Taser (4) _____ _____ _____ _____

5. Leapt (3) _____ _____ _____

6. Bleary (2) _____ _____

7. Stable (2) _____ _____

8. Starer (3) _____ _____ _____

REPLACE POTTERSVILLE

There's something not quite right about these film, TV, book, and song titles. You need to correct them by replacing the word POTTERSVILLE with the real location.

1. *A Tree Grows in POTTERSVILLE*

2. *April in POTTERSVILLE*

3. *Blue POTTERSVILLE*

4. *"POTTERSVILLE on My Mind"*

5. *"POTTERSVILLE Choo Choo"*

6. *"I Left My Heart in POTTERSVILLE"*

7. *Lost in POTTERSVILLE*

8. *"POTTERSVILLE, Here I Come"*

9. *WKRP in POTTERSVILLE*

A LOT OF CATS

Each time you see the 🐱 it stands for the consecutive letters CAT. Can you find all eighteen words in the grid—printed forward, backward, and diagonally—that contain CAT? For an extra-challenging brain workout, put a two-minute timer on this game and don't use the word list unless you get stuck.

```
        W                           G
    V   R                       P   T
    K   A   K               U   S   W
X   E   L  🐱   J       S   Y   L   J   E
Y   D   L   Z   N  🐱   L   A   O   N   R
Z   U   I   T   X   A   R   K  🐱   O   U
Z  🐱   P   ●  🐱   D   P   ●   I   L  🐱
V   E   R   Z   E   C   Z   C   O   H   I
Y   A   E   H   R   Y   H   O   N  🐱   R
B   R  🐱   Z       ●           P   Y   E   A
J   O   O   I   X   W   V   Y   T   D   C
    V   B   G   O   L   A  🐱   K   W
        X  🐱   E   N   S   G   J
        Y   K  🐱   Z   Z
```

Word List

❍ Bobcat	❍ Catalog	❍ Category	❍ Caricature
❍ Cattle	❍ Copycat	❍ Vacation	❍ Decathlon
❍ Catnap	❍ Educate	❍ Catalyst	❍ Caterpillar
❍ Scatter	❍ Location	❍ Cathedral	

❍ Cater
❍ Catch
❍ Catsup

Follow the Rules

If you follow each instruction precisely, you will discover the second half of the phrase: "Old age is not . . ." We've provided the first line, and the rest is up to you. A gold star to the solver who gets it right on the first try. This game is harder than you think.

1. With no spaces between words, write down the phrase: O L D   A G E   I S   N O T

2. Remove the third letter and place it at the end.

3. Swap the sixth and the tenth letters.

4. If Montana is in the Pacific Time Zone, place MT after the N. If not, place TM after the N.

5. Place an F in the beginning.

6. Remove the S and replace it with an H.

7. If Robert Redford is over seventy years old, place an R in the sixth position. If not, place a Y in the sixth position.

8. Remove the seventh letter and place it before the last T.

9. Place an I in the twelfth position.

10. Remove the first A and the last O.

11. Remove the third, fourth, and eighth letters.

O	L	D	A	G	E	I	S	N	O	T

Did you get the right answer?

FIDDLE FADDLE

All of the two-word phrases in this game begin with the initials F and F.

1. Her cookbook was written in 1896.

_____ _____

2. McDonald's or Burger King fare.

_____ _____

3. Dieters look for this designation on the foods they buy.

_____ _____

4. Smokey the Bear's target.

_____ _____

5. Fallen arches.

_____ _____

6. Footwear for the beach.

_____ _____

7. For this type of angling, the bait hovers over the water's surface.

_____ _____

8. Where huddles and touchdowns occur.

_____ _____

9. Spain's last dictator.

_____ _____

10. A desirable object that someone wants but should not have, like the apple in the Garden of Eden.

_____ _____

11. Carbon-rich energy sources formed by the decomposition of dead organisms.

_____ _____

12. Washington, Jefferson, or Franklin, for example.

_____ _____

13. The brief period after a parachutist jumps out of the plane but before he deploys his parachute.

_____ _____

14. Airline bonus program.

_____ _____

15. Clarence Birdseye's product.

_____ _____

16. An irresistibly attractive woman who leads men into dangerous situations.

_____ _____

PICTURE THEMES

The pictures in each column may seem like they have nothing in common. But if you look carefully, you'll see a theme emerge. Can you figure out the unique theme for each column of three pictures?

Column A

Column B

A _____

B _____

C _____ D _____

Major League Baseball Teams

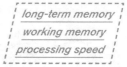

long-term memory
working memory
processing speed

How many of the thirty major league baseball teams can you name in one minute?

what's your movie song IQ?

Given a sampling of the lyrics, can you identify the movie from its famous song?

1. "A kiss on the hand might be quite continental . . ."

_____

2. "Moon River, wider than a mile . . ."

_____

3. "Summertime and the livin' is easy . . ."

_____

4. "Gonna fly now. Flying high now."

_____

5. "Raindrops on roses and whiskers on kittens . . ."

_____

6. "I could have spread my wings and done a thousand things . . ."

_____

7. "Some enchanted evening, you may see a stranger . . ."

_____

8. "Shall we dance? On a bright cloud of music, shall we fly?"

_____

9. "I'm gonna live forever, I'm gonna learn how to fly."

_____

10. "Well, you can tell by the way I use my walk . . ."

_____

11. "Every night in my dreams, I see you, I feel you . . ."

_____

12. "You and me, we sweat and strain . . ."

_____

---

 trivia

UNIQUE STATES

long-term memory
executive functioning

These questions focus on unique features or accomplishments of some U.S. states.

- What is the only U.S. state that borders only one other U.S. state?

- What is the only U.S. state whose name starts with two vowels?

- Which state was the first to grant women the right to vote?

- Which is the only U.S. state that consists entirely of two separate peninsulas?

APRIL IN HISTORY

This trivia quiz will stretch your long-term memory muscles.

753 B.C. According to legend, these twin brothers founded the city of Rome.

1492 Christopher Columbus received a commission from these monarchs to seek a westward ocean passage to Asia.

1775 Paul Revere rode twelve miles from Boston to this Massachusetts town to warn the colonists that the British were coming.

1861 The Civil War began when Confederate forces fired on this South Carolina fort.

1865 President Abraham Lincoln, while watching a play at this Washington, DC, theater, was shot by John Wilkes Booth.

1896 The first modern Olympic games, with athletes (male only) from fourteen countries competing in forty-three events, took place in this city.

1912 The luxury liner *Titanic,* which had left on its maiden voyage from this English port city, sank in the North Atlantic off Newfoundland.

1913 Swedish American inventor Gideon Sundback filed a patent for this device, which he called a "separable fastener."

1936 Bruno Hauptmann was electrocuted in Trenton, New Jersey, for this very high-profile crime.

1945 As Russian troops approached his Berlin bunker, Adolf Hitler committed suicide along with his wife of one day. What was her name?

1945 The nation mourned the passing of Franklin D. Roosevelt. What was the cause of his death?

1947 He broke the color barrier in baseball when he debuted with the Brooklyn Dodgers.

1953 American scientist James Watson and British scientist Francis Crick discovered the structure of this material—the biological building block that carries all the genetic information for living things.

1961 This Russian cosmonaut became the first human being ever to travel in space. The flight lasted 118 minutes from blastoff to landing and orbited the earth once.

1964 The African nations of Tanganyika and Zanzibar merged their territories and their names to form this new nation.

1968 At the age of thirty-nine, civil rights leader Martin Luther King Jr. was shot to death in this city.

1975 As the last U.S. helicopters left the country, this South Vietnamese capital surrendered to the Communist North Vietnam.

1986 An explosion and fire occurred in the No. 4 reactor at the Chernobyl nuclear power plant in this country.

1993 A fifty-one-day siege at the Branch Davidian compound near this Texas city ended when the building was set on fire by the people hiding inside.

1995 A truck bomb exploded outside the Alfred P. Murrah building in this city, killing 168 people and injuring many more.

1999 Two students from this Colorado high school went on a shooting rampage, killing thirteen people before taking their own lives.

trivia

FAMOUS DISASTERS

long-term memory
executive functioning

No corner of the world is immune to disaster. How many of these can you recall?

● This 1871 disaster began in the O'Leary's barn—but no one knows if the cow was to blame.

● The first time a disaster was captured live on film was this 1937 fiery event over Lakehurst, New Jersey. "Oh, the humanity!"

● What caused the 2004 tsunami (tidal wave) that left nearly 250,000 people dead and wiped out whole towns and villages in Southeast Asia?

● In A.D. 79, Mt. Vesuvius erupted near the Bay of Naples and buried two towns that would not be uncovered for nearly two thousand years. Can you name one of those two towns?

whatzit

How many clues do you need to guess what the WHATZIT is? One to three clues—Outstanding; three to seven clues—Very Good; seven to ten clues—Time to study up on your WHATZITs.

1. The WHATZIT originated in South America.

2. In the 1800s WHATZITs were considered food for livestock and the poor.

3. Today, the average American consumes more than six pounds of WHATZITs each year.

4. There are four types of WHATZITs grown in the United States: runner, Virginia, Spanish, and Valencia.

5. Astronaut Alan Shepard brought a WHATZIT with him to the moon.

6. Tom Miller pushed a WHATZIT to the top of Pike's Peak (14,100 feet), using his nose, in four days, twenty-three hours, forty-seven minutes, and three seconds.

7. About 1.5 percent of the U.S. population is allergic to WHATZITs, which are actually legumes, related to beans and lentils.

8. George Washington Carver, who researched and developed more than three hundred uses for WHATZITs, is considered "The Father of the WHATZIT Industry."

9. Two presidents, Thomas Jefferson and Jimmy Carter, were WHATZIT farmers.

10. The late conservative commentator William F. Buckley once said, "If WHATZIT butter were more expensive, it would be considered a gourmet food."

whoozy

How many clues do you need to guess who the WHOOZY is? One to three clues—Outstanding; three to seven clues—Very Good; seven to ten clues—Time to study up on your WHOOZYs.

1. WHOOZY was born into a wealthy New York family in 1884.

2. WHOOZY was tutored at home, and at the age of fifteen went to a finishing school near London.

3. WHOOZY returned home at age seventeen and became a social worker in the East Side slums of New York City.

4. When she was twenty, WHOOZY's uncle, the president of the United States, gave her away at her wedding.

5. WHOOZY's mother-in-law, who had vociferously opposed the marriage, dominated household matters until the couple moved away to Albany.

6. WHOOZY had four sons, one daughter, and one stillborn son.

7. In 1918 WHOOZY discovered (from letters she found in his suitcase) that her husband was involved in a four-year love affair. They didn't divorce, but maintained separate lives thereafter.

8. WHOOZY's husband was elected governor of New York in 1928.

9. When her husband was elected president of the United States in 1932, WHOOZY profoundly changed the role of the First Lady, continuing to speak out on behalf of the poor, women's rights, and in support of the civil rights movement.

10. WHOOZY died in 1962, two years after she was struck by a car in New York City, an occurrence that precipitated a steep decline in her health.

NAME MERGE

long-term memory

executive functioning

Given a clue for each of two famous people, can you figure out what name they share? For example: *Clarence Thomas Jefferson* or *Jesse James Cagney*.

1. Long-haired country music singer/songwriter famous for "On the Road Again"; and the first post-apartheid president of South Africa.

2. Dancing star of *Singin' in the Rain*; and Regis Philbin's last sidekick.

3. Cincinnati Reds player who admitted to betting on baseball; and mother of a Massachusetts political dynasty.

4. Art Garfunkel's singing partner; and the acerbic judge on *American Idol*.

5. Famous flag seamstress; and Monica's brother from the TV show *Friends*.

6. Romantic comedy actress who starred in *Sleepless in Seattle* and *You've Got Mail*; and the actor who was married to Farrah Fawcett and is Tatum's dad.

7. Famous Dutch diary writer; and legendary American architect who designed the Guggenheim Museum.

8. Yankee's legend dubbed "The Sultan of Swat"; and the second woman justice to serve on the Supreme Court.

9. Actor who played Opie Taylor and Richie Cunningham; and the pioneering sports journalist and announcer who would always "tell it like it is."

10. Cleft-chinned actor who played the title role in *Spartacus*; and World War II U.S. Army general active in the Pacific theater.

GEOGRAPHICAL DOUBLE ENTENDRES

This is a word game combined with a trivia game in which you name the geographical place—which is also a word for something entirely different.

long-term memory
working memory
executive functioning

1. A city in southwestern Georgia or . . . another word for prairies.

2. A county in Ireland or . . . a wine bottle stopper.

3. A city in the Mojave Desert or . . . sewing tools.

4. A city in Oregon or . . . female siblings.

5. An Irish city or . . . a short, often naughty, poem.

6. The former name of the Hawaiian Islands or . . . a common lunch food.

7. A river located mainly in Idaho or . . . a legless reptile.

8. A remote Polynesian island or . . . a key Christian holiday.

9. A town in New Mexico or . . . an old-time TV game show.

10. A city in Italy or . . . a luncheon meat.

---

 trivia

OHIO BORN

long-term memory
executive functioning

You don't have to be from Ohio to come up with names of these famous folks.

● This feminist leader and cofounder of *Ms. Magazine* was born in Toledo, Ohio, in 1934.

● Best known as the controversial owner of the New York Yankees, he was born in Rocky River, Ohio, in 1930.

● Born in Mt. Vernon, Ohio, this comedian was best known as Uncle Arthur on *Bewitched* and as the quick-witted "center square" of a popular game show.

● This flamboyant boxing promoter, noted for his unusual hairdo, was born in Cleveland in 1931.

COTTON CANDY

All of the two-word answers in this game begin with the initials C and C.

1. Visa or Diners Club.

_____ _____

2. Alan Funt's television series . . . Smile!

_____ _____

3. This NASA space center was renamed for President Kennedy in 1963, but reverted back to its original name a decade later.

_____ _____

4. Also called a flattop, this 1950s men's hairstyle is popular again.

_____ _____

5. The world's last manually-operated transportation system of this type is an icon of San Francisco, California.

_____ _____

6. This National League baseball team has played in Wrigley Field since 1916.

_____ _____

7. All you need for this child's game is a long piece of string and two hands.

_____ _____

8. Lunchmeats, such as bologna, ham, and corned beef.

_____ _____

9. One of the most creative and influential people of the silent film era, his best-known character was The Little Tramp.

_____ _____

10. In Lewis Carroll's _Alice in Wonderland,_ this feline character had a distinctive mischievous grin.

_____ _____

11. The object of this game is to move ten marbles from one point of a six-pointed star to the opposite point.

_____ _____

12. A numismatist.

_____ _____

What Do They Have in Common?

Each question contains a list of several items. Can you figure out what they have in common?

1. Snare, bass, conga, and tom-tom

2. Lou, Murray, Ted, and Sue Ann

3. Naan, brioche, and challah

4. Lux, Lava, and Zest

5. Cyan, ultramarine, and periwinkle

6. Morgan, Arabian, Pinto, and Appaloosa

7. Weissmuller, Spitz, and Phelps

8. Abyssinian, Siamese, and Burmese

9. Champion, Silver, and Trigger

10. Hitch, slip, or figure eight

11. Kildare, Casey, Quinn, and Welby

12. Toe loop, double axel, and triple lutz

13. Anguilla, St. Martin, Grand Cayman, and Aruba

WOWIE!

All the answers in this quiz contain at least two W's.

1. "When you're alone and life is making you lonely you can always go . . ."

_____

2. This small cart can make gardening a lot easier.

_____

3. A person who speaks out about illegal or unethical activity at his workplace.

_____

4. A gathering of Native Americans where they dance, sing, socialize, and honor Indian culture.

_____

5. A person who hides aboard a ship or airplane to obtain free transportation.

_____

6. A person who isn't asked to dance at a social event.

_____

7. Invented in England by Edwin Budding in 1827, this device was a superior alternative to a scythe in grooming sports grounds and elegant gardens.

_____

8. The magazine published by the Jehovah's Witnesses and often distributed in their door-to-door ministry.

_____

9. A collective term for duck, geese, and swans.

_____

10. A class of boxers who tip the scale at 140 to 147 pounds.

_____

11. These domed, rounded homes of early Native Americans were covered by grass, bark, hides, or cloth.

_____

12. You'll never quit smoking without this.

_____

13. Bumbling, clumsy, inelegant, uncomfortable.

_____

14. This is what you have to do to get food from the mouth to the stomach.

_____

just one letter

We're looking for one-letter answers in this game.

1. The symbol for sleep or snoring.

_____

2. President with a one-letter nickname.

_____

3. The symbol for the British pound and the Italian lira resembles this letter.

_____

4. What a fork in the road looks like.

_____

5. Just an average performance on an exam or test.

_____

6. Four of these make a club for rural youngsters.

_____

7. A double curve in the road.

_____

8. He made James Bond's gadgets.

_____

9. Universal donor blood type.

_____

10. A dash in printer's language.

_____

11. Chromosome that determines male gender.

_____

Alma's Shopping List

Alma is a great shopper, but a really bad speller. Every item on her shopping list is misspelled by one letter. Can you fix it? (*Note: All of the items on the list are common brand names or generic names for foods and other items that are found in a grocery store.*) For an extra brain boost, see how many answers you can get in one minute.

1. Popper   **8.** Sour

2. Beads   **9.** Plus

3. Peace   **10.** Beep

4. Handy   **11.** Wish

5. Baron   **12.** Spritz

6. Brainy   **13.** Grades

7. Money   **14.** Gloves

Compound Word

Each picture represents one half of a compound word. For example, if you combine *key* and *hole,* you get *keyhole.* How many of the twelve possible compound words can you find? For an extra brain boost, see how many compound words you can find in two minutes. (*Note: Each picture is used only once.*)

Search

1 _____
2 _____
3 _____
4 _____
5 _____
6 _____
7 _____
8 _____
9 _____
10 _____
11 _____
12 _____

va-va-voom!

All the answers in this word definition game begin with the letters VA.

1. An available hotel or motel room.

2. Where a bank keeps the money.

3. This injection produces immunity against a disease.

4. From the 1880s to the early 1930s these live variety shows were the most popular theatrical entertainment in the United States.

5. This is the low area of land between mountains.

6. According to folklore, they live by night and sleep by day—in coffins.

7. A space entirely devoid of matter . . . or a household appliance.

8. A person who wanders from place to place without a home or job.

9. A short length of curtain hung at the top of a window or over the top of a longer curtain.

10. A graduating student with the highest academic achievements.

11. Worth a great deal of money.

12. A style of beard.

13. In 1872, a chemist distilled unrefined petroleum to make this healing jelly.

14. To destroy or damage property for no particular reason.

TOUGHER GOING

HOMO**NYMS**

Homonyms are two or more words that are pronounced the same way but have different meanings and/or spellings. In this game, we supply the definitions, and you must not only provide the homonyms, but SPELL them correctly as well!

1. A hollow or empty space; and the entire thing.

_____   _____

2. Wound by scratching or tearing; and shopping center.

_____   _____

3. Forced something open using leverage; and dignity and self-respect.

_____   _____

4. Young bird's squeaky sound; and stingy and miserly.

_____   _____

5. A pudding-like dessert; and large mammal with antlers.

_____   _____

6. Golf course; and a wild cat, sometimes spotted, with tufted ears.

_____   _____

7. A bed on a train; and the beginning of a life.

_____   _____

8. From starting point to destination; and part of the plant that is underground.

_____   _____

9. A plank of timber; and wearied and uninterested.

_____   _____

10. Take hold suddenly and forcibly; and expanses of salt water.

_____   _____

U.S. Currency

As of 2010, the U.S. Mint produces twelve different denominations of currency (including paper bills and coins). How many can you name in one minute? And for a harder challenge, you can also try to name the image that is on the front of each bill and coin.

---

what's the missing number?

Fill in the missing number from this list of expressions and titles.

1. _____ *Minutes* (TV)

2. _____ minutes of fame

3. _____ Pennsylvania Avenue

4. _____ *Sunset Strip* (TV)

5. _____ wheel drive

6. _____ dollar question

7. _____ Heinz varieties

8. _____ finger discount

9. _____ keys on a piano

10. _____ *Arabian Nights*

11. _____ -wheeler

12. *The* _____ *Steps*

13. _____ *Degrees of Separation*

WHERE'S THE LANDMARK?

Identify the country connected with each famous landmark.

long-term memory
executive functioning
attention to detail

1 _____

2 _____

3 _____

4 _____

5 _____

6 _____

7 _____

8 _____

mum's the word

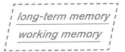

All the answers in this word definition game begin and end with the letter M.

1. A delicious fungus—but watch out for a poisonous one!

_____

2. The Guggenheim or the Louvre.

_____

3. Decorative initial on jewelry or towels.

_____

4. One thousand years.

_____

5. Screening test for breast cancer.

_____

6. The unintentional use of an incorrect word, as in: "The policeman comprehended the thief." (The word should be *apprehended*.)

_____

7. A large and stately edifice that houses a tomb or tombs.

_____

8. Violent and damaging disorder; chaos.

_____

9. A pipe with a bowl made of a soft, clay-like material that's often ornately carved.

_____

10. The chemical breakdown of food in the body to produce energy.

_____

11. A brief note or written message, especially in business or diplomacy.

_____

12. A teeny, tiny living thing, such as bacteria or viruses.

_____

13. A common road surface of broken stones and tar.

_____

14. To disfigure, wound, or disable.

_____

AKA Acronyms

Acronyms are a series of letters used in place of a word or name. How many of the acronyms below can you identify correctly?

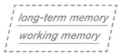

long-term memory

working memory

1. The Army listed the soldier as **MIA**, but he was really just **AWOL**.

2. Don's sister told him to **RSVP** to the invitation **ASAP**.

3. A background check showed that the applicant had both a **B and E** and a **DUI** on his record.

4. The **DJ** laughed when he was asked if he had a turntable that could play an **LP**.

5. At the end of a long week, Margaret's coworkers held a **TGIF** party, but it was strictly **BYOB**.

6. The **CFO** worried that the bottom line would be hurt if the company lost the **TM** on its most popular brand.

7. Joe had a low **GPA,** but he was still a **BMOC** because he played football.

8. Sally realized she had the wrong **SS** number on her **IRA**.

9. The couple decided it was time to buy an **HDTV** with an **LCD** screen.

10. The **RN** arrived on the accident scene before the **EMT**s and gave **CPR** to a teenager who wasn't breathing.

11. Jean couldn't remember if the documentary she wanted to see was going to be on **HBO** or **PBS**.

12. The young couple liked their bank's low rate on the **ARM;** but because they didn't have a big enough down payment, they would have to pay extra for **PMI**.

13. Since George was living in snowy Canada, he was hoping to buy a **VW** with **AWD**.

14. In 2005, the per capita **GNP** of the **UK** was $37,632.

What's the Question?

Remember "Where's the beef?" That famous question lived on long past its original use in a Wendy's commercial. Let's see how many questions, drawn from movies, songs, TV, and the news you can identify.

1. Bugs usually asks this question while he's chewing on a carrot.

2. In 1953, Patti Page asked about the price of a pet in this musical question.

3. The answer to this Abbott and Costello question is "Who."

4. "Why can't a woman be more like a man?" asked Henry Higgins in this popular musical.

5. "Who was that masked man?"

6. Peggy Lee made this existential question and song title a hit in 1969. (Maybe she "broke out the booze and had a ball" when the song reached the top ten.)

7. Finish this nightly public service announcement question from the 1960s: "It's eleven o'clock; do you know . . . ?"

8. The response to the title of this 1967 film starring Spencer Tracy and Katharine Hepburn was Sidney Poitier.

9. Hank Williams Jr. recorded the opening theme for *Monday Night Football,* which asked sports fans this question.

10. When Hamlet asks this question, he's trying to decide whether or not to commit suicide.

11. Taxi driver Travis Bickle, played by Robert De Niro, asks this question several times while looking in a mirror.

12. Which actress asked this question (and then answered it): "You know how to whistle, don't you, Steve? You just put your lips together and blow."

13. TV's Kojack, who was very fond of lollipops, asked this question at least once in every show.

HIDDEN COLORS

long-term memory
working memory
executive functioning

Can you identify the colors that complete the words in this list? For example, the color that completes" bo _ _ _om" is *red* (bo*red*om). For a more strenuous brain exercise, try covering up the definitions and solving the incomplete word without any hints.

1. Ch__ __ __ __ __maid   *This hard worker cleans up in a hotel.*

2. P__ __ __ __cutor   *Lawyer who conducts the case against a criminal defendant.*

3. __ __ __ __rium   *Home for guppies.*

4. __ __ __ __ __puff   *A yummy dessert . . . or a weak, ineffectual person.*

5. C__ __ __its   *List of names at the end of a movie.*

6. Comp__ __ __ __nt   *A polite expression of praise or admiration.*

7. Bo__ __ __y   *The scientific study of plants.*

8. T__ __ __ __worthy   *Honest, honorable, reliable.*

9. S__ __ __ __ __th   *Military plane built to be undetectable by radar.*

10. Stin__ __ __ __   *Fish with a long tail that ends with a barb.*

11. __ __ __ __fish   *A domesticated carp… often a child's first pet.*

12. Pi__ __ __ __st   *This holds the lemon meringue or banana cream.*

13. Im__ __ __ __ __   *To charge the holder of a public office with misconduct.*

---

 trivia

FIRST LADIES

long-term memory

executive functioning

Not every American president has been married while in office, but each has had a First Lady. Here are questions about four of them.

● She was the first First Lady to hire a press secretary. She also won an Emmy award for her televised tour of the White House.

● Her real first name was Thelma, though everyone called her Pat.

● Who were the two First Ladies who had only one child, both of whom were daughters?

● She was dubbed the "Secret President" for the role she played when her husband suffered a debilitating stroke in 1919.

*kn*ot too hard

All of the answers in this word definition game begin with the letters KN.

1. It's all the facts, information, and skills you've acquired through education and experience.

2. A canvas backpack.

3. Basically, it's an overweight hot dog.

4. Small, worthless decorative items.

5. Finger joints.

6. Official full name of New York's pro basketball team.

7. Types of this are bowie and Swiss Army.

8. It would be hard to open a door without this.

9. An extremely attractive woman; it's also a boxer's goal.

10. The name of Israel's legislative body.

INVENTIONS

long-term memory
executive functioning

A little technological history in this quiz.

● This undersea explorer and filmmaker was also involved in the invention of scuba gear, which made deep-sea diving possible.

● Nils Bohlin was working for this car company when he invented the modern seat belt in 1959, thus saving millions of lives.

● Elisha Gray Otis made skyscrapers possible with this invention in 1852.

● Alfred Nobel created the Nobel Prize to improve his legacy. He did not want to be remembered solely as the inventor of this destructive substance.

ODD MAN **OUT**

All of the items in each list have something in common except one thing. Your job is to figure out which item is the "Odd Man Out"—and why.

1. *Goldfinger*; *Live and Let Die*; *A Study in Scarlet*; *Dr. No*

2. Alex Rodriquez; Derek Jeter; Tom Brady; Randy Johnson; Jason Giambi

3. Snowflake; Elephant; Tree; Automobile

4. C; L; V; X; Z

5. Flounder; Shrimp; Lobster; Crab

6. Meg; Jo; Mary; Beth; Amy

7. URL; HTTP; PDF; ESP; WWW

8. Berlin; Brussels; Bonn; Baden-Baden

9. *On Golden Pond*; *The Devil Wears Prada*; *Kramer vs. Kramer*; *Sophie's Choice*

10. Huntington, WV; Trenton, NJ; Baltimore, MD; Richmond, VA

MAY IN HISTORY

This trivia quiz will stretch your long-term memory muscles.

1792   Twenty-four merchants met under a buttonwood tree on what is now Wall Street and formed this financial organization.

1844   This inventor tapped out the first ever telegraph message: "What hath God wrought?"

1859   This sound was heard in the city of London for the first time. After more than 150 years, it can still be heard four times every hour.

1869   A golden spike was installed in Promontory Summit, Utah, to mark the completion of this transportation achievement.

1915   A torpedo from a German U-boat hit this British ocean liner off the coast of Ireland, killing nearly twelve hundred passengers and crew.

1916   The cover of *The Saturday Evening Post* featured the first of more than three hundred cover illustrations by this artist.

1925   Substitute high school teacher John T. Scopes was arrested in Tennessee for teaching this subject.

1927   Aviator Charles Lindbergh took off from Roosevelt Field on Long Island, New York, on the first nonstop solo flight across the Atlantic Ocean. Where did he land almost thirty-four hours later?

1934   This criminal pair died in a hail of bullets when they were ambushed by police in Black Lake, Louisiana.

1934   The first quintuplets known to survive infancy were born in Ontario, Canada. What was their last name?

1953   Sir Edmund Hillary of New Zealand and Tenzing Norgay of Nepal were the first humans to accomplish this remarkable achievement.

1954   The U.S. Supreme Court issued the landmark ruling Brown v. Board of Education. What was the issue at stake in that case?

1960   The U.S. Food and Drug Administration approved the use of a drug called Envoid for this purpose—but only for married women.

1961   Forty-five million Americans watched this astronaut become America's first space traveler as he made a fifteen-minute flight aboard *Freedom 7,* launched from Cape Canaveral, Florida.

1970   National Guardsmen in this state opened fire on anti-war protesters at Kent State University, killing four students and wounding nine others.

1972   Arthur Bremer, a Wisconsin man looking for fame and recognition, shot this presidential candidate in a Maryland shopping mall.

1980   The World Health Organization announced that this devastating disease had been eradicated from the earth.

1994   This former political prisoner was elected president of South Africa in that country's first fully democratic election.

1994   The "Chunnel" officially opened, linking these two countries by train.

2005   Former FBI official W. Mark Felt revealed to *Vanity Fair* magazine this secret, which he had held for more than three decades.

2011   This elite U.S. military force captured and killed Osama bin Laden in Pakistan.

Three-Letter Anatomy

There are ten parts of the body with names that are only three letters long. How many can you name in one minute?

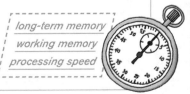

long-term memory
working memory
processing speed

IN THE KITCHEN

Word Finders are excellent brain exercises. Can you find all twenty-five kitchen-related items in the grid—printed forward, backward, and diagonally? For an extra-challenging brain workout, put a two-minute timer on this game and don't use the word list unless you get stuck.

```
D  N  R  E  T  A  R  G  R  S  A  T  W
M  I  C  R  O  W  A  V  E  T  E  O  Q
C  P  S  W  S  E  W  J  X  U  T  P  R
A  G  P  H  L  L  J  S  I  N  K  K  E
N  N  A  I  W  D  S  S  M  N  Z  C  T
O  I  T  S  O  A  A  N  I  U  X  O  S
P  L  U  K  B  L  S  F  O  V  G  R  A
E  L  L  Z  T  Y  E  H  V  O  Q  C  O
N  O  A  I  C  O  F  F  E  E  P  O  T
E  R  F  O  R  K  S  Q  N  R  Y  S  K
R  W  J  E  G  G  S  S  L  E  W  O  T
```

Word List

- Tea
- Salt
- Mug
- Eggs
- Grill
- Sink
- Nuts
- Knife
- Oven
- Ladle
- Mixer
- Forks
- Bowls
- Whisk
- Grater
- Spatula
- Spoons
- Towels
- Toaster
- Crock-Pot
- Rolling Pin
- Coffeepot
- Microwave
- Dishwasher
- Can Opener

rhyme ❖ time ❖

Each question in this game includes two definitions for two different words. The twist is, they will rhyme.

long-term memory
working memory

1. Extreme anger; and area in a theater where the play takes place.

_____

2. To reprimand or rebuke; and not young.

_____

3. Small garden area; and luxury boat.

_____

4. Juicy purple fruit; and rundown area of a city with substandard housing.

_____

5. Low-valued playing card; and a waterfowl known for flying in V-formation during migration.

_____

6. A spectral figure; and cooked bread.

_____

7. A soldier's water bottle; and the stimulant in tea and coffee.

_____

8. The capital of Arkansas; and a device that wakes you up.

_____

9. Veracity; and, as the saying goes, this is wasted on the young.

_____

10. Physics or chemistry; and dishwasher or refrigerator.

_____

11. Islands north of Cuba; and sleepwear.

_____

12. To swear or blaspheme; and Florence Nightingale's profession.

_____

DON'T BE BLUE

long-term memory

executive functioning

This quiz tests your knowledge of common expressions that use the word *blue*.

● Descriptive phrase for a manual laborer.

● You have this if you're related to royalty.

● Happening very rarely.

● Happening unexpectedly or suddenly.

● An architect's drawings.

● Archaic legislation that enforces religious or moral standards such as prohibitions on Sunday shopping or the sale of alcohol.

● The nickname for IBM.

● Term used for conservative Democratic office holders.

REPLACE THE
SPINACH

long-term memory
executive functioning

There's something wrong with these book, song, and movie titles. Can you fix them by replacing the word SPINACH with the correct food?

1. *Charlie and the SPINACH Factory* by Roald Dahl

2. *The SPINACH of Wrath* by John Steinbeck

3. *Green SPINACH and SPINACH* by Dr. Seuss

4. *Fried Green SPINACH at the Whistle Stop Café* by Fannie Flagg

5. *Goodbye, Mr. SPINACH* by James Hilton

6. *James and the Giant SPINACH* by Roald Dahl

7. "SPINACH Fields Forever" by John Lennon and Paul McCartney

8. *Mystic SPINACH* (Movie)

9. *A SPINACH Called Wanda* (Movie)

down to the wire

long-term memory

Fill in the blank space with the word (or words) that completes each expression.

1. _____ to the Marines

2. _____ the minute

3. _____ to the core

4. _____ to the people

5. _____ to the dogs

6. _____ to the fire

7. _____ to the occasion

8. _____ to the world

9. _____ to the rule

10. _____ to the city

11. _____ to the mob

something *old,* something *new*

All of the answers in this word definition game contain the letters OLD or NEW.

1. A type of salamander.

2. That furry green stuff that grows on cheese that's been around too long.

3. Low-melting alloy that is used to connect metal to metal.

4. A fig cookie . . . or a seventeenth-century physicist.

5. Another word for infant.

6. This decorative fish, which comes in all shapes, sizes, and colors, is actually a carp.

7. A temporary structure on the outside of a building, often used by construction workers.

8. You'll need this to play Pin the Tail on the Donkey.

9. You can always find horoscopes, classified ads, and op-eds in one of these.

10. You don't want to take a pan off the stove without one of these.

11. Many a new bride has been carried over this.

12. This word can precede *war* or *turkey*.

13. It's just another word for wallet.

14. A piece of tough fibrous tissue that connects muscle to bone or bone to bone. It's good to have in the body . . . but not in a steak.

DOUBLE TROUBLE

Compound words are made up of two smaller words, such as *hayloft* or *watchtower*. In this game, we give the second half of some compound words. You must identify the one word that precedes each of them to make a compound word. For example, given the words *weed, coast,* and *sick,* the one word that makes each a compound word is *sea* (*seaweed, seacoast,* and *seasick*).

1. Ball, glasses, lashes, witness

_____ (hint: e)

2. Shake, cuff, writing, some

_____ (hint: h)

3. Paste, pick, brush

_____ (hint: t)

4. Nail, print, tip

_____ (hint: f)

5. Cut, do, dresser

_____ (hint: h)

6. Ball, stool, note, locker

_____ (hint: f)

7. Ache, beat, burn

_____ (hint: h)

8. Storm, wash, teaser, child

_____ (hint: b)

9. Lights, quarters, lock, phones

_____ (hint: h)

10. Ground, stroke, fire, drop

_____ (hint: b)

11. Pit, chair, rest

_____ (hint: a)

12. Line, tie, lace

_____ (hint: n)

13. Screw, tack, nail

_____ (hint: t)

Political Quotes

Politics gives rise to many memorable sayings. Can you identify the speaker from these well-known quotes? For an extra brain challenge, try to remember the context of each quote.

long-term memory
executive functioning

1. "Yes, we can."

2. "Mission accomplished."

3. "I didn't inhale."

4. "Oh, the vision thing . . ."

5. "I took the initiative in creating the Internet."

6. "I'm not a crook."

7. "There you go again."

8. ". . . the only thing we have to fear is fear itself."

9. "The fundamentals of the economy are strong."

10. "I've looked on a lot of women with lust. I've committed adultery in my heart many times."

---

 trivia

NAME THE CONDIMENT

long-term memory

executive functioning

We use condiments all the time; but do you know what's in them?

● Tomatoes and corn syrup are the main ingredients in this common condiment.

● This condiment is made of not much more than egg yolks and vegetable oil.

● Vinegar, molasses, corn syrup, and anchovies are the main ingredients of this condiment first made by John Lea and William Perrins in Worcester, England.

● Apricot jam and applesauce usually make up this Asian condiment.

LAUNDRY LIST

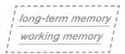

All of the two-word answers in this game begin with the initials L and L.

1. Nickname for famous pilot Charles Lindbergh.

_____ _____

2. Regulation to keep dogs from roaming free.

_____ _____

3. Baseball organization for youngsters.

_____ _____

4. Document that makes it legal for a restaurant to sell wine and beer.

_____ _____

5. Superman's girlfriend.

_____ _____

6. Term for a home phone that distinguishes it from a cell phone.

_____ _____

7. Claim to fame of Eugene V. Debs, Walter Reuther, and Jimmy Hoffa.

_____ _____

8. Female star of a play or movie.

_____ _____

9. Legislation requiring car manufacturers to repair, replace, or refund the cost of an automobile if it breaks down within a short time after purchase.

_____ _____

10. Paper with pre-punched holes for a three-ring binder.

_____ _____

11. Another term for crow's feet, or the wrinkles in the skin at the outer corner of your eyes.

_____ _____

IT'S A JOB

long-term memory
executive functioning

The individuals in each set of clues all shared the same profession. Do you know what it is in each case?

● Clarence Darrow, Johnny Cochran, F. Lee Bailey

● Michael DeBakey, C. Everett Koop, Benjamin Spock

● I. M. Pei, Frank Gehry, Frank Lloyd Wright

● Sally Ride, Buzz Aldrin, Neil Armstrong

FOREIGN CITIES

Can you come up with at least one non-American city for every letter of the alphabet? For an extra brain boost, see how many you can name in two minutes.

A _____   N _____

B _____   O _____

C _____   P _____

D _____   Q _____

E _____   R _____

F _____   S _____

G _____   T _____

H _____   U _____

I _____   V _____

J _____   W _____

K _____   X _____

L _____   Y _____

M _____   Z _____

a *bag* of tricks

All of the answers in this word definition game contain the consecutive letters BAG.

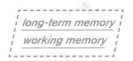

long-term memory
working memory

1. Surprisingly, many historians believe that this musical instrument originated in the Middle East, not in Scotland.

2. The capital of Iraq.

3. A seedy, run-down hotel or lodging.

4. A person who talks and talks and talks, but says little of value.

5. A long, thin loaf of French bread.

6. Nickname for a wealthy person.

7. This safety device was first introduced in American cars in the mid-1970s.

8. A small, round bread that likely originated in the Jewish area of Krakow, Poland, in the seventeenth century.

9. Northerners who went South after the Civil War to profit from the unsettled conditions during Reconstruction.

10. This root vegetable, called *swede* in England, originated in Scandinavia or Russia as a cross between the cabbage and the turnip. (Basically, it tastes like a turnip.)

11. This is an old-fashioned word for lower back pain.

12. An Italian custard dessert that is traditionally served with fresh figs, but in the U.S. is often served in a champagne glass with strawberries or blueberries.

TRIMBLE

Trimble is a trivia game and a word jumble combined. First, answer the trivia questions and cross out the letters of each answer in the letter grid. Then rearrange the remaining letters (those that have not been crossed out) to reveal another word or phrase related to the same theme.

Questions: The theme is *colors*, and the jumble consists of one word.

1. What was the name of the Lone Ranger's horse?

2. What was the color of Dorothy's magical slippers in *The Wizard of Oz*?

3. What was the color of the submarine in the Beatles song and animated movie?

4. What is the color of the third-place medal in the Olympics?

5. What color is Dr. Seuss's Grinch who stole Christmas?

6. What was the last name of the television journalist character played by Candice Bergen?

7. What was the color of Paul Bunyan's ox Babe?

8. Prisoners are often made to wear this color jumpsuit so that they will be easy to see if they escape.

9. This is the appropriate gift for a fiftieth anniversary.

10. What color is known worldwide as the signal for surrender or truce?

A	A	B	B	B	B	D	D	E	E
E	E	E	E	E	E	E	E	G	G
G	H	I	I	L	L	L	L	L	L
N	N	N	N	N	O	O	O	O	O
R	R	R	R	R	R	R	S	T	U
U	V	V	W	W	W	Y	Y	Z	

Add It Up

This game involves simple addition—but you have to figure out which numbers to add up.

1. Add the number of sides in a pentagon to the area code for Washington, DC.

_____

2. Add the year that Pearl Harbor was attacked to the year of the Cuban Missile Crisis.

_____

3. Add the number of U.S. states to the number of countries in the United Kingdom.

_____

4. Add the number of keys on a piano to the number of days in Hanukkah.

_____

5. Add the number of Supreme Court justices to the length of one term in office for a U.S. Senator.

_____

6. Add the number of days in a fortnight to the number of years in a score.

_____

7. Add the Roman numerals X plus C to V and give the answer in English.

_____

8. Add the boiling point of water (in Fahrenheit) to the normal temperature of the human body.

_____

HISTORY OF MEDICINE

long-term memory
executive functioning

How well do you know these medical milestones?

● This miracle drug was discovered when a dish in Alexander Fleming's laboratory was contaminated by a fungus.

● In 1885, nine-year-old Joseph Meister became the first person to survive rabies thanks to an experimental treatment by this French chemist and "Father of Microbiology."

● In the late nineteenth century, the Bayer Co. marketed two pain killers. One was an opiate, and the other was derived from willow bark. What names did Bayer give to these two drugs?

● This drug was a popular tranquilizer in Europe and Canada until it was connected to devastating birth defects.

by *land* and *sea*

All of the answers in this word definition game contain the word *land* or *sea*.

1. He collects the rent.

_____

2. The year is divided into four of these.

_____

3. Clams, oysters, haddock . . . collectively.

_____

4. A way to reclaim ground . . . and a place to dump the trash.

_____

5. A false spoken statement that damages a person's reputation.

_____

6. A little sports car doesn't have this.

_____

7. In coastal areas these are as common as pigeons.

_____

8. "No man is an _____" wrote John Donne.

_____

9. What you get when you sew two pieces of cloth together.

_____

10. The single most important safety feature in a car.

_____

11. Patients with gastrointestinal problems are often told to eat this kind of diet.

_____

12. In Hawaii, it's called a *lei*; or, it's the last name of Liza Minnelli's mother.

_____

13. In New York, it's the Empire State Building. In San Francisco, it's the Golden Gate Bridge.

_____

14. Reagan's win in 1984, Johnson's win in 1964, and Roosevelt's win in 1936. They sure were winners!

_____

wacky wordies

LOVERSTORN**LOVERS**

w**i**tness

❶ _____

❷ _____

THE SUN
everything

❸ _____

❹ _____

To solve these fun puzzles, look carefully at each frame, because the arrangement of the letters is a key clue to the familiar phrase contained within. For example, if the word *school* were placed high up in the frame, the answer would be *high school*. Or if the phrase "easy pieces" occurred five times in the frame, the answer would be *Five Easy Pieces*.

Lady *Lady* *Lady* *Lady* *Lady* *Lady*
Lady *Lady* *Lady* *Lady* *Lady* *Lady*
Lady *Lady* *Lady* *Lady* *Lady* *Lady*
Lady *Lady* *Lady* *Lady* *Lady* *Lady*
Lady *Lady* *Lady* *Lady* *Lady* *Lady*
Lady *Lady* *Lady* *Lady* *Lady* *Lady*

5 _____

6 _____

3 4 5 6 7 8 9 10
13 14 15 16 17 18
21 SAFETY 29
32 33 34 35 36
39 40 41 42 43

DANCING DANCING DANCING DANCING DANCING

7 _____

8 _____

Follow the Rules

To find out the ending to the phrase that begins "A light purse . . . ," carefully read each instruction below and do exactly what it says. The first answer has been provided. But beware, following the rules is not as easy as it seems.

1. With no spaces between words, write down the phrase: A LIGHT PURSE

2. Swap the first and third letters.

3. If San Francisco is the capital of California, place an S in the next-to-last position. If not, place an S in the third position.

4. Place an E in the eighth position.

5. If Thomas Jefferson was a vice president, place a V before the P. If not, place a V after the P.

6. Place a Y in the tenth position.

7. Place an A after the third vowel.

8. Change the twelfth letter to a C.

9. Remove the second, fifth, and seventh letters.

A	L	I	G	H	T	P	U	R	S	E

Did you get the right answer?

Initial Reaction

long-term memory
executive functioning

Many people, like O. J. Simpson and B. B. King, are known by their first and middle initials. How many people can you identify from their lesser-known full first two names?

1. James Pierpont, American banker

2. Phineas Taylor, American showman

3. Herbert George, English science fiction author

4. William Claude, American comedian and comic actor

5. Edward Estlin, twentieth-century American poet

6. John Ronald Reuel, English adventure/fantasy author

7. Samuel Ichiye, Japanese American U.S. senator from California

8. Edward Francis, American financier and stock brokerage founder

9. Alan Alexander, English children's author

10. Ieoh Ming, Chinese American architect

11. James Cash, American department store founder

12. Jerome David, reclusive American author

13. Burrhus Frederic, American psychologist/ researcher

14. Thomas Stearns, American-born poet, author of *The Wasteland*

15. Maurits Cornelis, Dutch graphic artist inspired by mathematics and geometry

---

 trivia

IT'S SPRING!

long-term memory
executive functioning

How well do you know your spring flowers?

● It's likely that this spring flower was first imported to Holland from Turkey in the 1500s.

● This spring flower, sometimes called a jonquil, looks a bit like a cup and saucer.

● This yellowing blooming shrub was named after Scottish botanist William Forsyth.

● "When lilacs last in the dooryard bloom'd," was poet Walt Whitman's elegy to this fallen U.S. president.

CATCH SOME ZZ'S

All of the answers in this quiz contain double Z's.

1. Woozy.

2. Jigsaw.

3. Winter whiteout.

4. Music of Davis or Coltrane.

5. Common word for a scavenger bird.

6. To steal money from your workplace.

7. The sound of bacon cooking in the pan.

8. To wolf down a beverage.

9. The lowest balcony of a theater.

10. A perfect example of onomatopoeia, thanks to the honeybee.

11. Shutterbugs that pursue celebrities.

12. Jimmy Durante's nickname.

13. Italian cheese used on pizza.

14. Headgear for a dangerous dog.

15. Spout for a garden hose.

16. The thick-walled part of a bird's stomach that contains stones to grind food.

CLASSIC RIDDLE
A WINDY DAY

As with many classic riddles, the answer lies in a detail that is omitted from the story.

It was a very stormy day. The wind gusted up to seventy-five miles per hour. Joseph entered his apartment and noticed that he had left the window wide open. A strong wind was blowing the curtains into the room. In front of the window was an empty table. Joseph saw some broken glass and a puddle of water on the floor near the table. Just a few inches away, Mike and Ike were lying dead on the floor. How did they die?

ODD MAN OUT

All of the items in each list have something in common except one thing. Your job is to figure out which item is the "Odd Man Out"—and why.

1. Brioche; Goulash, Naan; Pita; Lavash

---

2. Angora; Borzoi; Burmese; Persian

---

3. December 7, 1941; August 29, 2005; September 11, 2001; July 4, 1976

---

4. The Great Emancipator; The Great Communicator; Honest Abe; The Rail-Splitter

---

5. *Who's Afraid of Virginia Woolf?*; *Cleopatra*; *What Ever Happened to Baby Jane?*; *National Velvet*

---

6. Howdy Doody; Mickey Mouse; Lamb Chop; Charlie McCarthy

---

7. Columbia; Challenger; Zenith; Endeavor

---

8. Andrew; Glenda; Richard; Jesse; Michael; Reggie

---

9. Harvard University; Columbia University; Tufts University; Brandeis University

---

10. Pineapple; Lemon; Squash; Corn; Cauliflower

DOUBLE TROUBLE

Compound words are made up of two smaller words,

such as *hayloft* or *watchtower*. In this game, we give the first half of some compound words. You must identify the one word that follows each of them to make a compound word. For example, given the words *knuckle, moth,* and *basket,* the one word that makes each a compound word is *ball* (*knuckleball, mothball,* and *basketball*).

1. Mocking, jail, humming, blue

_____ (hint: b)

2. Cheese, wash, table, face

_____ (hint: c)

3. Birth, cobble, mile, tomb

_____ (hint: s)

4. Street, box, side, motor

_____ (hint: c)

5. Dog, drift, fire, Holly

_____ (hint: w)

6. Dough, hazel, pea, chest

_____ (hint: n)

7. Eye, fiber, hour, wine

_____ (hint: g)

8. Lady, bed, litter, shutter

_____ (hint: b)

9. Face, fork, chair, shop, up

_____ (hint: l)

10. Trouble, pace, match

_____ (hint: m)

11. Bread, chop, lip, match, slap

_____ (hint: s)

12. Back, junk, lumber, school

_____ (hint: y)

13. Cubby, fox, man, pigeon

_____ (hint: h)

14. Boom, home, shanty, down

_____ (hint: t)

15. Jelly, shell, gold, cat

_____ (hint: f)

U.S. Surnames

long-term memory
working memory
processing speed

The most recent U.S. census confirms what most of us already know: that Smith is the most common last name in the United States. How many of the other top twenty most common U.S. surnames can you name in one minute? (*Note: Statistics are according to the 2010 U.S. Census.*)

trivia

IN THE MIDDLE

long-term memory
executive functioning

Can you come up with these famous people's equally famous middle names?	● Francis Key	● Frank Wright
	● Ralph Emerson	● John Booth

word play

These are word "riddles." For most of them, if you read the question carefully, the answer will come easily.

1. What starts with "e" and ends with "e" and contains one letter?

_____

2. What "room" has no door, no windows, no floor, and no roof?

_____

3. What is found in the middle of Texas?

_____

4. What is the difference between here and there?

_____

5. What letter comes after "b" in the alphabet?

_____

6. This person is always wiring for money. Who is he?

_____

REPLACE THE ELBOW

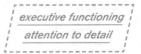

There's something wrong with these book and movie titles. Can you fix them by replacing the word ELBOW with the correct body part?

1. *The Man with the Golden ELBOW* by Nelson Algren

_____

2. *The Lovely ELBOWS* by Alice Sebold

_____

3. *Their ELBOWS Were Watching God* by Zora Neale Hurston

_____

4. *The ELBOW Is a Lonely Hunter* by Carson McCullers

_____

5. *The ELBOWmaid's Tale* by Margaret Atwood

_____

6. *ELBOWspray* (Movie and Musical)

_____

7. *BraveELBOW* (Movie)

_____

8. *Bury My ELBOW at Wounded ELBOW* by Dee Brown and Hampton Sides

_____

9. *The ELBOW of Our ELBOWS* by Thornton Wilder

_____

THE S HAVE IT

Can you identify these First Ladies just by looking at their eyes?

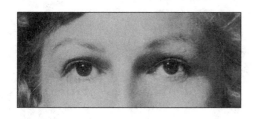

1 _____

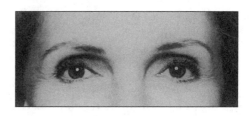

2 _____

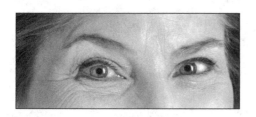

3 _____

4 _____

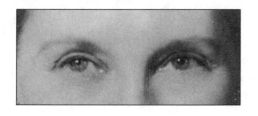

5 _____

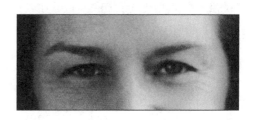

6 _____

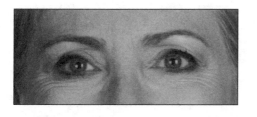

7 _____

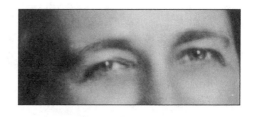

8 _____

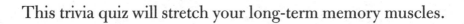

This trivia quiz will stretch your long-term memory muscles.

622 Muhammad, the founder of Islam, died in the city of Medina, located in this present-day country.

1692 Bridget Bishop was the first of twenty people to be executed for this crime in a Massachusetts town north of Boston.

1779 This Revolutionary War army general was court-martialed for plotting to hand over the U.S. fort at West Point, New York, to the British.

1876 Lt. Col. George Custer and his 7th Calvary were wiped out by Sioux and Cheyenne Indians in this famous Montana battle.

1885 This gift from France to honor the hundredth anniversary of the founding of the United States of America arrived by boat in New York Harbor.

1903 This business and manufacturing pioneer launched his Dearborn, Michigan, company with $28,000 in cash from a dozen investors. Within a couple of decades, his business grew into one of the largest and most profitable companies in the world.

1935 Bill Wilson and Dr. Bob Smith started this organization based on a twelve-step program of character development.

1944 The D-Day invasion of Europe took place as 156,000 Allied forces landed on the beaches of this French region.

1950 President Harry Truman ordered U.S. air and sea forces to this country to prevent the spread of Communism in Asia.

1953 This couple, convicted of conspiring to pass U.S. atomic secrets to the Soviet Union, was executed at Sing Sing Prison in upstate New York.

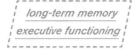

long-term memory
executive functioning

1963 This governor stood in front of a door at the University of Alabama in a symbolic attempt to block two African American students from enrolling in the school.

1966 The Supreme Court issued its landmark Miranda v. Arizona decision, which required police to do this before questioning a suspect.

1967 Lyndon Johnson nominated this Solicitor General to become the first African American justice on the Supreme Court.

1968 This Pop Art artist, known for his painted images of soup cans, was shot and nearly killed in his Manhattan studio.

1968 Senator Robert Kennedy was shot and mortally wounded in this Los Angeles hotel.

1973 This clean-cut White House lawyer began his testimony to the Senate Watergate Committee in which he would describe the cover-up of the Watergate break-in as "a cancer growing on the presidency."

1974 This new technique for saving choking victims was published in the *Journal of Emergency Medicine*.

1974 This ballet star ran three blocks to a waiting car in Toronto and thus effectively defected from the Soviet Union.

1997 Boxer Mike Tyson was disqualified from a heavyweight title fight for doing this.

1997 After 156 years of British rule, this colony was returned to China.

BEFORE THEY WERE PRESIDENT

long-term memory

executive functioning

Which U.S. presidents held these jobs before they were elected to the highest office in the land?

● Naval Officer, Farmer, and Governor of Georgia

● Haberdasher and County Judge in Missouri

● New York City Police Commissioner and Assistant Secretary of the Navy

● President of Princeton University and Governor of New Jersey

world of music

All of the geographical locations in these song lyrics are missing. Can you supply them?

1. Everybody's saying that there's nobody meaner than the
little old lady from _____.

2. Don't cry for me, _____.

3. The girl from _____ goes walking . . .

4. It's a long way to _____.

5. There is a rose in Spanish _____.

6. By the time I get to _____ she'll be rising.

7. Do you know what it means to miss _____?

8. Get your kicks on _____.

9. Woke up. It was a _____ morning and the first thing that I heard . . .

"C" ON THE MAP

long-term memory
executive functioning

You don't have to know everything about geography to succeed in this quiz . . . just those places whose names begin with the letter C.

● This Danish capital city is consistently on international lists as one of the cleanest and most livable cities in the world.

● This is the largest city on the Nile River.

● This Ohio city's airport is actually over the border in Kentucky.

● This is the second-largest nation in the world, yet it borders only one other country. Its two official languages are French and English.

● This is the most populous country in the Caribbean, and one of only five Communist states left in the world.

● This country's capital is Phnom Penh. It borders Thailand, Laos, and Vietnam, and in 1979, its savage dictator, Pol Pot, was deposed.

● This South American country is 2,700 miles long, but never more than 109 miles wide. It also lays claim to the world's southernmost city.

❓ CLASSIC RIDDLE
THE ELEVATOR RIDE

As with many classic riddles, the answer lies in a detail that is omitted from the story.

Mary is the first resident to move into a newly built apartment complex. She lives on the tenth floor. Every morning she takes the elevator to the ground floor and goes to work. Every evening, however, she gets off at the seventh floor and walks up three flights of stairs to her apartment. Why does she do this?

---

the *end*

All of the answers in this word definition game end with the word END.

1. To repair something.

2. To mix ingredients smoothly and inseparably.

3. This is what you do for a living if you make gimlets.

4. To take a lawbreaker into custody.

5. To create a false appearance, or act like nothing is wrong.

6. A comrade or chum.

7. To understand the nature or meaning of something.

8. A title of respect for a member of the clergy.

9. A monetary distribution to a stockholder.

10. To climb or go upward.

11. To irritate, insult, or behave in a disagreeable way.

12. To suggest someone for a job.

13. To behave as if stooping to the level of one considered inferior.

14. To hang by attachment to something above, like a chandelier.

Famous Movie Lines

How many of these memorable movie lines can you identify? Four stars if you can name the character, the actor who said the line, and the name of the film.

1. "I'm going to make him an offer he can't refuse."

2. "I'm as mad as hell, and I'm not going to take this anymore!"

3. "You can't handle the truth!"

4. "You're gonna need a bigger boat."

5. "I want to say one word to you. Just one word. Plastics."

6. "I'll have what she's having."

7. "I am big! It's the pictures that got small."

8. "La-dee-da, la-dee-da."

9. "As God is my witness, I'll never be hungry again."

10. "Get your stinking paws off me, you damned dirty ape!"

11. "Here's Johnny!"

12. "Open the pod bay doors, HAL."

13. "I feel the need—the need for speed!"

14. "Nobody puts Baby in a corner."

15. "I'm king of the world!"

THUMBS UP!

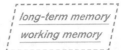

All the answers in this quiz begin with the letters TH.

1. Play venue.

2. Archaic word for *you*.

3. Seamstress's finger protector.

4. A person who studies religion.

5. A baker's dozen.

6. A roof covering of straw or a similar material.

7. Brand name for a vacuum flask.

8. Synonym finder.

9. Actor.

10. Bangkok's country.

11. M, in Roman numerals.

12. Do you remember your algebra? This is the word for a statement that has been proven to be true.

BY A LANDSLIDE

long-term memory
executive functioning

Every so often a president is elected by an overwhelming majority of votes. Can you recall these landslide victories?

● Democratic presidential candidate Walter Mondale won only his home state of Minnesota against this Republican.

● With a growing economy and a weak opponent, this Republican presidential candidate lost only Massachusetts and the District of Columbia in 1972.

● In 1964, Lyndon Johnson got the highest-ever percentage of the popular vote (61 percent) against this Republican senator.

● In 1936, U.S. voters, many of whom blamed the Republicans for the Great Depression, gave a landslide win to FDR over this Kansas governor.

Public Information

Most people know these two international symbols for *Ladies Room* and *Telephone*:

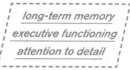
long-term memory
executive functioning
attention to detail

But do you know the meaning of the following less common symbols?

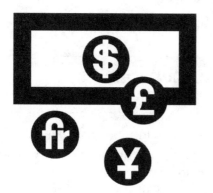

A _____

B _____

C _____

D _____

E _____

F _____

G _____

H _____

I _____

J _____

got an it*ch*?

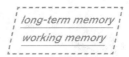

All of the answers in this word definition game end with the letters CH.

1. Seaside summertime playground.

_____

2. This will make your collar stand up.

_____

3. People from the Netherlands.

_____

4. The sound you hear when you bite into a piece of celery.

_____

5. A horse-drawn closed carriage used for traveling long distances.

_____

6. Archaic word for a country girl, servant girl, or strumpet.

_____

7. Zip, zero, nada.

_____

8. Also known as Bigfoot, this fabled ape-like creature is said to inhabit forests in the Pacific Northwest region of North America.

_____

9. A fink, stool pigeon, informant.

_____

10. For this sidewalk game, all you need is some chalk and a stone.

_____

11. Kiss.

_____

12. Satisfy your thirst.

_____

13. This is what happens if you don't lift the iron off the shirt.

_____

EXTREME GEOGRAPHY

long-term memory
executive functioning

Highest, lowest, hottest, coldest ... the earth is full of extremes. How well do you know your planet?

● Where is the highest spot on earth?

● What is the largest (in square miles) country on earth?

● What is the windiest continent on earth?

● In what North African country was the hottest temperature recorded?

TV Theme Songs

We provide a line from a television show theme song.
Can you name the show?

long-term memory
executive functioning

1. "Here's the story of a lovely lady . . ."

2. "A horse is a horse, of course, of course . . ."

3. "Well, we're movin' on up . . ."

4. "Come and listen to a story 'bout a man named Jed . . ."

5. "Boy, the way Glenn Miller played . . ."

6. "Thank you for being a friend . . ."

7. "Making your way in the world today . . ."

8. "There's a hold up in the Bronx . . ."

9. "Welcome back, your dreams were your ticket out . . ."

10. "Baby, if you've ever wondered . . . wondered whatever became of me . . ."

11. "I bet we've been together for a million years . . ."

12. ". . . schlemeel, schlemazel, hasenpfeffer incorporated . . ."

13. "The end of the Civil War was near when quite accidentally . . ."

14. "She was working in a bridal shop in Flushing, Queens . . ."

BORROWED FROM
India

All of the answers in this word definition game are common English words that originated in India.

1. Bedwear that's often flannel.

2. A thin bracelet with no clasp often worn in multiples.

3. Generic word for a sweet treat.

4. Actual money . . . not checks or credit cards.

5. A folding bed, often used for unexpected guests.

6. In ancient India, it meant "brother." In English it's a slang word for friend.

7. Another word for denim.

8. A common sweet citrus fruit.

9. Hair soap.

10. A humble little boat.

11. In Hindi, this means "wasteland" or "desert," but in English it's a dense, lush environment.

12. A tuxedo is incomplete without this.

13. Made from cane or beet, it's a dieter's nemesis.

14. This is a porch often found in the American south.

whoozy

long-term memory
executive functioning

How many clues do you need to guess who the WHOOZY is? One to three clues—Outstanding; three to seven clues—Very Good; six to eight clues—Time to study up on your WHOOZYs.

1. WHOOZY was born in 1809 in Boston. Orphaned at age two, he went to live with a childless couple in Virginia.

2. WHOOZY attended the University of Virginia but was expelled for not paying his gambling debts.

3. Accepted into West Point, WHOOZY only lasted one year. He intentionally got himself court-martialed for dereliction of duty.

4. At the age of 27, WHOOZY married his thirteen-year-old cousin in Baltimore. That same year he became editor of the *Messenger* but was soon fired due to drunkenness.

5. WHOOZY's talents as a writer began to receive increased recognition. In 1845, with the publication of his poem "The Raven," WHOOZY became a household name—though he only received nine dollars for the poem.

6. In 1847, WHOOZY's young wife died of tuberculosis. The next year he proposed marriage to and was accepted by poet Sarah Whitman; but due to his inability to stop drinking and his erratic behavior, the engagement was called off.

7. On October 6, 1849, WHOOZY was found near death on the streets of Baltimore. The cause was speculated to be alcoholism. He died the next day at the age of forty.

8. Some of WHOOZY's best-known stories are "The Telltale Heart," "The Pit and the Pendulum," "The Murders in the Rue Morgue," and "The Fall of the House of Usher."

---

 trivia

GUESS THE CATEGORY

long-term memory

executive functioning

The answers to these questions will give you a clue to this trivia category.

● Singing family in a 1970s situation comedy.

● Ken Kesey's book about a mental asylum. The movie starred Jack Nicholson.

● Author of *The Red Badge of Courage*.

● Famous English architect who designed London's St. Paul's Cathedral.

numerical titles

Can you fill in the missing number from each of these song, movie, and book titles?

1. "_____ Ways to Leave Your Lover"

2. *The House of the _____ Gables*

3. *A Tale of _____ Cities*

4. *Around the World in _____ Days*

5. *_____ Men and a Baby*

6. *Fahrenheit _____*

7. *_____ Is Enough*

8. "_____ Trombones"

9. *Ocean's _____*

10. *_____ Candles*

11. *Catch- _____*

12. *_____ Weddings and a Funeral*

13. *The _____ Steps*

14. *_____ Days of the Condor*

15. *North Dallas _____*

16. *The Crying of Lot _____*

17. *_____ Years of Solitude*

18. *_____ Coins in the Fountain*

19. *Slaughterhouse _____*

20. *_____ Dalmatians*

THIRTY>SECOND>MADNESS

States with Two-Word Names

How many of the ten states with two-word names can you name in thirty seconds?

_____   _____

_____   _____

_____   _____

_____   _____

_____   _____

What a Pair

Harvard and Yale, Thunder and Lightning, Coke and Pepsi are all common pairs . . . but what about *Wonder and Perrier?* If you redefine *Wonder and Perrier* correctly, you'll come up with the more familiar pairing *Bread and Water.* How many familiar pairs can you make from the clues below?

1. "Stop" to a film director . . . and arid.

2. TV's Mr. Serling . . . and a spool of film.

3. A bill passed by Congress . . . and a meal request to a waiter.

4. A method of curing meat . . . and reflective glass fixtures.

5. The person who transports your belongings to a new house . . . and a salt dispenser.

6. Court proceeding . . . and a mistake.

7. Light complexion . . . and a rectangle with four equal sides.

8. Long jacket . . . and to fasten with rope.

9. The opposite of multiply . . . and to vanquish.

10. A physical attack . . . and an energizer.

11. Clara, the "It Girl" . . . and a brand name of men's dress shirts since 1851.

12. A tune or aria . . . and the cha-cha.

13. Crazy or loco . . . and sliding metal bars that lock doors.

14. Macadam . . . and bird plumes.

15. A financial penalty or punishment . . . and a man unduly devoted to fashion.

JULY IN HISTORY

This trivia quiz will stretch your long-term memory muscles.

1789 Roughly one thousand French citizens stormed the Bastille—a critical turning point of the French Revolution. What was the Bastille?

1799 A black granite stone was discovered in Egypt that contained a legal decree in three written languages: ancient Greek, ancient Egyptian, and Hieroglyphics. What was the name of this stone, which finally enabled linguists to understand Hieroglyphics?

1804 Vice President Aaron Burr mortally wounded this former treasury secretary in a duel in Weehawken, New Jersey.

1826 John Adams and Thomas Jefferson, the second and third presidents of the United States, died on July 4 within hours of each other in their home states. Where did each die?

1897 This inventor was issued a U.S. patent for the radio.

1925 Adolf Hitler published this book, his personal manifesto.

1925 Two legendary lawyers faced off in Dayton, Tennessee, in the "trial of the century," in which high school science teacher John Scopes was accused of teaching evolution in violation of a Tennessee state law. Can you name these lawyers?

1946 This physician published a book that revolutionized the way children were raised for generations to come.

1948 This New York international airport was opened for business. It would later be called John F. Kennedy International Airport; but what did people call it for its first decade and a half?

1950 President Harry Truman authorized $15 million in military aid to this Southeast Asian country, signaling the beginning of U.S. involvement there.

1954 Marilyn Sheppard was found beaten to death in her Ohio home by her physician husband, Samuel Sheppard. He would eventually be convicted of the crime in a sensational murder trial. What television series did the Sheppard story inspire?

1961 This Nobel Prize–winning author used his favorite shotgun to commit suicide at his home in Ketchum, Idaho.

1966 Nineteen million senior citizens signed up for this new government program.

1969 Astronaut Neil Armstrong became the first man to set foot on the moon. What was his famous quote?

1969 Senator Edward Kennedy's Oldsmobile plunged off the Chappaquiddick Bridge on Martha's Vineyard, killing this twenty-eight-year-old female passenger.

1976 This fifteen-year-old Romanian gymnast became the first person in Olympic history to score a perfect 10 in gymnastics.

1978 Scientists around the world were waiting for news of the birth of Louise Brown in Oldham, England. Why?

1984 Democratic presidential candidate Walter Mondale named this New York congresswoman as his running mate, making her the first woman to run on a major party ticket.

1985 This Hollywood star became the first major celebrity to announce that he had AIDS, bringing much needed attention to this pandemic disease.

2008 Scientists reported that the Phoenix spacecraft had confirmed the presence of this in the soil of Mars.

RUSSIA

long-term memory

executive functioning

Here are four clues about Russia and Russians.

● Sergey Brin, one of the founders of this ubiquitous Internet search engine, was born in Moscow in 1973. His family emigrated to the U.S. six years later.

● This complex of buildings in Moscow was once the seat of the Soviet government and today houses Russia's presidential administration.

● This former KGB operative succeeded Boris Yeltsin in 2000 as the second president of Russia.

● She was born in Kiev in 1898; moved to Milwaukee when she was seven; moved to Palestine in 1921 after she got married; and became the fourth prime minister of Israel in 1969.

endings and beginnings

A compound word is made up of two smaller words, such as *stopwatch* or *panhandle*. In this game, we provide the first half of one compound word and the second half of another. Can you figure out the one word that completes them both? (If you get stuck, the first letter of the answer is provided in a hint.)

1. Slaughter _____ keeper (hint: h)

2. Butter_____shake (hint: m)

3. Bed _____ table (hint: t)

4. Child _____ wink (hint: h)

5. Cease _____ fighter (hint: f)

6. Lady _____ nail (hint: f)

7. Whirl _____ breaker (hint: w)

8. Laughing _____ broker (hint: s)

9. Birth _____ kicker (hint: p)

10. Card _____ walk (hint: b)

Who the What?

In this game, we supply the who and you must supply the what. For example: *Felix the _____*
Answer: *Cat*

1. Dora the _____

2. Jimmy the _____

3. Catherine the _____

4. Conan the _____

5. Oscar the _____

6. Ivan the _____

7. Joe the _____

8. Jack the _____

9. John the _____

10. André the _____

MERGE

long-term memory
executive functioning

Given a clue for each of two famous people, can you figure out what name they share? For example: *Clarence Thomas Jefferson* or *Jesse James Cagney*.

1. Astronaut and senator from Ohio; and one of the best-known bandleaders of the 1930s, whose plane disappeared over the English Channel in 1944.

2. Short story author of "The Gift of the Magi"; and Richard Nixon's secretary of state.

3. An openly gay liberal congressman from Massachusetts; and "Old Blue Eyes" from Hoboken, New Jersey.

4. Third president of the United States; and the first and only president of the Confederate States.

5. Author of "The Legend of Sleepy Hollow" and "Rip Van Winkle"; and the composer of "White Christmas" and "God Bless America."

6. The actor who played Colonel Potter in TV's *M*A*S*H*; and the actor who drove Miss Daisy.

7. In 1953, he was the first to scale Mt. Everest; and she's been a First Lady, a senator, and a secretary of state.

8. Actor who played George Costanza on *Seinfeld*; and the inventor of the telephone.

9. The actor famous for playing General Patton; and the "King of Ragtime" who composed the "Maple Leaf Rag" in 1899.

10. Author who introduced millions of children to Wonderland, the Cheshire Cat, and the Mad Hatter; and the actor who played Archie Bunker.

11. Broadway actress best known for playing Peter Pan; and prominent film director of *Taxi Driver*, *Raging Bull*, and *Goodfellas*.

PICTURE THEMES

These pictures may seem like they have nothing in common. But if you look carefully, you'll see a theme emerge. Can you figure out the unique theme for each column of three pictures?

Column A

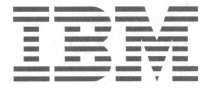

Column B

A _____

B _____

Column C

C _____

Column D

D _____

HIDDEN ANIMALS

Can you identify the animals that complete the words in this list? For example, the animal that completes "s_ _ _ ter" is *cat* (s*cat*ter). For a more strenuous brain exercise, try covering up the definitions and solving the incomplete word without any hints.

1. __ __ __ardly   *Lacking courage.*

2. G__ __ __mar   *The basic rules of language.*

3. T__ __ic   *Poisonous.*

4. Un__ __ __ __able *Intolerable, oppressive.*

5. Mi__ __ __ __ave   *An electromagnetic wave used in radar and cooking.*

6. __ __ __matic   *Having rigid opinions.*

7. Int__ _ _ _ __ous   *Term for a drug administered directly into the blood stream.*

8. S__ __ __ __holders   *People who own stock in a company.*

Alma's Shopping List

Alma is a great shopper, but a really bad speller. Every item on her shopping list is misspelled by one letter. Can you fix it? (*Note: All of the items on the list are common brand names or generic names for foods and other items that are found in a grocery store.*) For an extra brain boost, see how many answers you can get in one minute.

1. Cave

2. Union

3. Dream

4. Froth

5. Dime

6. Cheep

7. Chins

8. Sofa

9. Crept

10. Folders

11. Finger

12. Him

13. Break

14. Later

ODD MAN OUT

All of the items in each list have something in common except one thing. Your job is to figure out which item is the "Odd Man Out"—and why.

1. Hoover; Truman; Reagan; Eisenhower

2. Fedora; clog; bowler; cloche

3. Eyeglasses; elevator; shirt; remote control

4. Trafalgar Square; Left Bank; Covent Garden; Harrods

5. "It's Not for Me to Say"; "Misty"; "Chances Are"; "Folsom Prison Blues"

6. Barbados; Canary Islands; Cayman Islands; Turks & Caicos Islands

7. Brentwood; Crenshaw; Flatbush; Venice; Watts

8. *Singin' in the Rain*; *A Star Is Born*; *An American in Paris*; *On the Town*

9. Kreplach; cassoulet; wonton; pierogi

10. Tennis; squash; badminton; volleyball; Ping-Pong

11. Retractor; stethoscope; clamp; forceps

12. Guernsey; Jersey; Orkney; Ayrshire

PENCIL PLAY

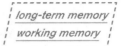

All of the two-word answers in this game begin with the initials P and P.

1. Spanish painter, sculptor, and cofounder of the Cubist movement, he lived most of his adult life in France.

_____

2. With the advent of cell phones, these are becoming rare.

_____

3. Popular during the 1950s, these calf-length trousers were also called clam diggers and Capri pants.

_____

4. Miser, cheapskate, skinflint, or tightwad.

_____

5. She was the tomboy in the comic strip _Peanuts_ . . . but was not named after the popular candy.

_____

6. The mischievous boy who lived on the small island of Neverland.

_____

7. Pretending to be dead or asleep in the face of a threat.

_____

8. Despotic leader of the Khmer Rouge in Cambodia.

_____

9. Gutenberg's mid-fifteenth century invention.

_____

10. Coveted award in journalism circles.

_____

11. The perfect ending to a Thanksgiving feast.

_____

12. Some Native American tribes smoked this in a ceremonial way to seal an agreement or a treaty.

_____

13. Table tennis.

_____

14. He used his magical musical instrument to lead the children of Hamelin, Germany away from town, and they were never seen again.

_____

Follow the Rules

Follow each instruction to find out the ending of the saying that begins "All mothers are . . ." We've provided the answer to the first instruction; the rest is up to you.

1. With no spaces between words, write down the phrase: A L L M O T H E R S A R E

2. Swap the second L with the second R.

3. If Florida is to the east of Puerto Rico, place an E at the end. If Florida is to the west of Puerto Rico, place a W at the beginning.

4. If a yard equals twenty-four inches, place YD after the M. If not, place IN after the M.

5. Place a K in the sixth position.

6. Double the ninth letter.

7. Place a G before the second A.

8. Swap the second and ninth letters.

9. Remove the consecutive letters O T H E R S and place them, in order, at the end.

10. Swap the fifth and eleventh letters.

11. Remove the first E and all A's and L's.

A	L	L	M	O	T	H	E	R	S	A	R	E

Did you get the right answer?

WORD PARTS

The word *menace* is defined as "a threat." In this game, however, we don't supply the definition of a word, but of its parts. For example, given the first clue "male adults," plus the second clue "the highest card in the deck," the answer is *menace (men + ace)*.

1. To ask for charity + the lowest cardinal number

_____

2. Car + pa's mate + facial spasm

_____

3. Slang for former spouse + plentiful

_____

4. Small hat + aptitude

_____

5. The total of a set of added numbers + the mother of Jesus

_____

6. Guys + to curse or use obscene language

_____

7. Mischievous child + atmosphere

_____

8. Headwear + a primary color

_____

9. A mongrel dog + not many

_____

10. Svelte + royal ruler

_____

---

 trivia

FOUR-SYLLABLE WORDS

long-term memory
executive functioning

All the answers in this quiz are four-syllable words.

● The largest specimen of this ferocious reptile was found in Louisiana and measured nineteen feet, two inches in length.

● The dictionary definition of this word is "disposed to preserve existing conditions, restore traditional ones, and oppose innovation."

● The march called "Pomp and Circumstance" by Sir Edward Elgar is heard often throughout May and June at this type of ceremony.

● Credit for this invention is often shared among John Logie Baird, Philo Farnsworth, and Vladimir Zworykin. Today, the average American home has 2.93 of these.

toponyms

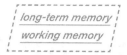
Toponym is just a fancy word for a place name. In this game we have a group of words that were derived from place names. For example, did you know that the French phrase *serge de Nîmes,* which means *"cloth of Nîmes"* (a city in France), is where the word *denim* came from?

1. A bathing suit named after the South Pacific atoll where atomic bombs were tested in the 1940s.

2. Ground beef named after a city in Germany.

3. A small yellow bird named after a string of islands off the northwest coast of mainland Africa.

4. A race of 26.2 miles named after a town in Greece.

5. A stiff paper for file folders or envelopes named after the capital city of the Philippines.

6. Worldwide sporting event named after the tallest mountain in Greece.

7. A very small, oily fish named after a Mediterranean island near Italy.

8. A small leafy green vegetable named after a city in Belgium.

9. A lightweight cotton fabric, usually with a colorful plaid design, named after a coastal city in southeastern India.

10. A rich sauce named after the Netherlands.

11. Men's formal wear named after a village in upstate New York.

12. A spicy chicken snack named after the city in New York where it originated.

13. A brimless hat named after a city in Morocco.

what's your movie song IQ?

Given a sampling of the lyrics, can you identify the movies that inspired them?

long-term memory
executive functioning

1. "Suicide is painless, it brings on many changes . . ."

_____

2. "Come on, babe, why don't we paint the town?"

_____

3. "Let's start at the very beginning, a very good place to start."

_____

4. "Did you ever know that you're my hero . . ."

_____

5. "When I was just a little girl, I asked my mother, what will I be . . ."

_____

6. "Start spreading the news, I'm leaving today . . ."

_____

7. "When you wish upon a star . . ."

_____

8. "Love, soft as an easy chair . . ."

_____

9. "If I should stay, I would only be in your way."

_____

10. "Round, like a circle in a spiral . . ."

_____

11. "The shadow of your smile, when you are gone . . ."

_____

---

 trivia

FATHER KNOWS BEST

long-term memory
executive functioning

Do you recognize these real or fictional dads from the names of their children?

● Father to Sondra, Denise, Theo, Vanessa, and Rudy.

● Father to George, Jeb, Neil, Marvin, Dorothy, and Robin.

● Father to Sonny, Fredo, Michael, and Connie.

● Father to Goneril, Regan, and Cordelia.

THE BLUES OR THE BLAHS

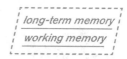
All of the answers in this quiz begin with the letters BL.

1. A severe snowstorm.

2. A person who tells secrets . . . or just talks too much.

3. Adipose tissue . . . especially for whales.

4. A small kitchen appliance.

5. McCarthy-era roster.

6. This breed of dog has a legendary sense of smell.

7. He was the British prime minister on September 11, 2001.

8. An afghan or coverlet.

9. All humans do this about ten times a minute.

10. Film clips that reveal funny or embarrassing mistakes.

11. The cheap seats in a baseball park.

12. The criminal offense of demanding money from a person in return for not revealing compromising information about him.

13. Zeppelin.

14. This Irish term describes talk that aims to charm, flatter, or persuade.

15. Sacrilegious speech about God or sacred things.

wacky wordies

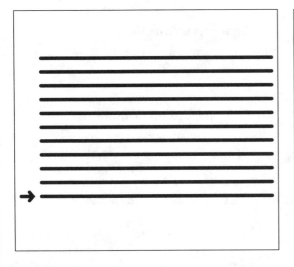

1. _____

2. _____

c i2i

3. _____

ar^{UP}ms

4. _____

To solve these fun puzzles, look carefully at each frame, because the arrangement of the letters is a key clue to the familiar phrase contained within. For example, if the word *school* were placed high up in the frame, the answer would be *high school.* Or if the phrase "easy pieces" occurred five times in the frame, the answer would be *Five Easy Pieces.*

drive THE ROAD

JOB **in** JOB

⑤ _____

⑥ _____

| 4 | 1 | 1 |

load

chin
chin

⑦ _____

⑧ _____

DISEASES

From A to Z, how many diseases, ailments, or conditions can you come up with in two minutes?

A _____

B _____

C _____

D _____

E _____

F _____

G _____

H _____

I _____

J _____

K _____

L _____

M _____

N _____

O _____

P _____

Q _____

R _____

S _____

T _____

U _____

V _____

W _____

X _____

Y _____

Z _____

SOBRIQUETS

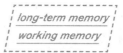

Unlike nicknames, which are generally used in place of a person's given name, sobriquets are used to describe a person's character, skill, strength, personality, achievement, or reputation. Sobriquets are usually bestowed by historians, journalists, press agents, critics, or the public, and can be either an honor or an insult. How many famous people can you name when given their sobriquets?

1. Satchmo

2. The Governator

3. Wilt the Stilt

4. Mr. Television

5. Broadway Joe

6. The Little Tramp

7. The Donald

8. The Juice

9. The Great One (Entertainment)

10. The Great One (Sports)

11. The Greatest (Sports)

12. Scarface

13. Bush's Brain

14. The Velvet Fog

15. The Wizard of Menlo Park

16. Charlie Hustle

17. Governor Moonbeam

18. Doctor Death

FOOD

long-term memory

executive functioning

A small buffet of clues about food.

● This culinary term for vegetables cut into matchstick-like strips is also a woman's name.

● Cereals such as wheat and oats come from this common plant family.

● Some types of sushi are rolled in a dark green wrap made of this.

● This gourmet fungus can be found near the roots of certain trees such as beech, hazel, and oak.

PUT ON YOUR THINKING CAP

All of the answers in this word definition game begin with the letters CAP.

1. The fine branching blood vessels that form a network between the veins and arteries.

2. London, Paris, and Washington, DC, are three examples.

3. A castrated rooster fattened for cooking.

4. Italian coffee prepared with espresso, hot milk, and steamed milk foam.

5. This describes a boat overturned in the water.

6. The part of a spaceship that contains the crew.

7. Kirk, Kidd, and Kangaroo all held this military rank.

8. To abduct or take custody of a person or creature by force.

9. The maximum amount that something can contain.

10. In the 1930s and 1940s, he directed *It Happened One Night, Mr. Smith Goes to Washington,* and that seasonal favorite *It's a Wonderful Life.*

11. A South American monkey named for an order of Franciscan monks known to wear brown capes with pointed hoods.

12. To charm; to attract and hold the interest of someone.

13. The tenth astrological sign, symbolized by the goat.

14. To give in; to stop resisting; to surrender.

15. The economic system in which a country's trade and industry are controlled by private owners for profit.

long-term memory
working memory

colorful people

In this quiz, the answers are famous people whose names contain a color, such as *Graham Greene* or *Elizabeth Barrett Browning*. (*Note: Some colors may be found in more than one answer.*)

1. He played Ben Cartwright from 1959 to 1973.

2. Debbie Reynolds won an Oscar in 1964 playing this famous *Titanic* survivor.

3. He was a prolific author of novels and stories of the Old West. One of the first millionaire authors, his bestselling western was *Riders of the Purple Sage*.

4. This former child star was appointed U.S. ambassador to Ghana in 1974 and to Czechoslovakia in 1989.

5. Candice Bergen played this fictional TV journalist from 1988 to 1998.

6. He was a left-handed power pitcher and the Cy Young Award winner of 1971 when he was with the Oakland Athletics.

7. Famed editor of *Cosmopolitan* magazine from 1965 to 1997 and author of *Sex and the Single Girl*.

8. Manfred von Richthofen, famed World War I German fighter pilot, was better known by this nickname.

9. Author of *The Joy Luck Club*.

10. He was the chairman of the Federal Reserve during the administrations of Ronald Reagan, George H. W. Bush, Bill Clinton, and George W. Bush.

11. Basketball pioneer and legendary coach of the Boston Celtics.

12. Captain Kangaroo's sidekick.

13. Author of the 2003 bestseller *The Da Vinci Code*.

family time

In this scene, there are seventy-three words **that begin with the letter T.** How many can you find?

working memory
executive functioning
attention to detail
multitasking
processing speed

twy this!

All of the answers in this word definition game begin with the letters TW.

1. This is an archaic word for two. It's also the pen name of Samuel Langhorne Clemens.

_____

2. The period between daylight and darkness.

_____

3. Eyebrow-thinning implement.

_____

4. To flicker, as light.

_____

5. This coarse wool with flecks of color originated in Scotland.

_____

6. To spin around quickly.

_____

7. An insignificant or despicable person; a bonehead, jerk, or nitwit.

_____

8. This sixteen-year-old British beauty made it fashionable to be skinny in the 1960s.

_____

9. To pinch, or to make a slight adjustment.

_____

10. A strong thread or string.

_____

11. A sudden but minor pain, spasm, or cramp.

_____

12. The social networking website that restricts user messages to 140 characters—about two sentences.

_____

---

 trivia

SOUP

long-term memory

executive functioning

If you like soup, you'll ace this quiz.

● Can you name two of the three most popular types of Campbell's soup sold in the U.S.?

● What is the main ingredient in gazpacho, a soup from Spain and Portugal?

● Gumbo is a Creole soup that is thickened with this vegetable.

● What are the two main vegetables in vichyssoise?

U.S. Presidents

long-term memory
working memory
processing speed

How many of the forty-four U.S. presidents can you name in one minute?

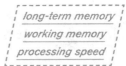

PUT THE LIST IN ORDER

long-term memory
working memory
executive functioning
multitasking

Put each list of four or five items in the order called for in the question.

① Put this list of Oscar-winning films in order of when they premiered, starting with the earliest:

____ **a.** *On the Waterfront*

____ **b.** *Gone with the Wind*

____ **c.** *It Happened One Night*

____ **d.** *Casablanca*

____ **e.** *Ben-Hur*

② Put this list of animals in order of their average life span, starting with the longest:

____ **a.** Alligator

____ **b.** Giant tortoise

____ **c.** Parrot

____ **d.** Horse

③ Put this list of historical events in order, starting with the earliest:

____ **a.** Plymouth Rock landing

____ **b.** Telephone patented

____ **c.** Shakespeare dies

____ **d.** Smallpox vaccine

④ Put this list of "math problems" in order, starting with the smallest number:

____ **a.** Months in a decade

____ **b.** Days in a fortnight

____ **c.** The number of minutes in four hours

____ **d.** Weeks in two years

⑤ Put this list of U.S. presidents in order by their height, starting with the tallest:

____ **a.** Richard Nixon

____ **b.** Thomas Jefferson

____ **c.** Ronald Reagan

____ **d.** Lyndon Johnson

____ **e.** Jimmy Carter

⑥ Put this list of television game shows in order of when they first premiered on TV, starting with the earliest:

____ **a.** *Jeopardy!*

____ **b.** *The Price Is Right*

____ **c.** *Hollywood Squares*

____ **d.** *Truth or Consequences*

____ **e.** *Family Feud*

⑦ Put the following planets in order of their size, starting with the largest:

____ **a.** Saturn

____ **b.** Mars

____ **c.** Jupiter

____ **d.** Earth

____ **e.** Mercury

⑧ Put this list of actors in order of their age, starting with the youngest:

____ **a.** Tom Hanks

____ **b.** Tom Cruise

____ **c.** George Clooney

____ **d.** Brad Pitt

____ **e.** Meryl Streep

9. Put this list of World War II military engagements in order of when they were fought, starting with the earliest:

____ **a.** The Battle of Midway

____ **b.** The Battle of the Bulge

____ **c.** The Attack on Pearl Harbor

____ **d.** The Battle of Iwo Jima

____ **e.** The Battle of Britain

10. Put this list of retail stores in order of when they first opened their doors, starting with the earliest:

____ **a.** Walmart

____ **b.** JCPenney

____ **c.** Brooks Brothers

____ **d.** Barnes & Noble

____ **e.** Sears

whose quote is it?

Can you guess who said (or wrote) the following quotes? For a more rigorous brain workout, cover up the hints on the right and answer the questions without them.

long-term memory
executive functioning

1. *"I may not get there with you. But I want you to know tonight that we, as a people, will get to the Promised Land."*   Civil Rights Leader

2. *"Genius is one percent inspiration and ninety-nine percent perspiration."*   Inventor

3. *"I hope I will be able to confide everything in you, as I have never been able to confide in anyone, and I hope you will be a great source of comfort and support."*   Diarist

4. *"A verbal contract isn't worth the paper it's written on."*   Movie Mogul

5. *"Don't look back. Something might be gaining on you."*   Baseball Player

6. *"I hold it, that a little rebellion now and then, is a good thing, and as necessary in the political world as storms in the physical."*   U.S. President

7. *"I cannot and will not cut my conscience to fit this year's fashions."*   Playwright

8. *"God does not throw dice with the universe."*   Scientist

9. *"Man, if you gotta ask, you'll never know."*   Musician

★ AUGUST IN HISTORY ★

This trivia quiz will stretch your long-term memory muscles.

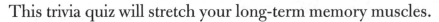

1859   Petroleum was discovered in this eastern state, leading to the world's first commercially successful oil well.

1888   A prostitute named Mary Ann Nichols was found murdered in London's East End. She is generally regarded as the first victim of this serial killer.

1902   Ogden Nash, an American poet known for his comic light verse, was born in Rye, New York. Can you finish his seven-word poem "Reflections on Ice-Breaking," which begins: "Candy is dandy . . ."

1902   This pioneering cookbook author opened the first cooking school in the United States. She advocated the use of standardized measurements in recipes.

1912   Edgar Rice Burroughs's classic novel was first published in serial installments in a magazine. What was the name of his title character, who became an instant cultural sensation, and one of the most famous fictional characters in the world?

1945   The U.S. detonated two atomic bombs over these two cities. After the second bomb, Japan surrendered unconditionally to allied leaders.

1947   When India gained independence after nearly two hundred years of British rule, several Muslim-majority regions were separated off, forming this new country.

1954   Time, Inc. published the first edition of this magazine with a cover photograph of a Milwaukee Brewers batter swinging at a New York Giants pitch.

1956   This influential American abstract painter, famous for pouring and dripping paint on canvas, died in a car crash while driving drunk.

1963   Which Washington, DC, landmark was Martin Luther King Jr. standing in front of when he gave his famous "I Have a Dream" speech?

1968 Anti-Vietnam War candidate Eugene McCarthy lost the Democratic presidential nomination to this war-supporting Minnesotan.

1974 On August 8, Richard Nixon announced his resignation. How many days later did he leave office?

1977 Elvis Presley was found dead at the age of forty-two on the bathroom floor of his Graceland mansion in this city.

1977 After less than two weeks in office, President Gerald Ford nominated this former governor to serve as vice president of the United States.

1980 This Polish union head led a workers' strike at the Lenin Shipyard in Gdansk—a job action that led to the creation of the Solidarity labor movement and to the eventual end of Soviet dominance over Poland.

1981 More than eleven thousand members of this government union went on strike. Forty-eight hours later, President Ronald Reagan fired them all.

1984 This diminutive author of *Breakfast at Tiffany's* and *In Cold Blood* died at age fifty-nine in the home of his friend Joanne Carson (ex-wife of Johnny Carson).

1997 Britain's Princess Diana left this hotel and was killed minutes later in a tragic car accident.

2005 Hurricane Katrina made landfall in Louisiana. Who was the mayor of New Orleans at the time?

---

trivia

MAYOR OF WHERE?

long-term memory
executive functioning

Given a list of mayors past and present, can you name the U.S. city they serve?

● John Lindsay, David Dinkins, Fiorello LaGuardia, and Rudy Giuliani

● Gavin Newsom, Dianne Feinstein, George Moscone, and Joseph Alioto

● Harold Washington, Jane Byrne, and Richard Daley

● Adrian Fenty, Anthony Williams, and Marion Barry

● James Curley, Kevin White, Raymond Flynn, and Thomas Menino

● Frank Rizzo, W. Wilson Goode, and Edward G. Rendell

● Maynard Jackson, Andrew Young, and Shirley Franklin

● Samuel Yorty, Thomas Bradley, Richard Riordan, and Antonio Villaraigosa

Compound Word

Each picture represents one half of a compound word. For example, if you combine *key* and *hole,* you get *keyhole.* How many of the twelve possible compound words can you find? For an extra brain boost, see how many compound words you can find in two minutes. (*Note: Each picture is used only once.*)

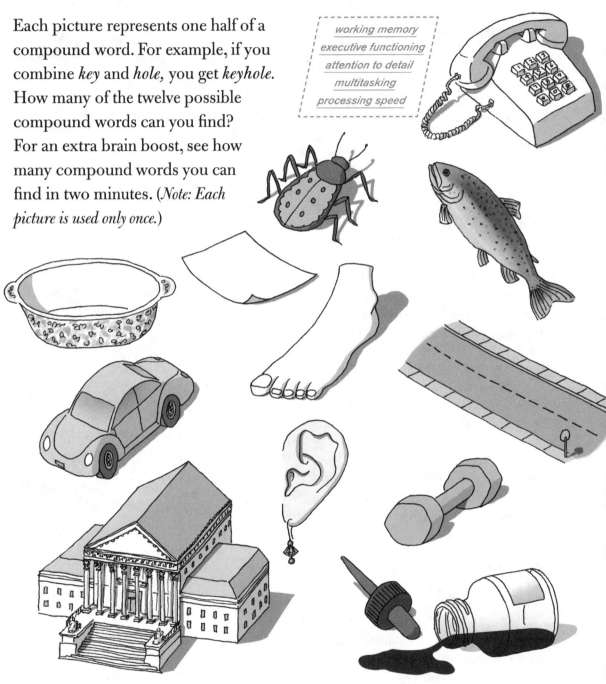

Search

1 _____
2 _____
3 _____
4 _____
5 _____
6 _____
7 _____
8 _____
9 _____
10 _____
11 _____
12 _____

british vs. american english

It has been said that America and Britain are two countries separated by a common language. How much "British" do you know?

1. Many Americans live in an *apartment*; many British people live in one of these.

2. If the lights go out in America, you would look for a *flashlight*; in England, you'd look for this.

3. In American supermarkets you use a *cart* to collect your purchases; in British supermarkets, you use this.

4. In America, you eat a *cookie*; in England it's called this.

5. In England, you might buy a bag of *crisps*; in America they're called this.

6. In American cars, you check the oil under the *hood*; in English cars you look under this.

7. When he's in England, Larry King wears *braces*; in America he wears these.

8. In America you fill your car with *gas*; in England you fill it with this.

9. If an English baby cries, you might give her a *dummy*; American babies get this.

10. In England, the hair that falls over the forehead is called a *fringe*; in America it's called this.

11. In American intersections you'd see a *yellow* traffic light; in England it's this color.

12. In England, you put a *plaster* on a small cut; in America it's called this.

13. In England, women get upset when they get a *ladder in their tights*; American women call it this.

14. You'd put a *diaper* on an American baby; this goes on a British baby.

15. In England, this reception improver is called an *aerial*; in America, it's called this.

16. In England, this person is a *news presenter*; in America he or she is called this.

17. In America, you buy medical supplies at a *pharmacy*; in England, you buy them here.

18. In America, you'll find a spare tire in the *trunk*; in England, you'll find it here.

19. In an English restaurant this is called an *aubergine*; in America it's called this.

20. In England, it's a *callbox*; in America it's called this.

21. In America, your group might rent a *bus* for a comfortable road trip; in England, you'd rent this.

22. In America, you'd find a *wrench* in most toolboxes; in England, you'd find this.

23. In England you might get an *engaged tone* when you call someone; in America it's called this.

24. In English winters you wear a *jumper*; Americans stay warm with this.

WHAT'S THE STORY?

long-term memory

executive functioning

Can you identify the classic stories from these brief plot descriptions?

● In a 1790 New York village, Ichabod Crane is run out of town by the Headless Horseman, leaving Brom Bones the only suitor of young Katrina Van Tassel.

● George and Lennie, two migrant field workers in California during the Great Depression, dream of settling on their own land someday. The dream is destroyed when Lennie, unaware of his own strength, kills a woman.

● Nick Carraway rents a bungalow between two mansions on Long Island. His cousin Daisy lives in one of the mansions. In the other lives a mystery man who hosts lavish parties, which he rarely attends.

● Poor spinster Hepzibah Pyncheon lives in a big gloomy house in Salem, Massachusetts. She opens a shop in a side room to support her brother, who is being released from prison after serving thirty years for murder.

PICK YOUR POISON

long-term memory
executive functioning

If these clues cause you problems, you'd better have the poison emergency number on hand.

● This symbol has been placed on containers of poisonous substances since the mid-1800s.

● This substance was added to paint to speed drying and resist moisture, but it was banned in 1977 because of its toxic effects.

● In ancient Greece, the philosopher Socrates was sentenced to death by drinking poison made from this plant.

● Adolf Hitler took a capsule of this poison just before shooting himself.

THIRTY › SECOND › MADNESS

Ivy League Colleges

> *long-term memory*
> *working memory*
> *processing speed*

The term "Ivy League" was first used in the 1930s in reference to an athletic conference of eight private northeastern universities. These schools are among the nation's oldest institutions of higher learning, and they are often ranked among the best universities in the world. How many of the eight Ivy League colleges can your players name in thirty seconds? (You'll get an extra brain boost if you can identify the city or town in which each school is located.)

_____

_____

_____

_____

_____

_____

WHO SAID IT?

long-term memory
executive functioning

Who said these newsworthy words? And for an extra brain challenge, what were the circumstances?

● "The number of casualties will be more than most of us can bear."

● "My fellow Americans, our long national nightmare is over."

● "I have found it impossible to carry the heavy burden of responsibility and to discharge my duties as King as I would wish to do without the help and support of the woman I love."

● "Always remember: others may hate you, but those who hate you don't win unless you hate them. And then you destroy yourself."

Chapter Six

CHALLENGING

ODD MAN OUT

long-term memory
working memory
executive functioning

All of the items in each list have something in common except one thing. Your job is to figure out which item is the "Odd Man Out"—and why.

1. North Carolina; Georgia; Florida; Pennsylvania

2. Cougar; rabbit; flamingo; falcon; impala

3. Chanterelle; shiitake; portobello; nori

4. Dinner; litter; noodle; orient; carrot

5. Beryllium; hollyhock; gladiola; delphinium

6. Tate; Nordstrom; Getty; Hermitage; Uffizi

7. Glasgow; Jupiter; Hollywood; Naples; Venice

8. TLC; WWW; IFC; ESPN

9. "My Favorite Things"; "Climb Ev'ry Mountain"; "Younger Than Springtime"; "Edelweiss"

10. Rho; omicron; alpha; omega; enigma

11. Colorado; Washington; California; Florida; New Jersey

12. Rosemary; basil; ginger; fennel

REPLACE THE SPINACH

There's something wrong with these titles. Can you fix them by replacing the word SPINACH with the correct food?

1. *The Big Rock SPINACH Mountain* by Wallace Stegner

2. *A Clockwork SPINACH* by Anthony Burgess

3. *The SPINACH Orchard* by Anton Chekhov

4. *The SPINACH Field* by Joseph Wambaugh

5. *A SPINACH in the Sun* by Lorraine Hansberry

6. "The SPINACH Man" by Lesley Bricusse and Anthony Newley

7. *What's Eating Gilbert SPINACH?* (Movie)

8. *The SPINACH Dumpling Gang* by Jack Bickham

9. *Like Water for SPINACH* by Laura Esquivel

ONE>MINUTE>MADNESS
Land Countries

How many of the twelve countries that end in *land(s)* can you name in one minute? (*Note: This list does not include countries that end in the word Island(s), as in Cayman Islands, Virgin Islands, Solomon Islands, and so on.*)

by the numbers

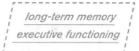
Here's a mix of knowledge questions with a little bit of math.

1. In what year did we celebrate the bicentennial of the signing of the Declaration of Independence?

2. How old is a woman four years shy of being a centenarian?

3. If the clock says 11:13 A.M., how many minutes are there until noon?

4. The military time of 1400 hours is what time on a normal twelve-hour clock?

5. How much would you pay for a two hundred-dollar chair advertised at 20 percent off?

6. How much is the emergency phone call number minus the number for directory assistance?

7. In Lincoln's Gettysburg Address, "Four score and seven years ago" is how long?

8. How much is the boiling point of water (in Fahrenheit) minus the freezing point of water (in Fahrenheit)?

9. How many inches is a half-foot plus a half-yard?

10. If you bought a baker's dozen of cookies and ate two, how many cookies remain?

11. If a British pound is worth $1.50 in U.S. currency, how many pounds can six dollars buy?

12. How many batters does a pitcher have to face to complete a perfect game in baseball?

13. How many degrees from his starting point is a soldier who turned about-face?

SLIPPERY SLOPE

All of the two-word answers in this game begin with the initials S and S.

1. He "met a pieman going to the fair."

_____

2. Federal agency that protects the president.

_____

3. This comic strip (and comic book) about a lowly army private debuted during World War II.

_____

4. Black and white footwear popular in the 1950s.

_____

5. Thoroughbred horse from the state of Washington that won the Triple Crown in 1977.

_____

6. Mixed drink stirrer.

_____

7. June 21, when the sun is at its northernmost point.

_____

8. A possession that demonstrates a person's social or economic prestige.

_____

9. Sometime you need this to reach the top shelf.

_____

10. Manual transmission.

_____

11. Infield position in baseball.

_____

12. This was the only way for a lady to ride a horse until breeches became more popular in the early twentieth century.

_____

13. Slang name for the maximum security prison about thirty miles north of New York City.

_____

14. This metal does not rust, which makes it perfect for cutlery, surgical instruments, and many other applications.

_____

more or less?

You may not actually know the answers to these questions, but life experience may help you reason them out.

1. Are there more humans or squirrels in the United States?

_____

2. Are there more hairs on an adult human's head (on average), or more feathers on a full-grown bald eagle?

_____

3. Was the average height of an American man in 1900 taller or shorter than the average height of an American woman today?

_____

4. Who has more television channels to watch: the average American household or the average British household?

_____

5. Are more Americans blind or deaf?

_____

6. Do more Americans claim a German heritage or an Irish heritage in the United States?

_____

Anagrams

The letters of each word in this list can be arranged in multiple ways to form other words. We provide the word and the number of anagrams that are possible to make.

1. Sepal (5)   _____   _____   _____   _____

2. Teals (5)   _____   _____   _____   _____

3. Warder (4)   _____   _____   _____   _____

4. Tinsel (4)   _____   _____   _____   _____

5. Padres (5)   _____   _____   _____   _____

6. Lusters (2)   _____   _____

7. Rattles (2)   _____   _____

8. Pertains (3)   _____   _____

What Do They Have in Common?

long-term memory
executive functioning
attention to detail

Each question contains a list of several items. Can you figure out what they have in common?

1. The heart, women's shoes, and gas station equipment

2. Shasta, Hood, McKinley, and Rainier

3. M&Ms, oysters, peanuts, and turtles

4. *National Velvet, Seabiscuit, King of the Wind,* and *Misty of Chincoteague*

5. Vichyssoise, bouillabaisse, gazpacho, and miso

6. Thimble, wheelbarrow, shoe, and battleship

7. Stockings, a marathoner, a car, and a political candidate

8. *Bitte, por favor,* and *prego*

9. Elwood P. Dowd, Jefferson Smith, Roger Hobbs, and George Bailey

10. Lettuce, a pin, a glass of beer, and a coin

11. Eric Blair, Samuel Clemens, and Charles Dodgson

12. Underwood, Olivetti, Royal, and Remington Rand

---

trivia
WHAT HAPPENED ON...?
long-term memory
executive functioning

We give the date. Can you figure out the event?

● December 7, 1941

● April 4, 1968

● April 15, 1912

● August 9, 1974

boo!

All of the answers in this word definition game begin with the letters BOO.

1. Moonshine, hooch.

_____

2. An Australian aboriginal hunting weapon.

_____

3. He'll take your bet . . . but it isn't legal.

_____

4. Abbreviated term for the huge generation of people born between 1946 and 1964.

_____

5. Someone who really likes to read.

_____

6. A remote or isolated area that is often described as "the middle of nowhere."

_____

7. To deal in illegal goods, especially the transportation and sale of intoxicating liquors.

_____

8. A supplemental dose of a vaccine to increase its effectiveness.

_____

9. A mobile lending library.

_____

10. The choice seats in a diner.

_____

11. The person who keeps track of a company's financial transactions.

_____

12. A location undergoing rapid growth due to sudden prosperity. This word would aptly have described Detroit when the automobile industry began to take off.

_____

13. A project that wastes time and money, particularly one that has failed long before it is shut down or completed.

_____

14. A rude, clumsy, unmannerly person.

_____

15. An obsequious or overly deferential person; a toady.

_____

long-term memory
executive functioning
attention to detail

FLAG  DAY

Can you name the countries these flags represent?

❶ _____

❷ _____

❸ _____

❹ _____

5 _____

6 _____

7 _____

8 _____

are you *decent?*

All of the answers in this word definition game begin with the letters DEC.

1. Coffee without the kick.

2. A glass container, usually with a stopper, for serving wine.

3. Dead, passed away.

4. A full complement of playing cards . . . or an unroofed porch, usually made of planks of lumber.

5. To mislead, swindle, or lie to someone.

6. To undermine an organization or government by removing its leaders. Literally, it means to cut the head off.

7. A two-day Olympic event in which competitors take part in ten athletic events.

8. The slow rotting of organic matter through the action of bacteria.

9. Unit that measures the intensity or volume of sound.

10. To opt, elect, or choose.

11. This helps clear blocked nasal passages when you have a cold.

12. To reduce, lessen, or dwindle.

13. This term describes something that is luxuriously self-indulgent.

14. Scientific term that describes trees that shed their leaves annually.

ALPHABETICAL GEOGRAPHY

long-term memory
executive functioning

We provide the letters, and you provide the name of the geographical location.

● Name one of the two countries that have an X in their name.

● Name the two four-letter countries that start with the same three letters. (Hint: They're both in the news a lot!)

● Name two of the four countries that begin with the letter V.

● Name the only South American country that ends in a U.

long-term memory
working memory
processing speed

ONE›MINUTE›MADNESS

Salad Days

You've got one minute to come up with as many one-word answers as possible to complete the phrase _____ *Salad*. We came up with nineteen.

_____ Salad   _____ Salad

_____ Salad   _____ Salad

_____ Salad   _____ Salad

_____ Salad   _____ Salad

_____ Salad   _____ Salad

_____ Salad   _____ Salad

_____ Salad   _____ Salad

_____ Salad   _____ Salad

_____ Salad   _____ Salad

_____ Salad

TV hometowns

We provide the name of a television show. Can you give the town (real or fictional) in which it was mainly set?

1. *The Andy Griffith Show*

2. *The Mary Tyler Moore Show*

3. *Frasier*

4. *The Sopranos*

5. *Murphy Brown*

6. *Everybody Loves Raymond*

7. *Laverne & Shirley* and *Happy Days*

8. *Mork and Mindy*

9. *Designing Women*

10. *The Golden Girls*

11. *Northern Exposure*

12. *Bonanza*

13. *The Ghost & Mrs. Muir*

14. *Green Acres*

15. *Gunsmoke*

16. *I Dream of Jeannie*

17. *St. Elsewhere*

18. *Ironside*

19. *Alice*

20. *Wings*

21. *Roseanne*

22. *Murder, She Wrote*

Political Quotes

Politics gives rise to many memorable sayings. Can you identify the speaker from these well-known quotes? For an extra brain challenge, try to remember the context of each quote.

1. "Where's the beef?"

2. "My friends . . ."

3. "That giant sucking sound . . ."

4. "We are all republicans—we are all federalists."

5. "Senator, you're no Jack Kennedy."

6. "A vast right-wing conspiracy."

7. "Have you no sense of decency, sir? At long last, have you left no sense of decency?"

8. "Trust, but verify."

IT'S GREEK TO ME

long-term memory
executive functioning

Four clues about Greeks and Greek Americans.

● He was a slave in ancient Greece who is credited with a famous collection of fables.

● This journalist and leading advisor to the Clinton campaign once considered following in his father's footsteps and becoming a Greek Orthodox priest.

● If he had won the 1988 presidential election, he would have become the nation's first Greek American president.

● He is considered the father of Western philosophy. Plato's "Dialogues" are the best surviving accounts of his teachings.

Capitonyms

A capitonym is a word that changes its meaning (and sometimes its pronunciation) when it is capitalized. In this game, you get two clues to identify the capitonym.

1. A large country . . . or fine dishes.

2. A boy's name . . . or a baby kangaroo.

3. A poet named Ezra . . . or currency in London.

4. A summer month . . . or inspiring reverence and admiration.

5. Biblical man of patience . . . or the work that one does.

6. Born in Warsaw . . . or to clean the silverware.

7. A legendary country singer . . . or what's in your wallet.

8. A popular toothpaste . . . or the peak of a wave.

9. An innovative computer maker . . . or a crispy fruit.

10. A caffeine-free soft drink . . . or a small supernatural being.

---

 trivia

HISPANIC HERITAGE

long-term memory

executive functioning

¿Usted conoce a estos hispanoamericanos famosos?

● Bob Vila, a Cuban American, was the first host of this popular PBS television series.

● Born Ramón Gerardo Antonio Estevez, by what name is this star of TV's *The West Wing* better known?

● Born Margarita Carmen Cansino, by what name was 1940s sex symbol and star of *Gilda* better known?

● This Puerto Rican–born Baseball Hall of Famer spent his career with the Pittsburgh Pirates. He died in a plane crash in 1972 while bringing aid to earthquake victims in Nicaragua.

whatzit

How many clues do you need to guess what the WHATZIT is? One to three clues—Outstanding; three to seven clues—Very Good; seven to ten clues—Time to study up on your WHATZITs.

1. WHATZITs are found on low, creeping shrubs or vines that thrive in conditions that would not support most other crops: acid soil, few nutrients, and low temperatures, even in summer.

2. Wisconsin is the leading producer of WHATZITs, with over half of U.S. production. WHATZITs are also a major commercial crop in Maine, Massachusetts, Michigan, Minnesota, New Jersey, Oregon, and Washington.

3. WHATZITs, one of only a handful of major fruits native to North America, were used by Native Americans in medicines, dyes, and a variety of foods.

4. There are 440 WHATZITs in one pound and 4,400 in one gallon of juice. WHATZITs are available in a wide variety of forms including fresh fruit, juice, sauce, and dried.

5. Recently, WHATZITs were given the commercial status as a "superfruit" because they are packed with nutrients such as antioxidants.

6. WHATZITs have been shown to help maintain a healthy urinary tract and can also help break down and prevent the formation of kidney stones.

7. Calling the berries "Sassamanash," natives may have introduced WHATZITs to starving English settlers who incorporated the berries into the first Thanksgiving in 1621 in Plymouth, Massachusetts.

8. Americans consume some 400 million pounds of WHATZITs each year. About 80 million pounds—or 20 percent—are gobbled up during Thanksgiving week.

★ SEPTEMBER IN HISTORY ★

This trivia quiz will stretch your long-term memory muscles.

1846 Dentist William Morton was the first person to publicly demonstrate the use of this anesthesia on a patient.

1901 Following the death of this president from an assassin's bullet, Theodore Roosevelt was sworn in as the twenty-sixth president of the United States.

1927 Jack Dempsey lost the World Heavyweight title to this rival boxer in a controversial fight that was known forever after as the "battle of the long count."

1939 World War II began when German forces invaded and soon conquered this European country.

1940 What did four teenagers discover while exploring a system of caves in the Lascaux region of southwestern France?

1952 This British-born silent film legend was prevented from entering the United States, where he had lived for forty years, because of his suspected Communist activity.

1957 Governor Orval Faubus called out the National Guard to prevent nine black students from entering Central High School in this city.

1957 *On the Road,* the book that has been called "the defining work of the postwar Beat Generation" was published. Who wrote this chronicle of mid-century American youth?

1959 During a visit to the U.S., Soviet Premier Nikita Khrushchev exploded with anger when he was told that he could not visit this then four-year-old California tourist site because authorities couldn't guarantee his safety.

1963 In one of the deadliest acts of the civil rights era, four young African American girls were killed when a bomb exploded during Sunday services at the 16th Street Baptist Church in this city.

1967   This Michigan governor said during a TV interview that he had undergone a "brainwashing" by U.S. officials during a visit to Vietnam two years earlier—a remark that is widely believed to have derailed his 1968 campaign for president.

1969   With the outcome of the Vietnam War still uncertain, this North Vietnamese leader died of heart failure in Hanoi. Six years later, Saigon, the former capital of South Vietnam, was renamed after this Communist hero.

1972   Tragedy unfolded during the Summer Olympics in this city when Palestinian terrorists took eleven members of the Israeli team hostage and murdered them the next day.

1976   The revolutionary who brought Communism to the People's Republic of China and led the country as Party chairman for twenty-seven years died in Beijing at the age of eighty-two.

1978   Following twelve days of secret negotiations at Camp David, a framework for peace between Egypt and Israel was signed by the leaders of those two countries and the United States. Can you name all three signers?

1982   Seven people in the Chicago area died after taking this over-the-counter pain reliever, which was later discovered to have been laced with cyanide.

2001   A series of coordinated suicide attacks by Al-Qaeda terrorists took nearly three thousand American lives and injured more than six thousand. Name the three key locations.

CANDY SLOGANS AND JINGLES

long-term memory

executive functioning

Who can forget these advertising jingles— or the candy they were selling?

● "The great American chocolate bar."

● "Sometimes you feel like a nut. Sometimes you don't." (Two candy bars.)

● "Gimme' a break. Gimme' a break. Break me off a piece of that (*blank blank*) bar."

● "Get the sensation."

rhyme ◆ time ◆

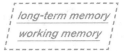

Each question in this game includes two definitions for two different words. The twist is, they will rhyme.

1. Fastener; and the meat of an adult sheep.

2. To remain in one place in the air; and lid for a container.

3. To import or export goods illegally; and to keep objects in the air by simultaneously tossing and catching them.

4. Percolator; and the paved area that surrounds just about every shopping mall.

5. Tony Blair's political party; and a person who lives nearby.

6. A play-on-words; and a Ruger or Luger.

7. State induced by hypnosis; and waltz or foxtrot.

8. Summertime toy weapon; and a four-bagger in baseball.

9. The quintessential American dessert; and it's now called middle school.

10. The dark shape and outline of someone against a lighter background; and early fighter for the women's right to vote.

11. A quick burst of light; and coins and dollars.

12. A sorcerer, like Merlin; and a type of reptile, like an iguana or chameleon.

13. The panda's favorite food; and South American country whose capital is Lima.

14. Loud, disruptive, clamorous noise; and the support arm for an adjustable bookshelf.

15. Passive restraint system in an automobile; and frequently, the physical consequences of a long flight.

Punctuation Marks

long-term memory
working memory
processing speed

How many of the sixteen punctuation marks used in English can you name in one minute? (Two are obscure.)

Presidential Nicknames

Can you name these U.S. presidents from their nicknames?

long-term memory
executive functioning

1. Mr. Nice Guy

2. The King of Camelot

3. Poppy

4. The Trust Buster, The Hero of San Juan Hill

5. Tippecanoe

6. The Sage of Monticello

7. Old Hickory

8. Old Kinderhook

9. Old Rough and Ready

10. The Schoolmaster

CHARTREUSE TITLES

Something is wrong with the following titles. You need to replace the word CHARTREUSE with the correct color.

long-term memory
executive functioning

1. *The Color CHARTREUSE*

2. *CHARTREUSEfinger*

3. *CHARTREUSE Submarine*

4. *"CHARTREUSEsleeves"*

5. *A Patch of CHARTREUSE*

6. *"CHARTREUSE River Valley"*

7. *The CHARTREUSE Pimpernel*

8. *The Unsinkable Molly CHARTREUSE*

9. *CHARTREUSE Hawk Down*

10. *I Am Curious CHARTREUSE*

11. *Island of the CHARTREUSE Dolphins*

12. *The CHARTREUSE Hill Mob*

13. *CHARTREUSE Gardens*

14. *CHARTREUSE Like Me*

15. *"CHARTREUSE Moon"*

---

 trivia

SAINTS

long-term memory

executive functioning

All the answers in this trivia quiz contain the word *saint*.

● The Twin City that fits this category.

● This peak is responsible for the deadliest volcanic eruption in U.S. history.

● In a New Orleans jazz funeral this song is played twice—first slowly, as a dirge while the coffin is on its way to the cemetery, then in a Dixieland style on the way back.

● The three main U.S. Virgin Islands that fit this category.

WISE WORDS

All of the two-word answers in this game begin with the initials W and W.

1. Where you'll find the administrative offices of the president of the United States.

2. A stretch of a river with a broken, foamy surface, often associated with rapids.

3. An "arm clock."

4. A Native American tribe, and a city in the southwest corner of Washington state.

5. Description of Moby Dick.

6. This tree isn't really sad—it just looks that way because it's often planted near water and its foliage trails downward.

7. This superhero, who debuted in 1941, was described by creator William Moulton Marston as a "distinctly feminist role model."

8. Built by King Herod in 20 B.C., this is a sacred gathering place for Jews in Jerusalem.

9. A porch or platform on the roof of a house, often used in early New England as a lookout for incoming ships.

10. An aviation pioneer.

11. An automotive raindrop remover.

12. Indecisive; lacking in strength and character.

13. An organization that greets newcomers to a neighborhood with gifts and local information.

14. Sounds made by men that are usually considered rude to women.

*ph*un times

All of the answers in this word definition game begin with the letters PH.

1. An irrational fear or aversion to something.

2. A person who donates money to good causes.

3. Mythical bird that rises from the ashes.

4. The process by which plants change light into food.

5. Title of the supreme ruler in ancient Egypt.

6. A hearty houseplant recognizable by its heart-shaped leaves.

7. Ghost, apparition, spirit.

8. This is the inflammation of a vein, usually in the legs, often associated with blood clots.

9. A man who has casual romantic relationships with many women.

10. Profession of Alfred Stieglitz and Margaret Bourke-White.

11. The branch of science concerned with the nature and properties of matter and energy.

12. This word, popularized by Walter Winchell, means "nonsense." It can also be an expression of disgust, disagreement, or contemptuous rejection.

13. These are the chemical signals in animals that trigger attraction between two members of the same species.

14. A person who studies, and often collects, postage stamps and related items.

DOUBLE TROUBLE

Compound words are made up of two smaller words, such as *hayloft* or *watchtower*.

In this game, we give the first half of some compound words. You must identify the one word that follows each of them to make a compound word. For example, given the words *knuckle, moth,* and *basket,* the one word that makes each a compound word is *ball* (*knuckleball, mothball,* and *basketball*).

1. Waste, wall, news, note

_____ (hint: p)

2. Grid, hem, wed, pad

_____ (hint: l)

3. Bottle, red, rubber, turtle

_____ (hint: n)

4. Bull, hot, sheep, watch

_____ (hint: d)

5. Brother, false, neighbor, mother

_____ (hint: h)

6. Milk, tumble, sea, rag

_____ (hint: w)

7. Citizen, flag, court, friend

_____ (hint: s)

8. Bread, clothes, front, neck

_____ (hint: l)

9. Fire, nut, safe, wise

_____ (hint: c)

10. Broad, fore, out, type

_____ (hint: c)

11. Bullet, water, oven, child

_____ (hint: p)

12. Knee, snow, white, ice

_____ (hint: c)

13. Bag, wind, drain, stove

_____ (hint: p)

14. Land, war, slum, over

_____ (hint: l)

wacky wordies

the π sky

15,840 ft. island

❶ _____

❷ _____

lev el house

LO head/heels **VE**

❸ _____

❹ _____

To solve these fun puzzles, look carefully at each frame, because the arrangement of the letters is a key clue to the familiar phrase contained within. For example, if the word *school* were placed high up in the frame, the answer would be *high school.* Or, if the phrase "easy pieces" occurred five times in the frame, the answer would be *Five Easy Pieces.*

5 _____

6 _____

study
———
C C C
C C

7 _____

8 _____

BY THE LETTER

Hidden in this grid—printed forward, backward, and diagonally—are the names of five 8-letter countries, four 7-letter baseball teams, seven 6-letter movies, twelve 5-letter animals, and five 4-letter body parts. For an extra-challenging brain workout, put a three-minute timer on this game, and don't use the word list unless you get stuck.

```
C A M B O D I A H O R S E
J O R I O L E S R U M E L
Z X L S Z S Z O H C Y S P
L E S O O M U N I C H C A
E L B N M H E V A L A O K
S T A R A B N A Z R A T I
R P O M A I I K G N U L S
E E L P A N D A D J V A T
T E G A A J V N H Y E N A
T H X I S C A N I H C D N
O S E O T H A I L A N D X
B R E W E R S E E K N A Y
```

Countries
- ○ Cambodia
- ○ Colombia
- ○ Pakistan
- ○ Scotland
- ○ Thailand

Baseball Teams
- ○ Brewers
- ○ Indians
- ○ Orioles
- ○ Yankees

Movies
- ○ Ben-Hur
- ○ Capote
- ○ Hamlet
- ○ Munich
- ○ Psycho
- ○ Splash
- ○ Tarzan

Animals
- ○ Bison
- ○ Horse
- ○ Hyena
- ○ Koala
- ○ Lemur
- ○ Llama
- ○ Moose
- ○ Otter
- ○ Panda
- ○ Sheep
- ○ Tiger
- ○ Zebra

Body Parts
- ○ Chin
- ○ Hand
- ○ Lung
- ○ Nose
- ○ Toes

Stinky Pinky

long-term memory
working memory

We have twentieth-century humorist George S. Kaufman to thank for this game (and for its unusual title). Each Stinky Pinky answer contains two words that rhyme—but you have to figure out what that answer is from an offbeat definition.

1. A naked place to sit

2. Chardonnay for a hog

3. Pastry for a cobra

4. An inexperienced monarch

5. A Baby Ruth bar dropped on the beach

6. A skinnier boxer

7. A colorless taxi

8. Person with an extreme dislike of restaurant servers

9. A conceited cumulonimbus

10. An additional large rabbit

11. Very watery bee juice

portmanteaus

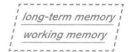
The word *portmanteau,* meaning suitcase, was given a new definition by Lewis Carroll (of *Alice in Wonderland* fame) to mean words that were made up of elements of two or more other words. Carroll was a prodigious coiner of portmanteaus, including *slithy* (from slimy and lithe) and *mimsy* (from miserable and flimsy). Portmanteaus can refer to most anything: geographical places (*Texarkana*), people (*Brangelina,* combining the names of Brad Pitt and Angelina Jolie), or things (*Blog,* from web log). Can you guess the two (or more) word origins of the following portmanteaus?

1. E-mail

2. Charbroil

3. Carjack

4. Gasahol

5. Guesstimate

6. Paratrooper

7. McMansion

8. Muppet

9. Smog

10. Squiggle

11. Spork

12. Bit (computer term)

13. Frankenfood

14. Moped

15. Slang

16. Caplet

17. Cyborg

blank of plank

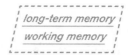
All of the familiar phrases in this quiz take the same form *(Blank) of (Blank),* as in *Ace of Spades* or *Nick of Time.* We provide the first word. Can you supply the last? It helps to know that the last word, in every case, will begin with the letter P.

1. Abuse of P _____

2. Bay of P _____

3. Bird of P _____

4. Book of P _____

5. Breach of P _____

6. Burden of P _____

7. Change of P _____

8. Coat of P _____

9. Crime of P _____

10. Cult of P _____

11. Horn of P _____

12. Invasion of P _____

13. Laws of P _____

14. Member of P _____

15. Mother of P _____

16. Pad of P _____

17. Piece of P _____

18. Plaster of P _____

19. Prince of P _____

20. Proof of P _____

21. Rites of P _____

WOMEN INVENTORS

long-term memory

executive functioning

How well do you know these contributions that women have made to modern life?

● Almost everyone has tried Ruth Wakefield's 1930 creation—a cooking accident that became America's most popular baked goodie.

● It's not surprising that Bette Nesmith Graham was a secretary when she invented this correction fluid.

● Mary Anderson patented this innovation for streetcars in 1905, but driving cars in bad weather is also easier, thanks to her.

● Patsy Sherman was a chemist at 3M when an accidental spill led to this invention, which protects fabrics from spills and stains.

BORROWED FROM
Irish

Although only about 350,000 people in the world can speak Irish Gaelic, we all know a few words that have been adopted into English and are commonly used. How much Gaelic do you know?

1. In both Irish and English, this is a marsh or area of wet, muddy ground that is too soft to hold anything heavy.

2. From the Irish *cailín* (pronounced *kai-LEEN*), this word means "young woman or girl."

3. This word, from the Irish phrase *go leor,* means "plenty" or "a lot."

4. Most everyone knows this Irish word for a mischievous elf.

5. In both English and Irish, this word means a large body of fresh water surrounded by land.

6. Pronounced *Baala an tee more* in Irish, this large eastern city's name means "big house."

7. In both languages, this is a small, crudely built shack.

8. In Irish it means "mud." In English, it means "a slovenly person."

9. This word has two meanings in both English and Irish. The first is a kind of shoe; the second is a strong regional accent. In English we commonly use it to describe a heavy Irish accent.

10. This means "poet" in both Irish and English—think Shakespeare.

11. In both languages, this means "small, tiny fragments"—especially after they've been smashed or exploded.

12. In Irish, this word literally means "water of life." In both languages, it's a popular alcoholic drink distilled from malted grain.

BUSINESS HISTORY

long-term memory

executive functioning

● In 1978 these two lifelong friends opened an ice cream parlor in Burlington, Vermont. In 2001 Unilever bought their company for over $300 million.

● At age seventeen, J. C. Hall started selling picture postcards. By 1916, he had made a business of it headquartered in Kansas City.

● William Jaird Levitt became widely credited as the father of modern suburbia when he built this development of more than seventeen thousand single-family homes for returning World War II veterans.

● Before his business could flourish, this innovator had to prove to a wary public that the elevator brakes he invented would work.

● This California company first made dollhouse furniture, and later the Chatty Cathy and long-time bestseller Barbie dolls.

● This company began in 1886 when a door-to-door book salesman gave perfume to women to entice them to buy his books. The perfume became more popular than the books.

● This company took its current name in 1947 when it began making car radios. Within a decade it was also producing one of the bestselling handheld transistor radios in the United States.

● High school dropout Hyman Golden started this company by selling apple and other fruit juice drinks to New York City health food stores. Sales skyrocketed when he added iced tea in 1987.

● He recognized the profit in making razor blades cheap enough to be disposable.

● He realized that air conditioning systems would not be successful if they didn't control humidity in addition to cooling the air.

● He said that he invented the outboard motor after having to row to shore on a Milwaukee lake to get ice cream for his girlfriend.

---

executive functioning

attention to detail

? CLASSIC RIDDLE
BOTTOMS UP

As with many classic riddles, the answer lies in a detail that is omitted from the story.

Jack and Jesse, twin brothers, went to a bar. They both ordered scotch on the rocks and were served identical drinks. Jack nursed his drink while Jesse gulped his down quickly. Within a few minutes of finishing their drinks, they both got sick. Jesse recovered, but Jack died. Why?

color coded

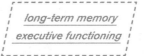

Many things are associated with colors—the Red Sox or the White House, for example. In this quiz we give the associations, and you must provide the colors.

1. What color is associated with breast cancer awareness and a famous panther?

2. What color is associated with a healthy tea and the end of a golf fairway?

3. What color is associated with the Democratic Party and IBM?

4. What color is associated with Mars and China?

5. What two colors are associated with Halloween?

6. What color is associated with a delivery company and a university in Providence, Rhode Island?

7. What color is associated with royalty and "The People Eater"?

8. What two colors are on the flags of Israel and Greece?

9. What color is associated with the interior of a cloud and the tongue of a convincing orator?

10. What color is associated with an annual California parade and an optimist's glasses?

11. What color is associated with the Protestants of Northern Ireland and autumn?

12. What two colors are associated with the U.S. Civil War?

HOMO**NYMS**

Homonyms are two or more words that are pronounced the same way but have different meanings and/or spellings. In this game, we supply the definitions, and you must not only provide the homonyms, but SPELL them correctly as well!

1. Calculates a total; and, classifieds.

_____   _____

2. The movement of the ocean; and, fastened with a rope.

_____   _____

3. Sicken; and, a bitter beer.

_____   _____

4. "Yes" to a politician or sailor; and, the visual organ.

_____   _____

5. Wept noisily; and, hairless.

_____   _____

6. Sandy shore; and, a large tree with smooth bark.

_____   _____

7. To strike repeatedly; and, a red root vegetable.

_____   _____

8. A large rock; and, more courageous, riskier.

_____   _____

9. Device to stop a vehicle; and, a rest from work.

_____   _____

10. Purchase; and, a phone conversation ender.

_____   _____

---

trivia

MARINE MATTERS

long-term memory

executive functioning

Sea creatures are the common thread in this trivia quiz.

● At 37.4 pounds and 2.1 feet long, this record-breaking crustacean was caught off Cape Cod, Massachusetts in 1974.

● Chinook, coho, and sockeye are all types of this highly valued food fish.

● The male (not the female) of this marine creature found in tropical and temperate waters carries the eggs until they mature.

● This bivalve was the source of wampum, the sacred beads sometimes used as currency by Native Americans in the northeast.

euphemisms

A euphemism is a mild, roundabout, or sometimes funny way of saying something that might otherwise be considered too blunt, painful, or offensive. Using the phrase "golden years" for old age is one example of a common euphemism. Euphemisms are sometimes also used to artificially soften the stark truth. A company might announce that it is "downsizing," rather than saying that it's going to lay off workers. In this game we give the euphemism, and you provide the meaning.

1. *Au naturel*

2. Powder your nose

3. Between jobs

4. Bun in the oven

5. Comfort station

6. To be economical with the truth

7. In reduced circumstances

8. Lose your lunch

9. Revenue enhancements

10. Unmentionables

11. Sanitation engineer

12. Chemical dependency

13. Enhanced interrogation techniques

14. Electronic surveillance

15. Job action

CLOTHING

From A to Z, how many articles of clothing can you come up with in two minutes?

long-term memory
working memory
executive functioning
processing speed

A _____

B _____

C _____

D _____

E _____

F _____

G _____

H _____

I _____

J _____

K _____

L _____

M _____

N _____

O _____

P _____

Q _____

R _____

S _____

T _____

U _____

V _____

W _____

X _____

Y _____

Z _____

pro and *con*

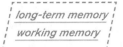

All of the answers in this word definition game begin with either the letters PRO or the letters CON.

1. To delay, postpone, or put off doing something.

_____

2. Any kind of competition or challenge where there is usually a winner and a prize.

_____

3. The "go-to" guy or gal in a hotel for just about anything you need.

_____

4. Bottled gas commonly used in barbecues.

_____

5. An Italian dry-cured ham that is sliced very thin and usually served uncooked.

_____

6. A person, such as an apprentice or student, who is helped or guided by someone else.

_____

7. Formerly called Zaire, its capital is Kinshasa.

_____

8. A huge fire that destroys a great deal of property or land.

_____

9. Tool used in math class to measure angles.

_____

10. Word for a person who favors traditional views and values and tends to oppose change.

_____

11. Fruits and vegetables.

_____

12. Can't, won't, and don't, for example.

_____

13. Person who writes the code that makes computers work.

_____

14. This describes a disease that's easily spread.

_____

15. Government attorney who institutes a legal case against defendants.

_____

16. A tricky question, like a riddle.

_____

What Do They Have in Common?

Each question contains a list of several items. Can you figure out what they have in common?

1. Burr, Barkley, Humphrey, and Rockefeller

2. Acute, right, and obtuse

3. *Night Watch, Water Lilies, The Starry Night,* and *American Gothic*

4. "The Sleeper," "Around the World," and "Walk the Dog"

5. A tree, a bank, and a library

6. Tiger, panda, and mako shark

7. Locks, a typewriter, and music

8. Gaeta, Spanish, and kalamata

9. Zippers, combs, gears, a saw, and a shark

10. Kampuchea, Ceylon, Siam, and Burma

11. Report cards, a slope, an elementary school, and meat

12. Wombat, wallaby, possum, and kangaroo

13. A book, a property owner, a song, and Queen Elizabeth

---

 trivia

TAKE YOUR VITAMINS

long-term memory

executive functioning

Here's a dose of trivia about those all-important vitamins.

● Ascorbic acid, plentiful in citrus fruits, is better known as this.

● Bananas, orange juice, and avocados are great sources of this dietary mineral, which is essential for maintaining the salt-fluid balance in the body.

● This vitamin, which comes from the sun, helps absorb calcium and prevent osteoporosis. It is also added to milk, yogurt, and other foods.

● Goiter and other thyroid diseases were drastically reduced when this dietary mineral was added to common table salt.

FILM BIOGRAPHIES

How many of the following film titles in the first column can you match to the real life person, named in the second column, portrayed in the film. For an extra brain boost, try to name the actor who portrayed the main character.

1. Raging Bull
2. Braveheart
3. The Ten Commandments
4. The Spirit of St. Louis
5. Lust for Life
6. The Pride of the Yankees
7. The Agony and the Ecstasy
8. Mommie Dearest
9. Immortal Beloved
10. Ray
11. Gorillas in the Mist
12. Good Night, and Good Luck.
13. Yankee Doodle Dandy
14. What's Love Got to Do with It
15. Walk the Line
16. Lady Sings the Blues
17. Bound for Glory

A. Johnny Cash
B. Dian Fossey
C. Michelangelo
D. Billie Holiday
E. William Wallace
F. Lou Gehrig
G. George M. Cohan
H. Moses
I. Tina Turner
J. Vincent van Gogh
K. Joan Crawford
L. Ludwig van Beethoven
M. Charles A. Lindbergh
N. Jake LaMotta
O. Edward R. Murrow
P. Woody Guthrie
Q. Ray Charles

---

trivia

HIGH SCHOOL READING LIST

Can you name these classic books—they're often required reading for high school students.

● Harriet Beecher Stowe's goal in writing this book was to convince her large Northern readership of the necessity of ending slavery.

● This outlaw was a popular English folk hero since medieval times. Howard Pyle compiled the traditional stories into a novel in 1893.

● In this classic Mark Twain novel, poor Tom Canty exchanges clothes with a wealthy royal boy, and for a while they live each other's lives.

● This is George Bernard Shaw's most beloved play, and is the basis for Lerner and Loewe's 1950s musical *My Fair Lady*.

u.s. citizen test

Applicants for U.S. citizenship are required to take a test to demonstrate their "knowledge and understanding of the fundamentals of the history, and of the principles and form of government of the United States." How well would you do if you had to take the test?

1. What are the first three words of the Constitution?

2. What are two of the three "inalienable rights" mentioned in the Declaration of Independence?

3. How many justices are on the Supreme Court?

4. Name three of the thirteen original states.

5. What do we call the first ten amendments to the Constitution?

6. What is *one* right (or freedom) guaranteed by the First Amendment?

7. How many U.S. Senators are there?

8. If both the president and the vice president can no longer serve, who becomes president?

9. Name the two longest rivers in the United States.

10. Name one (of five) U.S. territories.

11. How many amendments does the Constitution have?

12. Under our Constitution, some powers are exclusive to the federal government. What is one of these four powers cited in the Constitution?

long-term memory
executive functioning

a lot of bread

long-term memory
executive functioning
attention to detail

Can you identify the breads pictured here—and the countries, regions, or cultures they come from?

❶ _____

❷ _____

❸ _____

❹ _____

5 _____

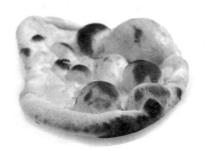

6 _____

7 _____

8 _____

Palindromes

Palindromes are words or phrases that read the same backward and forward. *Madam, I'm Adam* is a well-known palindrome. In this game, all of the answers are one-word palindromes.

1. A quick glance, or a chick's chirp.

2. A short, sharp, sound . . . from a car horn or a trumpet, for example.

3. A small child.

4. Dunce, nitwit, idiot.

5. Iranian rulers—before the Islamic revolution.

6. A technology that uses electromagnetic waves to detect objects in its path.

7. A principle or belief, especially one of the main principles of a religion or philosophy.

8. Legal proof of property ownership.

9. Pertaining to cities or citizenship; it's also a Honda car model.

10. A carpenter's tool used to ensure that a surface or edge has no part higher than another.

11. Novels or series of novels in which generations of people in a group or family are chronicled over many pages.

---

trivia

NOTABLE LASTS

long-term memory

executive functioning

This quiz explores some notable "lasts" in history.

● On December 25, 1991, the Soviet flag was removed from the Kremlin, and this last leader of the USSR resigned.

● On January 27, 2006, this company sent its last telegram.

● In January 1971, the last advertisement for this harmful product was aired on U.S. television.

● Frederik Willem de Klerk was the last leader of South Africa under this racist system.

Famous Movie Lines

How many of these memorable movie lines can you identify? Four stars if you can name the character, the actor who said the line, and the name of the film.

1. "The stuff that dreams are made of."

2. "Show me the money!"

3. "Why don't you come up sometime and see me?"

4. "Badges? We ain't got no badges! We don't need no badges! I don't have to show you any stinking badges!"

5. "I see dead people."

6. "Well, nobody's perfect."

7. "I'm walking here! I'm walking here!"

8. "This morning I shot an elephant in my pajamas. How he got into my pajamas, I'll never know."

9. "A boy's best friend is his mother."

10. "Gentlemen, you can't fight in here! This is the War Room!"

11. "No wire hangers, ever!"

12. "Life is a banquet, and most poor suckers are starving to death!"

13. "Carpe diem. Seize the day, boys. Make your lives extraordinary."

14. "Snap out of it!"

15. "My mother thanks you. My father thanks you. My sister thanks you. And I thank you."

OCTOBER IN HISTORY

This trivia quiz will stretch your long-term memory muscles.

1400   This "Father of English Literature," best remembered for writing *The Canterbury Tales,* died and became the first poet to be buried in Westminster Abbey.

1825   This waterway, which connected the Great Lakes with the Atlantic Ocean, was opened for commercial traffic.

1867   This country's flag was lowered in Sitka, Alaska, and replaced by the Stars and Stripes.

1917   The October Revolution (also called Red October) began when this Bolshevik leader (and later the first premier of the Soviet Union) seized government buildings in Petrograd.

1923   The more centrally located city of Ankara was named as the new capital of this country.

1939   A letter written by four leading scientists was delivered to President Franklin Roosevelt urging him to support the development of the atomic bomb. How many of the scientists can you name?

1945   President Harry Truman announced that the United States would share the secret of the atomic bomb technology with only these two countries.

1946   Ten high-ranking Nazi officials, including Joachim von Ribbentrop, Hermann Goering, and Rudolf Hess, were executed in this German city where their famous ten-month long trial was held.

1947   This Air Force test pilot became the first person to break the sound barrier, flying at Mach 1 speed over Southern California.

1961   This New York Yankee hitter broke the home run record set by Babe Ruth in 1927.

1962   President John F. Kennedy delivered a televised address announcing a full military blockade of Cuba. Why?

1975   *Saturday Night Live* debuted on NBC. How many of the original cast of seven can you name?

1980 During a presidential debate with incumbent Jimmy Carter, candidate Ronald Reagan asked voters this memorable question about their economic status.

1981 This President of Egypt was assassinated in Cairo—just three years after he won the Nobel Peace Prize for ending the conflict between Egypt and Israel.

1984 Baby Fae of Loma Linda, California, who was born with a severe heart defect, underwent an experimental transplant. She lived for twenty-one days with the heart of this animal.

1984 This Prime Minister of India was assassinated near her residence by two of her own security guards.

1985 This actor became the first major U.S. celebrity to die from complications due to AIDS, raising public awareness of the growing epidemic.

1987 After an intensely partisan and contentious Senate hearing, this Reagan Supreme Court nominee was rejected by a Senate vote of fifty-eight to forty-two.

2004 This baseball team "reversed the curse" and won the World Series for the first time since 1918.

---

trivia

SPEAK LATIN

long-term memory

executive functioning

Who says Latin is a dead language? We still use these Latin phrases.

● This motto of the U.S. Marine Corps means "Always faithful."

● This two-word Latin phrase means "Let the buyer beware."

● This two-word Latin phrase refers to the university that one attends or has attended.

● Widely considered the original motto of the USA, this three-word Latin phrase means "Out of many, one."

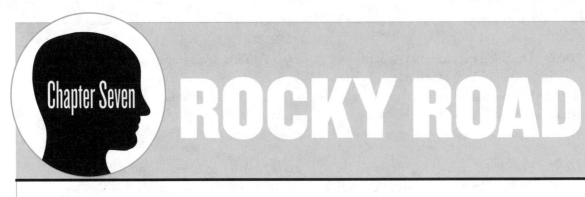

Chapter Seven

ROCKY ROAD

calculate the titles

To calculate the correct answer for each question, you have to figure out the missing number in each title and then add them together.

1. The _____ Faces of Eve plus

_____ Coins in the Fountain = _____

2. _____ Angry Men plus Catch-_____ = _____

3. A Tale of _____ Cities plus

Around the World in _____ Days = _____

4. Fahrenheit _____ plus

_____ Weddings and a Funeral = _____

5. _____ Leagues Under the Sea plus

The House of the _____ Gables = _____

6. _____ Dalmatians plus

_____ Degrees of Separation = _____

7. _____ Easy Pieces plus

_____ Men and a Baby = _____

8. _____ Arabian Nights plus

The _____ Musketeers = _____

9. North Dallas _____ plus

Slaughterhouse- _____ = _____

10. _____ Amigos plus

_____ Candles = _____

11. The _____ Steps plus

The Crying of Lot _____ = _____

long-term memory
executive functioning

endings and beginnings

A compound word is made up of two smaller words, such as *stopwatch* or *panhandle*. In this game, we provide the first half of one compound word and the second half of another. Can you figure out the one word that completes them both? (If you get stuck, the first letter of the answer is provided in a hint.)

long-term memory
working memory
executive functioning

1. Flash _____ bone   (hint: b)

2. Pad_____smith   (hint: l)

3. Sun _____ dream   (hint: d)

4. Foot _____ worthy   (hint: n)

5. Bob _____ calls   (hint: c)

6. Weather _____ read   (hint: p)

7. Pay _____ mate   (hint: c)

8. Drum _____ pin   (hint: s)

9. Cup _____ walk   (hint: c)

10. Black _____ box   (hint: m)

11. Paper _____ lifter   (hint: w)

executive functioning
attention to detail

? CLASSIC RIDDLE
A BAD MOVIE

As with many classic riddles, the answer lies in a detail that is omitted from the story.

Oliver and Olivia, a married couple, were the last patrons to be admitted to a sold-out movie. In the middle of the film, Oliver strangled Olivia. Although she was unable to scream, she did put up a struggle until she died a couple of minutes later. When the movie was over, Oliver took his wife's body home.

How did this crime occur without attracting anyone's attention?

two-part word game

long-term memory
executive functioning
attention to detail
multitasking

In Part One of this game you just have to answer the question correctly. In Part Two you need to replace one letter in the answer with an L (without changing the placement of any letters) to get a wholly different word.

1. Word that follows kidney, tomb, or rolling.

_____ _____

2. The number on the black ball in billiards.

_____ _____

3. In Jewish dietary laws, you don't mix meat with this.

_____ _____

4. The absence of war.

_____ _____

5. Fermenting agent that makes bread rise.

_____ _____

6. A small drink of whiskey.

_____ _____

7. Pisa's leaner.

_____ _____

8. Nancy Sinatra said these "were made for walking."

_____ _____

9. What cows do in grassy meadows.

_____ _____

10. A ladies' wallet or pocketbook.

_____ _____

11. Amtrak's rolling stock.

_____ _____

12. Ailing, unwell.

_____ _____

13. To put money away for a rainy day.

_____ _____

14. A practical joke or mischievous act.

_____ _____

15. An evil spirit or devil.

_____ _____

THINK TWICE

All of the two-word answers in this game begin with the initials T and T.

1. "She sells sea shells by the sea shore," for example.

_____

2. To discuss something frankly and straightforwardly—and not just on Thanksgiving.

_____

3. An improbable story, such as those about Pecos Bill and Paul Bunyan.

_____

4. British term for a dishcloth.

_____

5. Another word for a seesaw.

_____

6. You find these in a science lab, alongside the beakers and the Bunsen burners.

_____

7. The last three months of a pregnancy.

_____

8. The sometimes-long process of weaning a child from diapers.

_____

9. Too shy or embarrassed to speak.

_____

10. A tight-fitting strapless upper garment made of stretchy material.

_____

11. The little things that come in packages of plastic trash bags.

_____

12. An establishment created with the aim of attracting paying visitors, such as roadside attractions and gift shops.

_____

13. An organization that conducts research, issues reports, and engages in advocacy in areas such as social policy, political strategy, economic issues, etc.

_____

---

trivia

PRESIDENTS BEFORE AND AFTER

long-term memory
executive functioning

If you know your U.S. presidents, you'll ace this quiz.

● Who was president before and after Bill Clinton?

● Who was president before and after Richard Nixon?

● Who was president before and after Franklin Roosevelt?

● Who was president before and after John Adams?

The Shape of the States

How many of these U.S. states can you identify by their shape? (*Note: The states are not drawn to scale.*)

long-term memory
executive functioning
attention to detail

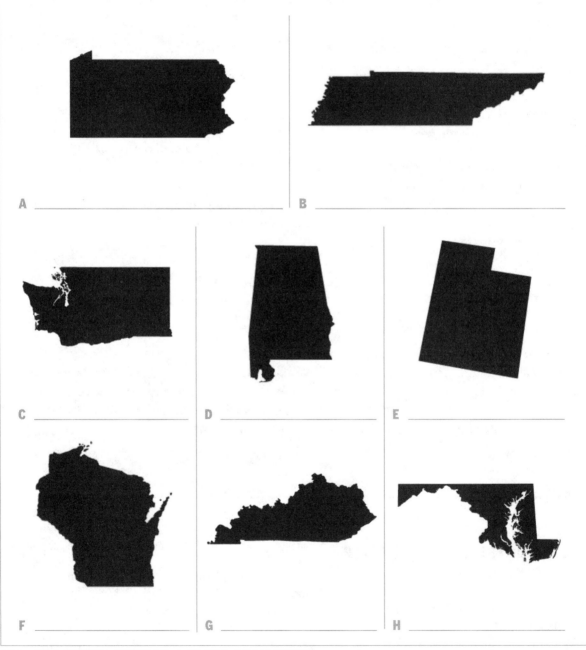

A _____

B _____

C _____

D _____

E _____

F _____

G _____

H _____

I _____

J _____

K _____

REPLACE THE
ARMADILLO

There's something wrong with these book and movie titles. Can you fix them by replacing the word ARMADILLO with the correct animal?

1. *The ARMADILLO, the Witch and the Wardrobe* by C. S. Lewis

_____

2. *The ARMADILLO Whisperer* by Nicholas Evans

_____

3. *Sweet ARMADILLO of Youth* by Tennessee Williams

_____

4. *The Little ARMADILLOS* by Lillian Hellman

_____

5. *The Night of the ARMADILLO* by Tennessee Williams

_____

6. *Island of the Blue ARMADILLOS* by Scott O'Dell

_____

7. *All the Pretty ARMADILLOS* by Cormac McCarthy

_____

8. *The Day of the ARMADILLO* by Nathanael West

_____

9. *The Red ARMADILLO* by John Steinbeck

_____

long-term memory
executive functioning

yo!

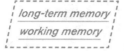

All of the answers in this game either begin or end with the letters YO.

1. People have been making and eating this dairy food—milk fermented by adding bacteria—for more than five thousand years.

_____

2. It's the fourth-most populated city in the state of New York—and the place where much of the action takes place in *Hello, Dolly!*

_____

3. A child, a kid . . . usually under thirteen years of age.

_____

4. A long, distressful, or dismal cry.

_____

5. People in the U.S. southwest know that this is the word for a flat, cracked stream bed that is usually dry except after heavy rains.

_____

6. An uneducated and unsophisticated person from the countryside.

_____

7. This becomes a fetus after two months of development in the womb.

_____

8. An old-fashioned way to express an undetermined distance or "over there." This word appears in the first line of the official song of the U.S. Air Force.

_____

9. This Japanese city near Tokyo has been a central port for foreign trade for more than a hundred and fifty years.

_____

10. This Day of Atonement is the holiest day of the year for Jews.

_____

11. This terrier dog is named after the northern English county where the breed was developed.

_____

12. This seven-mile stretch of pristine California territory became the nation's first national park.

_____

SOBRIQUETS

Unlike nicknames, which are generally used in place of a person's given name, sobriquets are used to describe a person's character, skill, strength, personality, achievement, or reputation. Sobriquets are usually bestowed by historians, journalists, press agents, critics, or the public, and can be either an honor or an insult. How many famous people can you name when given their sobriquets?

1. Deep Throat

2. The Queen of Mean

3. The Sultan of Swat

4. The Iron Lady

5. The Singing Cowboy

6. The Yankee Clipper

7. The Man of a Thousand Faces

8. The Teflon Don

9. The King of Swing

10. The First Lady of the American Stage

11. The Splendid Splinter

12. The Fab Four

13. The Lip

14. The Kingfish

15. Raging Bull

16. The Refrigerator

17. The Hollywood Madam

Follow the Rules

To find out the ending of the phrase that begins "Faithful friends . . ." just follow each instruction carefully. We've provided the first answer, and this warning: It's not as easy as you might think!

1. With no spaces between words, write down the phrase: F A I T H F U L F R I E N D S

2. Remove the twelfth letter and place it in the fourth position.

3. Change the first two F's to A's.

4. Remove the fifth letter and place it after the L.

5. If Ayn Rand wrote *Atlas Shrugged,* place an R after the second and third A. If not, do nothing.

6. If Abraham Lincoln was the twelfth president of the United States, place an L in the twelfth position. If Zachary Taylor was the twelfth president, place an O in the twelfth position.

7. Change the U to a D.

8. Remove the first I.

9. Remove the first and last letters.

10. Remove the eighth and twelfth letters.

F A I T H F U L F R I E N D S

Did you get the right answer?

MEMORABLE SMITHS

long-term memory
executive functioning

People named Smith are the subject of this quiz.

● She was the most popular female blues singer from the early 1920s until her death in a Mississippi car accident in 1937.

● Betty Smith was the author of this wildly popular 1943 novel about growing up poor in a New York City borough.

● Virtually every baby boomer remembers Buffalo Bob Smith, the host of this 1947–1960 kids' show which starred a freckled marionette.

● Appointed to the House of Representatives after the death of her husband in 1940, this Smith from Maine served ten years in the House and twenty-five years in the Senate.

HIT THE DECK

How many **one-word** answers can you come up with to complete the phrase that begins with *Hit the* _____? We came up with eighteen of them, including *Hit the deck*. For an extra brain boost, see how many answers you can come up with in one minute.

Hit the _____*deck*_____   Hit the _____

Hit the _____   Hit the _____

Hit the _____   Hit the _____

Hit the _____   Hit the _____

Hit the _____   Hit the _____

Hit the _____   Hit the _____

Hit the _____   Hit the _____

Hit the _____   Hit the _____

Hit the _____   Hit the _____

long-term memory
working memory
processing speed

whoozy

How many clues do you need to guess who the WHOOZY is? One to three clues—Outstanding; three to seven clues—Very Good; six to eight clues—Time to study up on your WHOOZYs.

1. WHOOZY was born in 1905 in Houston, Texas. At age eleven he built Houston's first radio transmitter, and at twelve he motorized a bicycle.

2. WHOOZY's mother died when he was seventeen, and his father died two years later, leaving him a company and a substantial inheritance.

3. At age twenty, WHOOZY moved to Hollywood to make a name for himself as a movie producer. He began dating some of Hollywood's elite actresses including Bette Davis, Ava Gardner, Olivia de Havilland, and Katharine Hepburn.

4. While still in Hollywood, WHOOZY started a new division of his father's company dedicated to the design and manufacture of airplanes.

5. As early as the 1930s WHOOZY showed signs of mental illness, primarily obsessive-compulsive disorder and frequent mood swings.

6. By the 1940s WHOOZY's behavior grew more bizarre. He moved from hotel to hotel and rarely ventured outside. Sometimes he would not bathe or cut his nails for weeks at a time.

7. WHOOZY died in 1976. An autopsy noted that he was in poor physical condition. X-rays revealed broken-off hypodermic needles embedded in his arms and severe malnutrition.

8. WHOOZY left a $2.5 billion estate and no will.

---

 trivia

WHAT'S THE ADDRESS?

long-term memory

executive functioning

You don't need a GPS to find these famous locations.

● What is the street address of the White House?

● What was the name of Scarlett O'Hara's family plantation?

● Where would you find the Breakers, the 70-room summer "cottage" built by Cornelius Vanderbilt?

● What is the New York street address of NBC headquarters and studios?

TV catch phrases

How many popular television programs can you identify from this list of iconic catch phrases?

1. "How sweet it is!"

_____

2. "Hi Ho, Silver!"

_____

3. "I'd like to buy a vowel."

_____

4. "Now cut that out!"

_____

5. "Good night, John Boy."

_____

6. "Is that your final answer?"

_____

7. "Stifle, Edith!"

_____

8. "Sock it to me."

_____

9. "Norm!"

_____

10. "You've got spunk. I hate spunk!"

_____

11. "Live long and prosper."

_____

12. "It's a common word, something you see every day."

_____

13. "Say kids, what time is it?"

_____

14. "This tape will self-destruct in five seconds."

_____

long-term memory
executive functioning

PICTURE THEMES

The pictures in each column may seem like they have nothing in common. But if you look carefully, you'll see a theme emerge. Can you figure out the unique theme for each column of three pictures?

Column A

Column B

A _____

B _____

Column C

C _____

Column D

D _____

Finish the Quote

Can you finish these well-known quotations?

1. Yogi Berra: "When you come to a fork in the road . . ." (2 words)

_____

2. Patrick Henry: "I know not what course others may take, but as for me . . ." (7 words)

_____

_____

3. Abraham Lincoln: "A house divided against itself . . ." (2 words)

_____

4. Benjamin Franklin: "There never was a good war or . . ." (3 words)

_____

5. Thomas Edison: "Genius is one percent inspiration and . . ." (3 words)

_____

6. Richard Nixon: "When the President does it, that means that . . ." (4 words)

_____

7. Ralph Waldo Emerson: "Do not go where the path may lead, go instead where there is no path . . ." (4 words)

_____

8. Mark Twain: "I never let my schooling interfere with . . ." (2 words)

_____

9. Martin Luther King Jr.: "I have a dream that my four little children will one day live in a nation where they will not be judged by the color of their skin but . . ." (6 words)

_____

_____

Anagrams

The letters of each word in this list can be arranged in multiple ways to form other words. We provide the word and the number of anagrams that are possible to make.

1. Please (2) _____ _____

2. Lemons (2) _____ _____

3. Capitol (2) _____ _____

4. Darters (3) _____ _____ _____

5. Dearths (4) _____ _____ _____ _____

6. Terrains (4) _____ _____ _____ _____

7. Cautioned (2) _____ _____

8. Emigrants (2) _____ _____

9. Discounter (2) _____ _____

 trivia

PERSON OF THE YEAR

long-term memory
executive functioning

Every year *Time* magazine selects a Person (or sometimes a group, organization, or object) of the Year who, "for better or for worse . . . has done the most to influence the events of the year." Can you recall these winners?

● He was named "Person of the Year" in 1991 for "revolutionizing news coverage."

● He got the title in 1938 for building a massive army and for his "defiant, ruthless foreign policy."

● In 1966, the title was given not to a single person but to this entire group of people who ranged in age from two to twenty.

● In 2001 the title was given to this "icon of steadfastness in the midst of chaos."

ick!

All of the answers in this word definition game contain the consecutive letters ICK.

1. A small cucumber preserved in a vinegar or brine solution.

2. Garbanzo beans.

3. What striking workers do to persuade others not to enter a building.

4. To argue frequently about petty or trivial things.

5. This disease, often characterized by bowed legs, was very common until the 1920s when its cause was found to be a vitamin D deficiency.

6. One of the most popular candy bars, it consists of peanut nougat, topped with peanuts and caramel, and covered in chocolate.

7. A very heavy, slightly sweet dark rye bread of German origin.

8. Hard woven plant material often made into patio furniture.

9. This Japanese word translates as "human-powered vehicle." Made of bamboo, it was often used to transport the social elite.

10. In *Oliver Twist,* this was the Artful Dodger's occupation.

11. Moniker or epithet.

DOUBLE TROUBLE

Compound words are made up of two smaller words, such as *hayloft* or *watchtower*. In this game, we give the first half of some compound words. You must identify the one word that follows each of them to make a compound word. For example, given the words *knuckle, moth,* and *basket,* the one word that makes each a compound word is *ball* (*knuckleball, mothball,* and *basketball*).

1. Tomb, gall, gem, stepping   (hint: s)

2. Crew, hair, upper, short   (hint: c)

3. No, some, home, busy   (hint: b)

4. Pepper, pop, barley   (hint: c)

5. Band, grand, hand, under   (hint: s)

6. Center, mantel, hair, time   (hint: p)

7. Arm, head, waist, contra   (hint: b)

8. Ear, head, micro, speaker   (hint: p)

9. Tender, bare, club, hot   (hint: f)

10. Band, cheer, ring   (hint: l)

11. Gum, horse, snow   (hint: s)

12. Cross, hang, push, take   (hint: o)

13. Space, witch, hover, needle   (hint: c)

14. Heart, side, sun, wind   (hint: b)

working memory
executive functioning

TRIMBLE

Trimble is a trivia game and a word jumble combined. First, answer the trivia questions and cross out the letters of each answer in the letter grid. Then rearrange the remaining letters (those that have not been crossed out) to reveal another word or phrase related to the same theme.

Questions: The theme is *people named John*, and the jumble consists of two words.

1. This John hosted *The Tonight Show* for thirty years.

2. This John, a movie icon, starred in *The Searchers* (1956), *Rio Grande* (1950), and *True Grit* (1969).

3. This John founded the Standard Oil Company in 1870 and is often considered the richest man that ever lived.

4. This John is famous for his mastery of the game of tennis and for his confrontational on-court behavior.

5. This John lost the 2004 presidential election to George W. Bush.

6. This John starred in *Saturday Night Fever, Grease,* and *Welcome Back, Kotter.*

7. This John painted, catalogued, and described the birds of North America.

A	A	A	A	A	B	C	C	C	D	E	E
E	E	E	E	E	E	F	H	J	K	K	L
L	L	L	M	N	N	N	N	N	N	N	N
O	O	O	O	O	O	O	R	R	R	R	R
R	R	S	T	T	U	U	V	W	Y	Y	

art and *sol*

All the answers in this word definition game begin with the letters ART or SOL.

1. These blood vessels carry blood away from the heart.

_____

2. Joint disease.

_____

3. Firm, dense, and stable in shape.

_____

4. Examples of this part of speech are *a, an,* and *the.*

_____

5. To find the answer to a problem.

_____

6. Having the ability to speak fluently and coherently.

_____

long-term memory
working memory

7. In archaeology, these are found items of cultural interest that were made by a human being.

_____

8. Trade union instrumental in the collapse of Communism in Poland.

_____

9. *Not* the real thing—like plastic Christmas trees or saccharine.

_____

10. Large caliber guns used by the military on land.

_____

11. A speech given by a lone character in a play.

_____

12. A state of seclusion or isolation, either chosen or enforced.

_____

★ NOVEMBER IN HISTORY ★

This trivia quiz will stretch your long-term memory muscles.

1604 This play by William Shakespeare was first performed at Whitehall Palace in London. It features an African prince/general in the Venetian military, his wife Desdemona, and the villainous Iago.

1869 This waterway between the Mediterranean Sea and the Red Sea was opened to shipping traffic. Ten years in construction, it enabled ships to travel from Europe to Asia without having to go around Africa.

1883 Four standard time zones were established for the continental United States under pressure from this industry.

1918 At the eleventh hour, on the eleventh day, of the eleventh month, this came to an official end.

1922 The entrance to the ancient tomb of this "Boy King" was discovered in Egypt.

1938 Nazis looted and burned seventy-five hundred Jewish businesses and homes, destroyed 267 synagogues, and killed or rounded up more than twenty-five hundred Jewish men in Germany and Austria. By what name is this violent night known?

1942 A fire in the Cocoanut Grove nightclub in this city killed nearly five hundred people, including cowboy film star Buck Jones.

1945 The yearlong "Trial of the Major War Criminals" before the International Military Tribunal commenced in this German city. Twenty-two captured Nazi leaders were tried, including Martin Bormann, Hermann Goering, and Rudolf Hess.

1959 This English professor and son of a Pulitzer Prize–winning poet confessed to a House subcommittee that he had been given the correct answers in the TV game show *Twenty-One*.

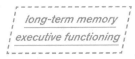

long-term memory
executive functioning

1962   The United Nations passed a resolution condemning this brutal South African system of racial segregation.

1963   President John Kennedy was killed and this Texas governor was injured while riding in a motorcade in Dallas, Texas.

1966   He became the first African American elected to the U.S. Senate.

1968   Richard Nixon won the presidency, defeating Vice President Hubert H. Humphrey and this third party candidate.

1973   President Nixon's personal secretary was questioned by a federal court about eighteen-and-a-half minutes that had been erased from a key Watergate audiotape. What was the secretary's name?

1978   Mayor George Moscone and City Supervisor Harvey Milk were shot to death inside this city's City Hall.

1979   Three days after he urged all Iranians to expand their attacks against the U.S. and Israel, militants seized the U.S. Embassy in Tehran and took sixty-three hostages.

1980   American TV viewers finally learned that Kristin Shepard, the sister-in-law played by Mary Crosby, was the one who committed this famous TV crime.

1986   Attorney General Edwin Meese revealed that the U.S. government secretly sold arms to Iran and then gave the profits to a rebel group in this country that was trying to overthrow the government.

1991   This Los Angeles Lakers basketball star announced that he had tested positive for the AIDS virus and was retiring.

1999   This six-year-old Cuban refugee was found floating in an inner tube off the Florida coast by sport fishermen—an event that would spark a seven-month, high profile custody battle between his Cuban and U.S. relatives.

---

trivia

GOING FOR GOLD

long-term memory

executive functioning

They're all gold medal winners. Can you name their sport?

● Jean-Claude Killy, France (1968)

● Sonja Henie, Norway (1928, 1932, 1936)

● Eric Heiden, USA (1980)

● Herb Brooks, USA (1980)

TV catch phrases

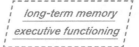

How many popular television programs can you identify from this list of iconic catch phrases?

1. "An' a one . . . an' a two . . ."

_____

2. "Just the facts, ma'am."

_____

3. "And the survey says . . ."

_____

4. "I'm Larry. This is my brother Darryl. And this is my other brother Darryl."

_____

5. "I know nothing!"

_____

6. "Marcia, Marcia, Marcia!"

_____

7. "Good night, and good luck."

_____

8. "Kiss my grits."

_____

9. "Remember to have your pet spayed or neutered."

_____

10. "The balcony is closed."

_____

11. "Would you believe . . ."

_____

12. "Up your nose with a rubber hose."

_____

13. "Let's be careful out there!"

_____

14. "I pity the fool."

_____

15. "Danger, Will Robinson!"

_____

16. "And now, for something completely different . . ."

_____

Stinky Pinky

We have twentieth century humorist George S. Kaufman to thank for this game (and for its unusual title). Each Stinky Pinky answer contains two words that rhyme—but you have to figure out what that answer is from an offbeat definition.

1. Azure paste

2. A stupid finger

3. A fast present

4. A tropical fruit dance

5. A forbidden hair wash

6. A canine from a muddy, peat-filled area

7. Bozo with a tan

8. Fisticuffs between flying toys

9. A tennis tool cover

10. A peppy Thanksgiving food

11. A cacophonous gathering of people

Border States

How many of the thirteen U.S. states that border Canada can you name in one minute?

ODD MAN OUT

All of the items in each list have something in common except one thing. Your job is to figure out which item is the "Odd Man Out"—and why.

1. *The Nutcracker*; *Swan Lake*; *Carmen*; *The Sleeping Beauty*

2. Jocund; blithe; morose; rapturous

3. South Africa; Jamaica; Japan; Canada; New Zealand

4. Vivid; birds; spare; sibling; victim

5. *Uncle Tom's Cabin*; *Huckleberry Finn*; *To Kill a Mockingbird*; *The Color Purple*

6. New York City; Los Angeles; Dallas; Philadelphia; Boston

7. Awkward; etiquette; igloo; office; able; image

8. Japan; Mexico; Jordan; Great Britain; Monaco

9. *Mary Poppins*; *Miracle on 34th Street*; *A Fish Called Wanda*; *To Sir, with Love*

10. Brass; plumber; bomb; debt; comb

11. Chorizo; paella; moussaka; gazpacho

12. Pocket; obeyed; fear; alarm; handsome

13. Warren Beatty; Anne Bancroft; Gene Hackman; Faye Dunaway

14. London; Oslo; Warsaw; Asmara; Ankara

geographical name game

Complete the names of these famous real and fictional people, whose first or last name can also be found on a map. Try it first without using the hints.

1. Abraham _____
Capital of Nebraska

2. Bob _____
Hometown of Bill Clinton

3. Irving_____
Capital of Germany

4. Jack _____
Capital of the United Kingdom

5. Michael _____
Capital of Mississippi

6. Christopher _____
Capital of Ohio

7. Joe _____
"Big Sky" state

8. John_____
Capital of Colorado

9. Oscar_____
Capital of Wisconsin

10. Dick_____
City in northern England

11. Grover _____
Second-largest city in Ohio

12. Janet _____
Second-largest city in Nevada

13. Denzel _____
Capital of the United States

14. _____ Clift
Capital city of Alabama

15. _____ Henderson
City called *Firenze* in Italy

16. _____ Williams
Home state of Nashville and Memphis

17. _____ Clinton
A very hip section of London

18. _____ Jones
Home state of South Bend and Ft. Wayne

19. _____ O'Keefe
Gone with the Wind state

20. _____ Fats
"Land of 10,000 Lakes"

long-term memory
executive functioning

kangaroo words

A Kangaroo Word is a word that contains letters of another word, in the correct order (though not necessarily contiguous), that has the same meaning. For example, the word *acrid* contains the word *acid,* and both words have similar meanings. The word *expurgate* contains its synonym *purge*. In this game, we provide the longer word. Can you find the shorter one? (*Note: The longer word is called the "kangaroo," and the shorter word is called the "joey," which is the name for a baby kangaroo that lives in its mother's pouch.*)

1. Astound

2. Chocolate

3. Container

4. Capable

5. Amicable

6. Damsel

7. Belated

8. Allocate

9. Cartoon

10. Disappointed

11. Observe

12. Encourage

13. Evacuate

14. Municipality

15. Instructor

16. Strives

17. Separate

18. Fabrication

Follow the Rules

Following rules is harder than it seems. All you have to do to find the ending to the saying that begins "Rain does not fall . . ." is to precisely follow each instruction. We've provided the first answer. Can you get to the end without making a mistake?

1. With no spaces between words, write down the phrase: R A I N D O E S N O T F A L L

2. Swap the first and ninth letters.

3. Place an O before every N and T.

4. Remove the eighth letter and place it in the next-to-last position.

5. Remove the first E and place it in the seventh position.

6. If Iowa is northeast of Nebraska, place NE in the eighteenth and nineteenth positions. If Iowa is southwest of Nebraska, place IA in the second and third positions.

7. Remove the first A and the last L.

8. If the word "they" is an adjective, add AD in the beginning. If the word "they" is a pronoun, remove the letters IT.

9. If Katie Couric used to be an anchor on *Good Morning America,* add a K in the third position and a C in the ninth position. If Diane Sawyer used to be an anchor on *Good Morning America,* remove the letters D and S.

R A I N D O E S N O T F A L L

Did you get the right answer?

BEATLES TUNES

Hidden in this grid—printed forward, backward, and diagonally—are words and phrases from the titles of twenty-six popular songs recorded by the Beatles. Fill in the missing words in the song list on the next page, then find them (the missing words only) in the grid. For an extra-challenging brain workout, put a three-minute timer on this game.

E	H	O	L	D	Y	O	U	R	H	A	N	D
R	R	X	Y	R	R	E	B	W	A	R	T	S
E	E	E	F	N	O	R	W	E	G	I	A	N
P	S	T	H	E	U	S	S	R	W	E	D	X
P	O	W	X	T	L	O	N	G	V	Y	N	E
I	L	I	F	E	G	L	W	O	B	R	A	N
R	A	C	C	O	O	N	L	G	Z	I	T	I
T	T	H	A	T	W	E	I	G	H	T	S	R
B	A	B	Y	X	M	R	E	D	Z	A	I	A
A	D	A	O	R	G	N	I	D	N	I	W	M
C	A	N	N	O	D	A	M	T	U	A	T	B
K	E	E	W	A	S	Y	A	D	E	J	T	U
I	T	B	E	T	H	E	W	A	L	R	U	S

Word List

- ____, It's You
- Back in ___ _____
- Can't Buy ___ _____
- Carry _____ _____
- Day _____
- Eight _____ __ _____
- Eleanor _____
- Get _____
- Hey _____
- I Am ____ _____
- I Saw Her _____ _____
- I Want to _____ _____ _____
- I'm a _____
- If I _____
- In My _____
- Lady _____
- Let ___ __
- _____ Tall Sally
- Lovely _____
- _____ Wood
- Paperback _____
- Rocky _____
- _____ Fields Forever
- The Long and _____ ___
- _____ _____ Shout
- Yellow _____

REPLACE THE SWAMP

There's something wrong with these book, song, and movie titles. Can you fix them by replacing the word SWAMP with the correct geographical feature?

1. *SWAMP of the Dolls* by Jacqueline Susann

_____

2. *Brokeback SWAMP* by Annie Proulx

_____

3. *A SWAMP Runs Through It* by Norman Maclean

_____

4. "Sitting on the Dock of the SWAMP" (song by Otis Redding)

_____

5. "The Lady of the SWAMP" by Sir Walter Scott

_____

6. *Under the SWAMP* by Malcolm Lowry

_____

7. *The SWAMP Book* by Rudyard Kipling

_____

8. *On the SWAMP* by Nevil Shute

_____

9. *Spoon SWAMP Anthology* by Edgar Lee Masters

_____

10. *SWAMPS in the SWAMP* by Ernest Hemingway

_____

what comes next?

long-term memory
executive functioning
attention to detail

Can you figure out the next logical item in each series of items? For example, if the list included *Red, Orange, Yellow, Green* . . . , then the next logical item, as determined by the color spectrum, would be *Blue*.

1. Steve Allen, Jack Paar, Johnny Carson . . .

2. Gold rings, calling birds, French hens, turtle doves . . .

3. December, November, October, September . . .

4. Maine, Maryland, Massachusetts . . .

5. L, LX, LXX, LXXX, XC . . .

6. One day, 48 hours, three days . . .

7. 1, 5, 10, 25 . . .

8. Asia, Africa, North America, South America . . .

9. Mercury, Venus, Earth, Mars . . .

10. Q, W, E, R, T . . .

11. Alpha, beta, gamma . . .

12. 2, 3, 5, 7, 11 . . .

13. 7, 8, 9, *, 0 . . .

14. Mondale, Bush, Quayle . . .

ALPHABETICAL WORLD TOUR

long-term memory
executive functioning

How well do you know the countries of Europe—alphabetically?

● Name two of the three European countries that begin with the letter I.

● Name three of the seven European countries that begin with the letter S.

● What country that starts with the letter T lies partially in Europe and partially in Asia?

● Name the two European countries that begin with the letter P.

rhyme ❖ time ❖

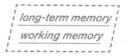
Each question in this game includes two definitions for two different words. The twist is, they will rhyme.

1. Something unexpected; and to dress in a way that changes or hides your true appearance.

2. Microbe or bacteria; and to wriggle or twist the body, especially when nervous or uncomfortable.

3. To express an opposing opinion; and home state of Al Gore and Davy Crockett.

4. A greeting; and author of *Civil Disobedience* and *Walden*.

5. A marine mollusk; and a baby goat.

6. To refuse to allow, to prohibit; and the capital city of Spain.

7. A menu of individual dishes; and military decoration for those wounded in action.

8. A puffy baked custard; and sherbet without dairy.

9. Scottish wool flecked with colors; and to mix bread dough.

10. A promise or vow; and a piece of pie or cheese.

11. Device that controls the flow of fuel to an engine; and a glass container.

12. Bright, brilliant, intense; and furiously angry.

13. Orange melon; and gazelle or impala.

14. It follows *pea* and *coco*; and golf swing.

what's your movie song IQ?

Given a sampling of the lyrics, can you identify these movies from their hit songs?

1. "Clang, clang, clang went the trolley."

2. "Who is the man that would risk his neck for his brother man . . ."

3. "You better shape up, 'cause I need a man . . ."

4. "Love lift us up where we belong . . ."

5. "Tumble out of bed and stumble to the kitchen . . ."

6. "If you get caught between the moon and New York City . . ."

7. "Now I've had the time of my life."

8. "Getting to know you, getting to know all about you."

9. "The night is bitter, the stars have lost their glitter . . ."

10. "Heaven, I'm in heaven . . ."

11. "Would you like to swing on a star . . ."

12. "Get your motor runnin'. Head out on the highway . . ."

long-term memory
executive functioning

par for the course

All of the answers in this word definition game begin with the letters PAR.

1. Emergency-wear for a test pilot.

_____

2. Common house pet called a budgie in England and Australia.

_____

3. The Eskimo word for this winter wear is *anorak*.

_____

4. Candles are usually made of this waxy substance.

_____

5. An umbrella-like device that protects the user from the sun.

_____

6. Although this bird nests on the ground, it's possible you'd find one roosting in a pear tree.

_____

7. In ancient times, this material made from animal skins was used as paper. Today, the more common version is made from vegetable pulp and is often used in baking.

_____

8. The main ingredient in this drug, once used to calm fretful children and to ease teething, diarrhea, or coughing, was opium. Today, it's classified as a narcotic and little used.

_____

9. This root vegetable looks like a white carrot.

_____

10. The House of Lords and the House of Commons make up this legislative body in England.

_____

11. Medically trained professional usually charged with providing emergency on-scene treatment and the transport of patients to the hospital.

_____

12. To imitate a work with deliberate exaggeration for comic effect.

_____

13. These curved brackets set off a word or clause in a sentence and indicate that it is an afterthought.

_____

NAME MERGE

Given a clue for each of two famous people, can you figure out what name they share? For example: *Clarence Thomas Jefferson* or *Jesse James Cagney.*

1. She played Rhoda Morgenstern; and she wrote *To Kill a Mockingbird.*

2. She played Auntie Mame on Broadway and in film during the 1950s; and he is the Australian actor who starred in *Gladiator.*

3. African American stand-up comedian who spent three years on *Saturday Night Live;* and 1950s romantic comedy heartthrob who often costarred with Doris Day.

4. He played the scientist "Doc" Emmett Brown in the *Back to the Future* movies; and he starred in *Seahunt* and was father to actors Beau and Jeff.

5. She was best known as a panelist on *What's My Line?*; and he wrote "The Star-Spangled Banner."

6. He sang "Hello Muddah, Hello Faddah"; and he played George Jefferson in TV's *All in the Family* and its spinoff series *The Jeffersons.*

7. Convicted assassin of Martin Luther King Jr.; and author of *Fahrenheit 451* and many science fiction short stories.

8. Great Balls of Fire! He was a rock 'n' roll pioneer in the 1950s until scandal involving his marriage to his thirteen-year-old cousin nearly ended his career; and the physician and researcher who wrote *Lives of a Cell: Notes of a Biology Watcher* in 1974.

back to *back*

All of the answers in this word definition game either begin or end with the word BACK.

1. The spine.

2. Large baleen whale known for its beautiful songs.

3. An ancient board game for two players with fifteen moveable pieces for each player.

4. Slang term for U.S. paper money.

5. The accumulation of uncompleted work that needs to be dealt with.

6. A sedan with a large upward-swinging door in the rear.

7. A person who sabotages a friend.

8. For many teething babies, this baked product was their first taste of real food.

9. A return to former glory, such as when an actor's career has failed and is then revived by a hit movie.

10. Remote and usually uninhabited regions of Australia.

11. A sudden, vivid memory from the past.

12. Improper or illegal payment for a favor; it's also called graft or payola.

WORKING WOMEN

long-term memory
executive functioning

See if you can identify these accomplished women.

● She was the first female astronaut in space and, at age thirty-two, the youngest astronaut to orbit the earth.

● Although *Little Women* was her best-known work, she wrote 270 other books.

● Near death in 1866, she turned to the Bible and recovered—an experience that led her to start the Christian Science Church in 1879.

● The daughter of missionaries, she grew up in China and wrote about American and Chinese culture. In 1938 she became the first woman to win the Nobel Prize in Literature.

BORROWED FROM
Arabic

Did you know that *apricot, crimson, hazard, jar,* and *tariff* were all originally Arabic words? In this game, you'll discover even more common English words that have been borrowed from Arabic.

1. Morning beverage.

2. This is the only number that's neither positive nor negative.

3. A frozen dessert usually made of fruit or fruit juices.

4. This crop was the backbone of the pre–Civil War southern economy.

5. John Wilkes Booth or Lee Harvey Oswald, for example.

6. Musical instrument, typically with six strings, which is the primary instrument used in flamenco, folk, country, rock, and pop music.

7. It's a fruit . . . and a bad automobile.

8. Makeup for eyelashes.

9. In this branch of mathematics, kids learn about polynomials and symbols for unknown numbers. For example: *3x + 1 = 10.*

10. A colorless, flammable liquid; it's the intoxicating constituent in beer, wine, and other spirits.

11. This word puts an end to any chess game.

12. Many scientists believe our craving for this sweet substance has led to the obesity epidemic in the United States.

13. The original Arabic word means "raw silk," but we use it more often to describe the loosely woven cloth used to dress wounds.

14. This word describes a light purple color—or the shrub that blooms in May with an abundance of fragrant, light purple flowers.

15. An annual booklet that's usually published in calendar form and often contains weather and climate information.

16. The art of knotting ropes and other textiles. It's used to make hammocks, belts, plant hangers, wall hangings, etc.

17. A percussion instrument that usually has a drum skin for hitting and metal discs along the edge that jingle when shaken.

---

18. The original meaning of this word was "a storage place for arms and ammunition." Today it's more commonly used for a weekly or monthly publication.

---

19. A type of yarn spun from the long hair of an angora goat. Although soft and fluffy, it can be irritating to the skin.

---

20. The highest rank that can be achieved in the U.S. Navy or Coast Guard.

---

21. Both a common legume . . . and the character from *The Little Rascals* who had slicked back hair and an enormous cowlick.

---

22. The tallest of all land mammals, it stands nearly six feet tall when it's born.

---

23. These small, shiny discs are sewn or woven into clothing for decoration.

---

24. You can't play tennis without one of these in your hand.

ONE > MINUTE > MADNESS
Cabinet Members

The U.S. president is advised in matters ranging from farming to the military by the members of his Cabinet. How many of the sixteen Cabinet level positions can you name in one minute? (*Note: All except two of the positions begin with the title "Secretary of . . . ."*)

---

long-term memory
working memory
processing speed

SOBRIQUETS

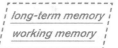
We learned earlier about sobriquets, which, unlike nicknames, are generally used in place of a person's given name and describe their character, skill, strength, personality, achievement, or reputation. Sobriquets are usually bestowed by historians, journalists, press agents, critics, or the public, and can be either an honor or an insult. But sobriquets are not just given to people. In this game we've provided the sobriquet and you must name the place or organization to which it refers.

1. The City of Brotherly Love

2. The Great White North

3. Tinseltown

4. The Land of the Rising Sun

5. The Great White Way

6. The City of Light (or The City of Love)

7. The Emerald Isle

8. The Steel City

9. The Eternal City

10. The Gray Lady

11. The Grand Old Party

12. The Old Bailey

13. Brew City

14. The Antipodes

15. The Beeb (or Auntie Beeb)

16. The Fourth Estate

17. The Old Lady of Threadneedle Street

laureates in literature

Given the year they won the Nobel Prize, their home nation, and their most famous works, can you name these past winners of the Nobel Prize for Literature? (All of them wrote in the English language.)

1. 1907, United Kingdom. *The Jungle Books; Just So Stories; Kim; The Man Who Would Be King; Gunga Din*

_____

2. 1925, Ireland. *Pygmalion; Major Barbara; Saint Joan; Man and Superman*

_____

3. 1930, United States. *Babbitt; Main Street; Arrowsmith; Elmer Gantry*

_____

4. 1936, United States. *Mourning Becomes Electra; The Iceman Cometh; Long Day's Journey Into Night; A Moon for the Misbegotten*

_____

5. 1948, United Kingdom. *The Love Song of J. Alfred Prufrock; The Waste Land; Murder in the Cathedral; Old Possum's Book of Practical Cats*

_____

6. 1949, United States. *The Sound and the Fury; As I Lay Dying; Absalom! Absalom!; The Reivers*

_____

7. 1954, United States. *The Sun Also Rises; A Farewell to Arms; For Whom the Bell Tolls; The Old Man and the Sea*

_____

8. 1962, United States. *Of Mice and Men; The Grapes of Wrath; Cannery Row; Travels with Charley*

_____

9. 1969, Ireland. *Waiting for Godot; Endgame; Happy Days; Krapp's Last Tape*

_____

10. 1983, United Kingdom. *Lord of the Flies; Darkness Visible; To the Ends of the Earth*

_____

11. 1993, United States. *Sula; Song of Solomon; Tar Baby; Beloved*

_____

long-term memory
executive functioning

Where's the Skyline?

long-term memory
executive functioning
attention to detail

Match the city image with its nickname.

A _____

B _____

C _____

D _____

E _____

1. Beantown

2. The Windy City

3. The Big Pineapple

4. The Big Apple

5. The Golden Gate City

6. The City of Angels

7. The Emerald City

F _____

G _____

che*que* this out!

All of the answers in this word definition game end with the letters QUE.

1. A small, usually upscale shop that caters to a select clientele.

_____

2. A type of nineteenth- and early twentieth-century entertainment that featured popular music, low comedy, and striptease artists like Gypsy Rose Lee.

_____

3. An Islamic house of worship.

_____

4. Not transparent; unable to be seen through.

_____

5. A feeling of irritation or resentment.

_____

6. A sticky deposit on your teeth or in your arteries.

_____

7. This type of dance club became very popular in the 1970s.

_____

8. Slightly shocking or sexually suggestive.

_____

9. Abrupt or offhand in manner and/or speech.

_____

10. This describes a woman who is quite tall and dignified.

_____

11. Ugly, gross, monstrous.

_____

12. To hand-sew smaller pieces of fabric on top of a larger piece of fabric to decorate it or to make a design.

_____

13. Highly ornate seventeenth- and eighteenth-century style of architecture, music, and art.

_____

14. A region (and its people) that straddles the border between France and Spain.

_____

whoozy

How many clues do you need to guess who the WHOOZY is? One to three clues—Outstanding; three to seven clues—Very Good; seven to ten clues—Time to study up on your WHOOZYs.

1. WHOOZY was born in 1934 in Connecticut.

2. Of Lebanese descent, WHOOZY has spoken Arabic since childhood.

3. WHOOZY graduated from Princeton in 1955 and from Harvard Law School in 1958.

4. After WHOOZY served in the U.S. Army (for six months), he moved to Washington, DC, to work for Secretary of Labor Daniel Patrick Moynihan.

5. WHOOZY never married, telling one colleague in his later years that he chose his career over family life.

6. WHOOZY's 1964 book *Unsafe at Any Speed,* focusing on the Chevy Corvair, was about the U.S. automakers' resistance to building safer cars.

7. In reaction to the book, General Motors tried to discredit WHOOZY by tapping his phones, investigating his past, and hiring prostitutes to trap him in compromising situations.

8. WHOOZY's work on auto safety led to the creation of the National Highway Traffic Safety Administration, which quickly mandated seatbelts and safer windshields in all automobiles.

9. Not known for his sense of humor, WHOOZY nonetheless hosted *Saturday Night Live* in 1977.

10. WHOOZY ran for president in 1996 and again in 2000 on the Green Party ticket. Many Democrats blame him for Al Gore's loss in 2000, claiming that he took precious Florida votes away from Gore.

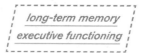

long-term memory
executive functioning

What Do They Have in Common?

Each question contains a list of several items.
Can you figure out what they have in common?

long-term memory
executive functioning
attention to detail

1. A college graduate, an angle, a thermometer, and a bad burn

2. A pen, a decimal number, a sharp knife, and a game score

3. Aldrich Ames, Julius Rosenberg, Nathan Hale, and Mata Hari

4. The doctor's office, a map, a fish, and music

5. Nixon succeeds LBJ, the "Miracle Mets" win the World Series, and Neil Armstrong walks on the moon

6. Eyeglasses, a bed, and a bowling competition

7. Adelie, Gentoo, king, and emperor

8. An ice cream parlor, dog walkers, and front loaders

9. A girl scout, a flat tire, and a quilt

10. Ronald Reagan, John Wayne, Louis Armstrong, and John F. Kennedy

DOUBLE TROUBLE

Compound words are made up of two smaller words, such as *hayloft* or *watchtower*. In this game, we give the first half of some compound words. You must identify the one word that follows each of them to make a compound word. For example, given the words *knuckle, moth,* and *basket,* the one word that makes each a compound word is *ball* (*knuckleball, mothball,* and *basketball*).

1. Awe, hand, lone, whole, irk   (hint: s)

2. Choke, house, with, thresh   (hint: h)

3. Cook, hard, silver, soft   (hint: w)

4. Dart, black, wash, bill   (hint: b)

5. Lunch, night, rag, life   (hint: t)

6. Crack, touch, count, show   (hint: d)

7. Every, no, else, some   (hint: w)

8. Copy, forth, up, birth   (hint: r)

9. Fare, ink, stair   (hint: w)

10. Brush, cease, wild, camp   (hint: f)

11. Further, any, never, ever   (hint: m)

12. Eye, back, whip   (hint: l)

13. Blow, work, wipe, strike   (hint: o)

14. Ear, fire, spark   (hint: p)

15. Foot, door, lock, side   (hint: s)

16. Horse, will, man, super   (hint: p)

17. Bed, hard, slip, under   (hint: c)

18. Pop, pass, left, push   (hint: o)

FOUR-SYLLABLE WORDS

From A to Z, how many four-syllable words can you come up with in two minutes?

long-term memory
working memory
executive functioning
processing speed

A _____

B _____

C _____

D _____

E _____

F _____

G _____

H _____

I _____

J _____

K _____

L _____

M _____

N _____

O _____

P _____

Q _____

R _____

S _____

T _____

U _____

V _____

W _____

X _____

Y _____

Z _____

It's a Lul*u*!

All of the answers in this word definition game end with the letter U.

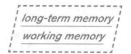

1. Chest of drawers.

2. List of restaurant offerings.

3. A Hawaiian feast or party.

4. Good-bye, to a Frenchman.

5. A marshy wetland along the Gulf Coast.

6. A ballet skirt.

7. Collection of clothing and household linens for a bride.

8. Hindu word for a very wise teacher.

9. Unrehearsed, spontaneous, improvised.

10. The term North Americans use for reindeer.

11. Off-white or light beige color.

12. A large flightless bird native to Australia.

13. Short Japanese poem with three lines and seventeen or fewer syllables.

14. Soybean curd, an Asian food favored by vegetarians.

15. A Japanese martial art.

TRIMBLE

Trimble is a trivia game and a word jumble combined. First, answer the trivia questions and cross out the letters of each answer in the letter grid. Then rearrange the remaining letters (those that have not been crossed out) to reveal another word or phrase related to the same theme.

Questions: The theme is *authors*, and the jumble consists of two words.

1. Last name of the author of *The Shining* and *Misery*.

2. Last name of the author of *The Grapes of Wrath* and *Of Mice and Men*.

3. Last name of the author of *A Farewell to Arms* and *The Sun Also Rises*.

4. Last name of the author of *The Naked and the Dead*, and *The Executioner's Song*.

5. Last name of the author of *Roots* and coauthor of *The Autobiography of Malcolm X*.

6. Last name of the author of *Interview with the Vampire* and *The Tale of the Body Thief*.

7. Last name of the author of *Lust for Life* and *The Agony and the Ecstasy*.

A	A	A	A	B	C	C	E	E	E	E
E	E	E	G	G	G	H	H	H	H	I
I	I	I	I	I	J	K	K	L	L	M
M	M	N	N	N	N	N	O	O	R	R
R	S	S	S	T	T	W	Y	Y		

eponyms

An eponym is a noun that is associated with a person's name. For example, calling someone a "Benedict Arnold" means that he's a traitor. Some eponyms are a little less obvious: The Barbie Doll takes its name from Barbara Handler, the daughter of the doll's inventor. It's also common for a disease, such as Alzheimer's, to take the name of the researcher who first identified it. How many eponyms do you know?

1. A measurement of loudness (volume), named after the inventor of the telephone.

2. Long, baggy pants worn under skirts in the nineteenth century, named after the women's rights activist who popularized them.

3. A landlocked South American country, named after a nineteenth-century South American hero and independence fighter.

4. Term for a womanizer, derived from the name of an eighteenth-century Italian "ladies' man" who was uniquely skilled in the art of seduction.

5. Comic book superhero's young sidekick, named after an English folk legend outlaw.

6. A type of tuba, named after the bandmaster, composer, and American "March King" who popularized its use.

7. A widely used Italian term that describes photographers who specialize in candid photos of celebrities, derived from a character in the 1960 film *La Dolce Vita*.

8. The refusal to buy or handle a particular product as a political protest, named after a British land agent who was ostracized by tenant farmers in Ireland when he refused to reduce rents after a particularly bad growing season.

9. The strip of hair grown by a man in front of his ears, named after a uniquely bearded soldier, who was also a businessman and politician from Rhode Island.

10. A classification system to organize books in a library, named after the American librarian who invented it.

NAME MERGE

Given a clue for each of two famous people, can you figure out what name they share? For example: *Clarence Thomas Jefferson* or *Jesse James Cagney*.

1. Guitar player and pioneer of the electric guitar; and the cowriter of "I Want to Hold Your Hand," "Can't Buy Me Love," and "A Hard Day's Night."

2. The beheaded Queen of Scots; and E. B. White's mouse who was adopted by a human family in this classic children's story.

3. *60 Minutes* reporter who retired at age ninety; and the deep-voiced actor who won an Academy Award in 1932 for his role in *The Champ*.

4. Nineteenth-century outlaw, bank robber, train robber, and gang leader; and the imposing actor who is the voice of Darth Vader in *Star Wars* and who also booms out, "This is CNN."

5. British author of *Women in Love* and *Lady Chatterley's Lover;* and the North Dakota–born "champagne music" bandleader.

6. He won an Oscar in 1965 for a dual role in *Cat Ballou* opposite Jane Fonda; and he is a Manhattan-born multi-award winning composer of songs such as "The Way We Were" and "Nobody Does It Better."

7. The fourteenth president of the United States, largely considered a failure; and the handsome Irish-born actor who played Remington Steele on TV and James Bond in four films between 1995 and 2002.

8. He played the Penguin in the 1960s TV series *Batman*; and she played Elise Keaton in *Family Ties*.

9. Perennial presidential candidate and leader of the Rainbow Coalition; and abstract artist known for his technique of dripping paint on the canvas.

CLASSIC LIT

Hidden in this grid—printed forward, backward, and diagonally—are words and phrases from the titles of twenty-five classic works of literature. Fill in the missing word(s) in the titles, then find them (the missing words only) in the grid. When you have found all the titles, rearrange the remaining letters and the answer will be the bestselling book of all time. For an extra-challenging brain workout, put a three-minute timer on this game.

I	L	E	E	D	U	T	I	L	O	S	F	O
E	F	K	I	T	E	Y	E	F	F	L	D	P
I	R	U	A	W	B	A	G	D	M	L	R	U
G	G	C	R	R	R	R	N	N	I	O	I	N
H	A	A	A	Y	E	A	H	U	C	D	B	I
T	T	G	B	E	R	N	T	O	E	E	G	S
Y	S	E	N	A	L	A	I	H	E	H	N	H
F	B	D	W	L	O	T	V	N	G	T	I	M
O	Y	T	A	H	E	H	T	O	A	D	K	E
U	H	E	I	G	H	T	S	I	B	O	C	N
R	E	H	T	F	O	D	R	O	L	O	O	T
K	A	R	A	M	A	Z	O	V	E	L	M	T
A	T	T	I	F	F	A	N	Y	S	B	A	H

- ○ _____ _____ Peace
- ○ Valley of _____ _____
- ○ The Grapes of _____
- ○ God's _____ _____
- ○ The Cat in _____ _____
- ○ The _____ Runner
- ○ _____ _____ and Men
- ○ King _____
- ○ Wuthering _____
- ○ Madame _____
- ○ Anna _____
- ○ In Cold _____
- ○ The Great _____
- ○ The _____ ___ _____ Rings
- ○ Crime and _____
- ○ The Brothers _____
- ○ The Sound and the _____
- ○ One Hundred Years ___ _____
- ○ Breakfast ___ _____
- ○ The House of the Seven _____
- ○ The _____ of the Baskervilles
- ○ Anne ___ _____ Gables
- ○ To Kill ___ _____
- ○ Nineteen _____-_____
- ○ I Know Why the _____ Bird Sings

word play

These are word "riddles." For most of them, if you read the question very carefully, the answer should come easily.

1. What part of the newspaper do angry people like best?

_____

2. If yesterday had been Wednesday's tomorrow, and tomorrow is Sunday's yesterday, what day would today be?

_____

3. What asks no questions but gets lots of answers?

_____

4. This is the only type of cheese that is made backward. What kind is it?

_____

5. What seven-letter word becomes longer when the third letter is removed?

_____

6. Besides living and breathing, what is everyone doing at the same time?

_____

executive functioning
attention to detail

all *a's*

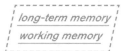

All of the answers in this word definition game begin and end with the letter A.

1. Hello, in Honolulu.

2. Fear of heights.

3. Fragrant odor.

4. Where you would find Wasilla and Denali.

5. Condition caused by a red blood cell or hemoglobin deficiency.

6. Celestial light show that is fairly common at high latitudes.

7. Home country of Arnold Schwarzenegger, Adolf Hitler, and Mozart.

8. A female friend, in Spanish.

9. The key ingredient in smelling salts.

10. A type of memory loss often used as a plot line in soap operas.

11. This "magical" word has a total of five A's.

12. Related to a camel and smaller than a llama, this Peruvian animal's hair is made into a very soft, luxurious wool fiber.

13. A single-celled organism.

14. A dangerous condition in which the supply of oxygen to the body is severely reduced or cut off entirely.

T PLUS THREE

long-term memory
working memory

All of the answers in this quiz are four-letter words that begin with T.

1. This breakfast cereal is for kids, not rabbits.

_____

2. Dorothy's dog.

_____

3. The astronauts' favorite drink.

_____

4. A South African cleric and 1984 Nobel Peace Prize winner.

_____

5. Having a sharp or bitter taste.

_____

6. The Oakland Raiders or Pittsburgh Steelers.

_____

7. Basically, this food is made from coagulated soy milk.

_____

8. A blue-green color.

_____

9. Roman garment.

_____

10. Prime Minister of Japan for most of World War II.

_____

11. Insect responsible for Lyme disease and tularemia.

_____

12. Collective term for equipment used in horseback riding, including the saddle and bridle.

_____

13. This is the largest and lowest-pitched brass instrument.

_____

---

 trivia

GEOGRAPHICAL FOODS

long-term memory
executive functioning

Foods are often closely tied to cultures and locations for a variety of reasons, as you'll see in this quiz.

● Ice cream covered in meringue and briefly baked in a hot oven. This dessert's name was coined in a New York restaurant in 1876 to honor a newly acquired U.S. territory.

● Broiled or grilled marinated flank steak that is cut against the grain in thin strips. This U.S. dish is unknown in the European city it's named for.

● This soft, mildly sweet spread was branded with this U.S. city's name because it was considered the home of top quality food in 1880.

● This food originated in the English region it's named after, but in the U.S. it's known as popovers.

Compound Word

Each picture represents one half of a compound word. For example, if you combine *key* and *hole,* you get *keyhole.* How many of the twelve possible compound words can you find? For an extra brain boost, see how many compound words you can find in two minutes. (*Note: Each picture is used only once to create an answer.*)

working memory
executive functioning
attention to detail
multitasking
processing speed

Search

1 _____
2 _____
3 _____
4 _____
5 _____
6 _____
7 _____
8 _____
9 _____
10 _____
11 _____
12 _____

the *long* and the *short* of it

All of the answers in this word definition game contain either the word LONG or the word SHORT.

1. An alternate route that takes less time.

_____

2. This breed of cattle, a symbol of Texas, is appropriately named.

_____

3. Crisco, for example.

_____

4. To be given insufficient money back when you've paid for something.

_____

5. On every world map, these are the north-south lines that divide the earth into equal parts.

_____

6. This hard, crumbly cookie is most associated with Scotland.

_____

7. This shape is best described as a stretched-out circle or square.

_____

> long-term memory
> working memory

8. Many amateur hobbyists use this type of radio to broadcast and listen to other amateurs in faraway places.

_____

9. Defensive position in baseball between second and third base.

_____

10. This measurement of distance, which equals one-eighth of a mile, is rarely used today except in horse racing.

_____

11. A person's weak points, deficiencies, or flaws.

_____

12. To lengthen the time, draw out, or extend the duration of something.

_____

13. To be unmindful of future consequences; lacking in forethought.

_____

14. A person employed in a port to load and unload ships.

_____

famous "fathers"

Every American knows that George Washington is the "Father of Our Country," but how many other famous "fathers" do you know?

1. He became the "Father of Antibiotics" quite by accident.

2. For his cutting-edge ideas on the origins of man, he is known as the "Father of Evolution."

3. We all know that George Washington is the father of this country; but who is considered the "Father of India"?

4. All new physicians pledge an oath based on the writings and practices of this ancient Greek "Father of Medicine."

5. The process of purifying milk was named after this French "Father of Bacteriology."

6. Although he wrote *The Canterbury Tales* in Middle English, he is considered the "Father of English Literature."

7. Excommunicated by the Roman Catholic Church for his radical ideas, this German theologian became the "Father of Protestantism" in the early sixteenth century.

8. Two writers, one British (1866–1946) and one French (1828–1905), have each been called the "Father of Science Fiction." Can you name one of them?

9. Can you name either the "Father of the A-Bomb" or the "Father of the H-Bomb"?

10. If you remember math from high school, you can probably name this ancient Greek "Father of Geometry."

11. The first over-the-counter mouthwash was named after this British "Father of Antiseptics."

whoozy

How many clues do you need to guess who the WHOOZY is? One to three clues—Outstanding. Three to seven clues—Very Good. Seven to ten clues—Time to study up on your WHOOZYs.

1. WHOOZY is an American woman who was born on February 27, 1980.

2. WHOOZY's academic abilities were evident early on; she was promoted directly to the fourth grade from the second grade, skipping the third grade entirely.

3. WHOOZY became a vegetarian at age twelve.

4. Born in the south, WHOOZY attended middle school and high school in Washington, DC.

5. WHOOZY attended Stanford University in California, majoring first in chemistry but switching to history in her junior year.

6. WHOOZY received her Master's degree in international relations at Oxford University in England.

7. In 2003 WHOOZY moved to New York City to work at McKinsey & Company, a management consulting firm that advises businesses and governments around the world.

8. WHOOZY had been romantically linked to actor Jake Gyllenhaal, but in 2010 she married Marc Mezvinsky, an investment banker at Goldman Sachs.

9. In November of 2011, WHOOZY was hired as an on-air correspondent for NBC.

10. WHOOZY's mother was the junior senator from New York from 2000 to 2008, when she then became Secretary of State under Barack Obama. WHOOZY's father became president of the United States in 1992, when she was twelve years old.

long-term memory
executive functioning

whatzit

long-term memory
executive functioning

How many clues do you need to guess what the WHATZIT is? One to three clues—Outstanding; three to seven clues—Very Good; seven to ten clues—Time to study up on your WHATZITs.

1. The WHATZIT was invented in the 1950s by a Frenchman named Arthur Granjean, who called it *L'Ecran Magique*.

2. WHATZITs were manufactured in Bryan, Ohio from 1960 until the company moved the plant to China in 2001.

3. In England, the WHATZIT was first marketed as "the DoodleMaster."

4. An instant hit with the baby boom kids, in 2003 the WHATZIT was named to the Toy Industry Association's list of the one hundred most creative toys of the twentieth century.

5. Traditionally available only in gray and black, a color version of the WHATZIT was introduced in 1993.

6. If you open up a WHATZIT and look inside, you will find a mixture of extremely fine aluminum powder and beads on a plate of glass. A stylus (or pen tip) moving through the powder leaves a dark trail behind.

7. Perhaps because of the increasing popularity of television, the shape of WHATZITs was similar to the shape of a television, with a main screen and two knobs.

8. Drawing a curved line on your WHATZIT involves the careful turning of both knobs together.

9. WHATZITs have influenced a generation of artists who now work in print and animation.

---

 trivia

"Z" ON THE MAP

long-term memory

executive functioning

All of the answers in this quiz are locations with a Z in their name.

● Located in northeast Israel, this little village was the hometown of Mary, Joseph, and Jesus.

● This is the only U.S. state with a Z in its name.

● This country, which has a long history of neutrality in world affairs, has a Z in its name—as does its largest city.

● Which two South American countries have a Z in their names?

HOMONYMS

Homonyms are two or more words that are pronounced the same way but have different meanings and/or spellings. In this game, we supply definitions, and you must not only provide the homonyms, but SPELL them correctly as well.

1. In one side and out the other; and, propelled something into the air.

2. Permitted; and, audibly, not silently or in a whisper.

3. Visitor; and, estimated or conjectured.

4. To express approval or admiration; and, appeals to God.

5. To cause liquid to flow from a container; and, a tiny opening in the skin.

6. 3.14159; and, a dessert often filled with fruit.

7. A figure or character that represents something else; and, a percussion instrument, usually made of brass.

8. One rank lower than a brigadier general; and, a piece of corn.

9. An inedible vegetable that is often used for decorative purposes; and, pierced with a bull's horn or tusk.

---

trivia

CHEESY

long-term memory
executive functioning

You may enjoy eating cheese, but how much do you know about this culinary treat?

● This is the most widely eaten cheese in the world. It shares its name with the village in southwest England where it originated.

● A wheel of this hard Italian cheese (primarily a grating cheese) weighs seventy-five pounds and must be cut by a saw.

● This very soft French cheese is sprayed with a mold related to penicillin and then aged to form its edible white crust.

● This U.S. cheese, first made by friars in Northern California, was popularized over a hundred years ago by businessman David Jacks, who first mass marketed it.

OCCUPATIONS

From A to Z, how many occupations or professions
can you come up with in two minutes?

A _____

B _____

C _____

D _____

E _____

F _____

G _____

H _____

I _____

J _____

K _____

L _____

M _____

N _____

O _____

P _____

Q _____

R _____

S _____

T _____

U _____

V _____

W _____

X _____

Y _____

Z _____

PUT THE LIST IN ORDER

Given a list of four or five items, put them in the correct order required by the question.

① All of these countries are in the World Tourism Organization's 2006 list of top ten tourist destinations (measured by tourist arrivals). Put them in order, starting with the most popular destination:

____ **a.** China

____ **b.** Spain

____ **c.** United States

____ **d.** France

____ **e.** Italy

② Put this list of colleges and universities in order of how many students (total number) are enrolled, starting with the school with the largest student population:

____ **a.** Princeton University

____ **b.** City College of New York

____ **c.** Brigham Young University

____ **d.** Boston University

____ **e.** West Point

③ Put this list of liquid measurements in order of amount, starting with the smallest:

____ **a.** 3 quarts

____ **b.** 32 tablespoons

____ **c.** 5 pints

____ **d.** ½ gallon

④ Put these U.S. states in order of when they were admitted to the Union, starting with the earliest:

____ **a.** Kentucky

____ **b.** Ohio

____ **c.** California

____ **d.** Arizona

____ **e.** West Virginia

⑤ Put this list of books in order of when they were first published, starting with the earliest:

____ **a.** *The Diary of a Young Girl* by Anne Frank

____ **b.** *The Catcher in the Rye* by J. D. Salinger

____ **c.** *Elmer Gantry* by Sinclair Lewis

____ **d.** *Gone with the Wind* by Margaret Mitchell

____ **e.** *To Kill a Mockingbird* by Harper Lee

⑥ Put this list of U.S. islands in order of size from largest (most square miles) to smallest, starting with the largest:

____ **a.** Long Island, New York

____ **b.** Kodiak Island, Arkansas

____ **c.** Martha's Vineyard, Massachusetts

____ **d.** Hawaii, Hawaii

____ **e.** Manhattan, New York

⑦ Put this list of worldwide telecasts in order of how large the audience was, starting with the largest worldwide audience:

____ **a.** Funeral of Michael Jackson, 2009

____ **b.** *Apollo* Moon Landing, 1969

____ **c.** 2010 World Cup Final

____ **d.** Funeral of Princess Diana, 1997

____ **e.** Funeral of Pope John Paul II, 2005

⑧ Put this list of movies in order of how many Academy Awards they won, starting with the most Oscar-winning movie first:

____ **a.** *My Fair Lady,* 1964

____ **b.** *West Side Story,* 1961

____ **c.** *Ben-Hur,* 1959

____ **d.** *Schindler's List,* 1993

⑨ Put this list of plays in order of how long they ran on Broadway, starting with the longest-running:

____ **a.** *Arsenic and Old Lace*

____ **b.** *South Pacific*

____ **c.** *Oklahoma!*

____ **d.** *The Phantom of the Opera*

____ **e.** *Cats*

---

trivia

WHO, WHAT, AND WHERE

long-term memory

executive functioning

Just the facts, ma'am (or sir)— we're looking for who, what, or where.

● **Who** wrote *The Great Gatsby*?

● **Who** sang "Mona Lisa," the number-one song on the *Billboard* charts for two months in 1950?

● **Who** was Robert Kennedy's bodyguard on the night he was shot? A former football star, he captured the shooter's gun and subdued him.

● **Who,** according to the Bible, said: "He that lives by the sword, will die by the sword"?

● **What** sport was invented in 1891 by a YMCA instructor who wanted something to keep boys active in the winter?

● **What** new technology was developed between 1942 and 1945 in a secret Army project code named "The Manhattan Project"?

● **What** violent organization, founded in Tennessee in 1865, was glorified in D. W. Griffiths's 1915 film *Birth of a Nation*?

● **What** is the name of the pigment that determines our skin and eye color?

● **Where** was Woodstock, the three-day music festival that attracted half a million hippie concertgoers, held in the summer of 1969?

● In **what** state is the geographical center of the contiguous (lower forty-eight) United States?

● **Where** is your coccyx?

● **Where** can the Sea of Serenity and the Sea of Tranquility be found?

DECEMBER IN HISTORY

This trivia quiz will stretch your long-term memory muscles.

1903 Wilbur and Orville Wright conducted the world's first airplane flight from this North Carolina town.

1911 This Norwegian explorer became the first person to reach the South Pole, beating both Robert Scott and Ernest Shackleton.

1936 King Edward VIII of England abdicated the throne to be with the woman he loved. Who was she?

1941 December 7 was described by President Franklin Roosevelt as "a day that will live in infamy." Why?

1944 This bandleader was lost forever when his U.S. Army plane disappeared in bad weather over the English Channel.

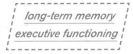

long-term memory
executive functioning

1947 John Bardeen, Walter Brattain, and William Shockley ushered in the electronics age with this invention.

1954 The U.S. Senate voted to condemn this Wisconsin Republican for "conduct that brings the Senate into dishonor and disrepute."

1955 Rosa Parks refused to give up her seat to a white man on a bus in this city, sparking a yearlong bus boycott by African Americans.

1957 Elvis Presley received his draft notice for the U.S. Army. In which foreign country did Presley spend eighteen months of his two-year army stint?

1963 This crooner's son was kidnapped (at age nineteen) from a Lake Tahoe hotel room. He was released two days later after the payment of a $240,000 ransom.

1967 This surgeon, in Cape Town, South Africa, performed the first human heart transplant.

1975 This follower of Charles Manson was sentenced to life in prison for her attempt on the life of President Gerald Ford.

1980 This rock music legend was shot and killed outside his apartment building in New York City.

1981 Elizabeth Jordan Carr was born in Norfolk, Virginia. Why was this news?

1985 Dian Fossey, famous for her studies of this African mammal, was found murdered at her research station in Rwanda.

1985 This rock 'n' roll heartthrob, who grew up on his parents' television show in the 1950s, was killed in an airplane fire and subsequent crash.

1988 A terrorist bomb on Pan Am Flight 103 exploded in mid-air, killing 259 people aboard the plane. In addition, eleven people in this Scottish town were also killed when large sections of the plane fell to earth.

1992 This British Prime Minister announced to the British parliament the formal separation of Prince Charles and Princess Diana.

2000 George W. Bush claimed the presidency over this rival, after the U.S. Supreme Court halted the Florida recount of votes.

2001 Richard Reid, a passenger on an American Airlines flight, was subdued by flight attendants and passengers when it was discovered that he was trying to ignite a bomb hidden in this unusual place.

2006 This deposed leader was hanged uttering his final words: "I bear witness that there is no god but God, and I testify that Mohammed is the Messenger of God."

trivia

IRELAND
long-term memory
executive functioning

You don't need the luck of the Irish to do well in this quiz.

● This unofficial anthem of Ireland has been called one of the most touching "good-bye" songs ever written.

● The island of Ireland is split between Northern Ireland and the Republic of Ireland. Can you name both capital cities?

● Ireland's flag is orange and green with white in the middle. The white stands for the hope of peace between the orange and green. What do the orange and green colors represent?

● St. Patrick has been credited with banishing these reptiles from Ireland—although there is no scientific evidence that Ireland ever had them.

What's the Question?

Remember "Where's the beef?" That famous question lived on long past its original use in a Wendy's commercial. Let's see how many questions, drawn from movies, songs, TV, movies, and the news you can identify.

1. Finish this musical question from the Monotones in 1958: "I wonder, wonder, who m'bado oo oo . . ."

2. The answer is: "Young girls picked them, every one." What is the 1960s anti-war musical question?

3. The baseball player mentioned in this Simon and Garfunkel question once replied: "I'm here. I've always been here."

4. If you were a *Mad Magazine* fan, you'd surely know this question—the slogan for the magazine's human mascot Alfred E. Newman.

5. For Tony Micelli, the answer to this TV series title question was "Angela Bower."

6. Only "The Shadow" knew the answer to this question.

7. This famous advertising question translates into Spanish as *"Toma leche?"*

8. This musical question was the title of a PBS children's game show about geography.

9. In the 1940s and '50s, this Dayton Allen catchphrase question became a cultural phenomenon that Allen used in television commercials and as the basis for novelty toys, a book, and a record.

10. Name the Shakespeare character who uttered this question: "What light through yonder window breaks?"

long-term memory
executive functioning

Capitonyms

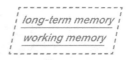

long-term memory
working memory

Earlier we learned that a capitonym is a word that changes its meaning (and sometimes its pronunciation) when it is capitalized. In this game, we provide the definitions for words that, when capitalized, are also common first names. From each definition, can you provide a well-known person with that name? For example: *What tool is used to fix a flat tire?* The answer is: Jack *Nicholson* (or anyone named *Jack*).

1. A precious gem from an oyster.

Pearl   (Bailey)

2. The night before an event or occasion.

Eve

3. A slang term for the bathroom.

Loo

4. A small shaving cut.

Nick   (Nolte)

5. A small wire nail.

Brad (Pitt)

6. A pal or chum.

FRIEND

7. The head of a college or college department.

Dean (Martin)

8. A strong belief.

tenet

9. A root spice often used in making cookies and dessert breads.

GINGER   (ROGERS)

10. Elegance and poise.

11. A long, spearlike weapon.

12. Short for a voice-amplifying tool.

mike

13. A stream of light.

beam

14. A bird that lays blue eggs.

oriole

15. The colored part of the eye.

iris

16. A vehicle used to transport goods or small groups of people.

lorry

17. The biological unit that controls inherited characteristics.

18. A winner, conqueror, or champion.

wacky wordies

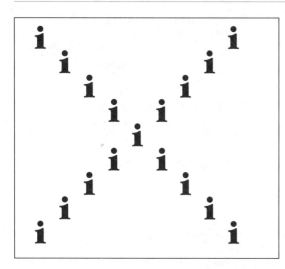

1 _____

2 _____

thoughts
thoughts ⇦

heaven heaven heaven
heaven heaven heaven
hea**l**'**m****ven**

3 _____

4 _____

To solve these fun puzzles, look carefully at each frame, because the arrangement of the letters is a key clue to the familiar phrase contained within. For example, if the word *school* were placed high up in the frame, the answer would be *high school*. Or if the phrase "easy pieces" occurred five times in the frame, the answer would be *Five Easy Pieces*.

one   the other

one   the other
one   the other
one   and   the other
one   the other
one   the other
one   the other

the law ^B

❺ _____ ❻ _____

HAR
MO
NY

❼ _____ ❽ _____

rhyme ❖ time ❖

Each question in this game includes two definitions for two different words. The twist is, they will rhyme.

1. Retribution; and circular monument in England.

_____

2. To expunge; and hug.

_____

3. Elegance and poise; and the long bar on a typewriter keyboard.

_____

4. Tiny shrimplike creatures that whales eat; and talent or competent ability.

_____

5. Small baked treat; and illegal bet taker.

_____

6. Non-rusting metal; and the main control device of a car.

_____

7. Linked railroad cars; and a hank of yarn.

_____

8. A very thin slice of cake; and Missouri or Hudson.

_____

9. Old-fashioned or out-of-date; and unfinished.

_____

10. The shape of a ball or the earth; and the opposite of courage.

_____

11. Prim or stiff, not casual; and standard or typical.

_____

12. Your sinuses during a cold; and seized by the police.

_____

13. Brag; and an apparition.

_____

14. Liquid blown through the air in tiny drops; and to unravel or wear at the edges.

_____

15. Putty used to fill holes in a wall; and a defensive move in football.

_____

16. Lettuce for Caesar salad; and what a candidate must do to get elected.

_____

Follow the Rules

It seems like a simple game—just follow each instruction to change one word or phrase into a related word or phrase. Caution! It's harder than you think.

1. With no spaces between words, write down the phrase: C O U N T   Y O U R   F R I E N D S

2. Place an L in the sixth position.

3. Place a Y before and after the D.

4. If the answer to the Spanish math problem *uno y ocho* is *nueve,* place an N in the ninth position. If not, do nothing.

5. Remove all the U's.

6. Remove the first and the tenth letters.

7. If Abraham Lincoln was a Democrat, swap the first and last letters. If not, do nothing.

8. Place an A after the second R and before the last Y.

9. Remove the third, eighth, and twelfth letters.

C O U N T Y O U R F R I E N D S

Did you get the right answer?

FIND THE WORDS

at the beach

In this scene, there are ninety words **that begin with the letter S.** How many can you find?

working memory
executive functioning
attention to detail
multitasking
processing speed

RAZZMATAZZ!

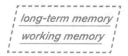
All the answers in this quiz end with the letter Z.

1. This Yiddish word for a clumsy or awkward person is also commonly used in English.

2. A colorful cotton fabric with a glazed finish, mostly used for curtains or upholstery.

3. Fake, artificial, or false.

4. A thin pancake filled with cheese, similar to a crepe, but of Jewish or Slavic origin.

5. Effervescence, bubbles, froth.

6. O. J. Simpson used to run through airports in commercials for this company.

7. This Mark won seven gold medals at the 1972 Munich Olympic Games, a record that held until 2008.

8. A popular ballroom dance that likely began in Austria in the sixteenth century.

9. To spray a liquid in quick, short bursts.

10. A communal settlement in Israel, typically a farm.

11. This semiprecious crystal, the second most abundant mineral on earth, is used in very accurate clocks and watches.

12. Russian for "human," this is the name of the Soviet Union's original human spaceflight program.

WHAT'S THE NEXT LINE?

long-term memory
executive functioning

These classic lines are unfinished. Can you provide the words that complete them?

- "How do I love thee?"

- "All the world's a stage . . ."

- "The woods are lovely, dark, and deep . . ."

- "Once upon a midnight dreary . . ."

- "Listen, my children and you shall hear . . ."

- "Grow old along with me . . ."

DOUBLE TROUBLE

Compound words are made up of two smaller words,

such as *hayloft* or *watchtower*. In this game, we give the second half of some compound words. You must identify the one word that precedes each of them to make a compound word. For example, given the words *weed, coast,* and *sick,* the one word that makes each a compound word is *sea* (*seaweed, seacoast,* and *seasick*).

1. Stairs, town, fall, size   (hint: d)

2. Drum, muff, phone, ache   (hint: e)

3. Headed, weight, house   (hint: l)

4. Hole, handle, power, slaughter (hint: m)

5. Back, bridge, strings   (hint: d)

6. Coat, cast, board, dose   (hint: o)

7. Ship, wood, ware, headed   (hint: h)

8. Door, fuse, hale, mate, stall   (hint: i)

9. Brush, liner, port, craft   (hint: a)

10. Arm, cast, close, go   (hint: f)

11. Board, hole, note, stone   (hint: k)

12. Boy, hide, lick, poke   (hint: c)

13. Box, bar, paper, storm   (hint: s)

14. Over, nail, out, man   (hint: h)

15. Fare, lord, lock, ship   (hint w)

16. Light, scraper, line, diver   (hint: s)

17. Coat, cock, shooter, nut   (hint: p)

18. Room, house, ship, yard   (hint: c)

PUT THE LIST IN ORDER

Given a list of four or five items, put them in the correct order required by the question.

① Put this list of world religions in order of when they were founded, starting with the oldest:

___ **a.** Buddhism

___ **b.** Hinduism

___ **c.** Christianity

___ **d.** Judaism

___ **e.** Islam

② Put this list of Monopoly properties in order of how much they cost (with no houses or hotels), starting with the most expensive:

___ **a.** Water Works

___ **b.** Marvin Gardens

___ **c.** Park Place

___ **d.** Connecticut Avenue

③ Put this list of beverages in order of when they were introduced, starting with the oldest beverage:

___ **a.** Kool-Aid

___ **b.** Coca-Cola

___ **c.** Instant Coffee

___ **d.** Tang

④ Put this list of nineteenth-century historical events in order of when they happened, starting with the earliest:

___ **a.** U.S. Purchases Alaska

___ **b.** The Pony Express

___ **c.** California Gold Rush

___ **d.** Ellis Island Opens

⑤ Put these ancient civilizations in order of when they first rose to prominence, starting with the oldest:

___ **a.** Ancient Egypt

___ **b.** Ancient Greece

___ **c.** The Roman Empire

___ **d.** Aztec

⑥ Put the following list of highest-rated network telecasts in order by the percent of American households that watched, starting with the highest percent watched:

___ **a.** O. J. Simpson Verdict

___ **b.** "Lucy Goes to the Hospital"

___ **c.** Elvis Presley on *The Ed Sullivan Show*

___ **d.** The Beatles on *The Ed Sullivan Show*

⑦ Put this list of U.S. presidents in order of age at the time of his inaugural, starting with the youngest:

___ **a.** Franklin Roosevelt

___ **b.** Bill Clinton

___ **c.** Barack Obama

___ **d.** George W. Bush

⑧ Put these world cities in order of their geographical location from north to south, starting with the northernmost:

___ **a.** Stockholm, Sweden

___ **b.** Washington, DC

___ **c.** Paris, France

___ **d.** Fairbanks, Alaska

___ **e.** Cairo, Egypt

9 Put this list of desserts in order of their calories, starting with the food with the most calories:

____ **a.** Hershey's Milk Chocolate Bar

____ **b.** Buttered popcorn, one cup

____ **c.** Apple pie, small slice

____ **d.** Dunkin' Donuts glazed donut

____ **e.** Ben & Jerry's vanilla ice cream, half a cup

10 Put these twentieth-century historical events in order by when they occurred, starting with the earliest:

____ **a.** Penicillin Discovered

____ **b.** The *Hindenburg* Explodes

____ **c.** Wright Brothers' First Flight

____ **d.** The *Titanic* Sinks

____ **e.** Elvis Presley Born

? CLASSIC RIDDLE
REWARD AND PUNISHMENT

Sometimes if you read the riddle carefully, the answer is right in front of you.

George Elwood was a night watchman for a large company in London. One morning, as George was finishing his shift, his boss told him, "I'm going on a business trip to Norway tomorrow. My flight leaves at noon from Heathrow Airport." Upon hearing this, George became alarmed and advised his boss to take the boat instead. "Why should I?" asked the boss. "Because last night," George explained, "I dreamed that a plane to Norway crashed just after takeoff from Heathrow." Being superstitious, the boss decided to take the boat. When it finally docked in Norway, he learned that the plane he was going to take had indeed crashed. Upon his return to the office, the boss gave a substantial reward to George. And then, he fired him. Why?

trivia

THE PRESIDENTS
long-term memory

executive functioning

How well do you know these unique facts about the U.S. presidents?

● He was the only president to serve in both World War I and World War II.

● They were the only president and vice president team who were not elected to the office.

● He was the first sitting president to give a speech on television.

● He was the only president to have a Ph.D. degree.

● He was the first (and only) president to resign from office.

● He was the first president born in the twentieth century.

● Surprisingly, this president, born in 1924, was the first U.S. president born in a hospital.

● He was the first president to die in the White House—after only thirty-one days in office.

A RIVER RUNS THROUGH IT

long-term memory
executive functioning

Rivers often play an important role in the life and economy of cities around the world. Given the city, can you name its river?

● What river runs through Paris?

● What river runs through Cairo?

● What river runs through London?

● What two rivers run on either side of Manhattan in New York City?

● What river runs through Baghdad?

● What river runs through Budapest and Vienna?

● What river runs through Montreal?

● What river runs through Rome?

opening lines

Can you identify the famous novels that begin with these first lines? For an extra brain boost, try to name the author as well.

1. "Call me Ishmael."

2. "It is a truth universally acknowledged, that a single man in possession of a good fortune, must be in want of a wife."

3. "It was a bright cold day in April, and the clocks were striking thirteen."

4. "It was the best of times, it was the worst of times, it was the age of wisdom, it was the age of foolishness, it was the epoch of belief, it was the epoch of incredulity, it was the season of Light, it was the season of Darkness, it was the spring of hope, it was the winter of despair."

5. "I am an invisible man."

6. "If you really want to hear about it, the first thing you'll probably want to know is where I was born, and what my lousy childhood was like, and how my parents were occupied and all before they had me, and all that David Copperfield kind of crap, but I don't feel like going into it, if you want to know the truth."

7. "Somewhere in La Mancha, in a place whose name I do not care to remember, a gentleman lived not long ago, one of those who has a lance and ancient shield on a shelf and keeps a skinny nag and a greyhound for racing."

8. "He was an old man who fished alone in a skiff in the Gulf Stream and he had gone eighty-four days now without taking a fish."

9. "It was a pleasure to burn."

10. "I was born in the Year 1632, in the City of York, of a good Family, tho' not of that Country, my Father being a Foreigner of Bremen, who . . . lived afterward at York, from whence he had married my Mother, whose Relations were named Robinson, a very good Family in that Country, and from whom I was called Robinson Kreutznaer . . ."

11. "Mr. Jones, of the Manor Farm, had locked the hen houses for the night, but was too drunk to remember to shut the popholes."

12. "Scarlett O'Hara was not beautiful, but men seldom realized it when caught by her charm as the Tarleton twins were."

13. "When he was nearly thirteen my brother Jem got his arm badly broken at the elbow."

14. "When Mr. Bilbo Baggins of Bag End announced that he would shortly be celebrating his eleventy-first birthday with a party of special magnificence, there was much talk and excitement in Hobbiton."

15. "All children, except one, grow up."

"M" ON THE MAP

long-term memory

executive functioning

All the answers in this quiz are places that begin with the letter M.

● This is the second largest city in Australia.

● This city is spelled *Mockba* in Cyrillic, the written language of its country.

● This Italian city, headquarters for Gucci, Armani, Versace, etc., is a world fashion and design capital.

● This "Lost City of the Incas" is located eight thousand feet above sea level in Peru.

● This North American city takes its name from Mount Royal, the three-peaked hill around which it was built.

● The name of this body of water comes from the Latin meaning "in the middle of the earth." Today, twenty-one countries border it.

● This country, located off the southeast coast of Africa, is the fourth-largest island in the world and is known for its unique plant and animal life.

long-term memory
executive functioning
attention to detail

FLAG  DAY

If you can identify these national flags, you're flagtastic!

❶ _____

❷ _____

❸ _____

❹ _____

5 _____

6 _____

7 _____

8 _____

The Greek Alphabet

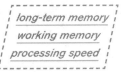

long-term memory
working memory
processing speed

You might be surprised by how many Greek letters you know—especially if you think back to the names of fraternities and sororities. How many of the twenty-four letters of the Greek alphabet can you name in one minute?

_____   _____   _____

_____   _____   _____

_____   _____   _____

_____   _____   _____

_____   _____   _____

_____   _____   _____

 trivia

BUGS

long-term memory
executive functioning

This quiz tests your knowledge of germs, insects, and sundry creepy crawlies.

● This insect has killed more people than all wars ever fought, through the spread of diseases like yellow fever and malaria.

● One of the Plagues of Egypt in the Bible was a swarm of these insects, which ate all the crops.

● These insects cause more damage to American homes than tornadoes and hurricanes combined.

● Known for its beauty, this is the only insect able to fly as far as twenty-five hundred miles to its winter home in Mexico.

● Thousands of people are infected yearly with Lyme Disease thanks to this tiny bug.

● The bubonic plague, or Black Death, was spread by this bug, which carried it from rats to humans.

399 Games

SOLUTIONS

CHAPTER ONE

page 1: It's Playtime
1. Playground
2. Timecard (or time clock)
3. Ragtime
4. Playboy
5. Timeout
6. Display
7. Playpen
8. Summertime
9. Overtime
10. Screenplay
11. Timetables
12. Playbill
13. Playoffs
14. Downplay

Page 2: Thirty-Second Madness: Federal Holidays
1. New Year's Day (January)
2. Birthday of Martin Luther King Jr. (January)
3. Washington's Birthday (Presidents Day is also correct.) (February)
4. Memorial Day (May)
5. Independence Day (July)
6. Labor Day (September)
7. Columbus Day (October)
8. Veterans Day (November)
9. Thanksgiving Day (November)
10. Christmas Day (December)

page 2: Letter Speller
1. C (sea)
2. I (eye)
3. K (Kaye)
4. O (owe)
5. P (pea)
6. B (bee)
7. Q (cue)
8. T (tea)
9. U (ewe)

page 3: Run the Alphabet—Animals
(*Other correct answers are possible.*)
A: Aardvark, Alligator
B: Badger, Baboon
C: Camel, Crow
D: Donkey, Dog
E: Emu, Elk
F: Ferret, Fish
G: Gopher, Grizzly Bear
H: Hamster, Hyena
I: Iguana, Impala
J: Jaguar, Jackal
K: Kitten, Koala
L: Llama, Lamb
M: Mink, Muskrat
N: Newt, Nightingale
O: Ocelot, Orangutan
P: Puma, Porcupine
Q: Quarter Horse, Queen Bee
R: Raccoon, Reindeer
S: Skunk, Squirrel
T: Tiger, Toad
U: Urchin, Unicorn
V: Vulture, Vole
W: Woodpecker, Walrus
X: X-Ray Fish, Xerus
Y: Yellowjacket, Yorkshire Terrier
Z: Zebra, Zebra Fish

page 4: Famous Movie Lines
Character; Actor; Film (Year)
1. Rhett Butler; Clark Gable; *Gone with the Wind* (1939)
2. Terry Malloy; Marlon Brando; *On the Waterfront* (1954)
3. Rick Blaine; Humphrey Bogart; *Casablanca* (1942)
4. Harry Callahan; Clint Eastwood; *Sudden Impact* (1983)
5. Norma Desmond; Gloria Swanson; *Sunset Boulevard* (1950)
6. Margo Channing; Bette Davis; *All About Eve* (1950)

7. Travis Bickle; Robert De Niro; *Taxi Driver* (1976)
8. The Captain; Strother Martin; *Cool Hand Luke* (1967)
9. Lt. Col. Kilgore; Robert Duvall; *Apocalypse Now* (1979)
10. Jennifer Cavalleri; Ali MacGraw; *Love Story* (1970)
11. Virgil Tibbs; Sidney Poitier; *In the Heat of the Night* (1967)
12. Arthur "Cody" Jarrett; James Cagney; *White Heat* (1949)
13. Knute Rockne; Pat O'Brien; *Knute Rockne, All American* (1940)
14. Hannibal Lecter; Anthony Hopkins; *The Silence of the Lambs* (1991)
15. Dorothy Gale; Judy Garland; *The Wizard of Oz* (1939)
16. Jimmy Dugan; Tom Hanks; *A League of Their Own* (1992)

page 5: The Shape of the States

A. Idaho
B. Maine
C. New Jersey
D. Michigan
E. Oklahoma
F. Illinois
G. Louisiana
H. Ohio
I. Virginia

page 6: Rhyme Time

1. New; and dew
2. Funny; and money
3. Guess; and press
4. Breeze; and freeze
5. Drum; and numb
6. Search; and church
7. Rind; and blind
8. Crowd; and plowed
9. Split; and quit
10. Bank; and spank
11. Yellow; and Jell-O
12. Jump rope; and Bob Hope
13. Brave; and shave
14. Beaver; and fever

page 6: Trivia—"I" Countries

- Italy
- India
- Ireland
- Iran

page 7: Finish the Jingle

1. "... egg." (American Egg Board)
2. "... is Folgers in your cup." (Folgers Coffee)
3. "... in perfect harmony." (Coca-Cola)
4. "... 'cause a Band-Aid's stuck on me." (Band-Aids)
5. "... it's O-S-C-A-R." (Oscar Mayer)
6. "... Nestlé's makes the very best ... chocolate." (Nestlé)
7. "... she's a Pepper, we're a Pepper, wouldn't you like to be a Pepper too?" (Dr Pepper)
8. "... lettuce, cheese, pickles, onions on a sesame seed bun." (McDonald's)
9. "... and away go troubles down the drain." (Roto-Rooter)
10. "... like somethin' from the oven, and Pillsbury says it best." (Pillsbury)
11. "... State Farm is there." (State Farm Insurance)
12. "... in your Chevrolet." (General Motors/ Chevrolet)
13. "... oh, what a relief it is." (Alka-Seltzer)
14. "... like a cigarette should." (Winston)
15. "... double your fun with Doublemint, Doublemint, Doublemint gum." (Wrigley's Doublemint Gum)
16. "... the San Francisco treat." (Rice-A-Roni)
17. "... with the helpful hardware man." (Ace Hardware)

page 8: January in History

1820 Antarctica
1848 A nugget of gold, which sparked the California Gold Rush of 1849
1870 A donkey
1892 Ellis Island
1922 Insulin
1942 Carole Lombard
1945 Fluoride
1952 Dave Garroway
1953 Lucille Ball
1954 Joe DiMaggio and Marilyn Monroe (She filed for divorce less than a year later.)
1959 Alaska

1959 Clint Eastwood
1962 Ernie Kovacs
1973 Roe v. Wade
1974 Speed limit signs (The
    maximum speed limit on
    all the nation's highways
    was reduced to fifty-five
    miles per hour.)
1976 The Concorde
1981 Iran
1991 Kuwait
1994 Nancy Kerrigan, who
    went on to win the
    silver medal in the 1994
    Olympics
2009 The Hudson River

page 9: Alma's Shopping List

1. Shrimp
2. Windex
3. Snickers
4. Corn (Pork *is also correct.*)
5. Crab
6. Pampers
7. Carrots
8. Skippy
9. Milk
10. Cookies
11. Waffles (Ruffles *is also correct.*)
12. Butter
13. Pasta
14. Jell-O

page 10: Stinky Pinky

1. Jackie's khakis
2. Shy fly
3. Cheap sheep
4. Drunk skunk
5. Bill's pills
6. Dirt shirt
7. Dumb gum
8. Weird beard
9. Cute fruit
10. Bing's rings
11. Sick chick
12. Fish wish
13. Smart art
14. Lox box

page 11: Big Bang

1. Bumble Bee
2. Bell Bottoms
3. Big Ben
4. Baby Boomer
5. Bad Breath
6. Balance Beam
7. Baby's Breath
8. Burning Bush
9. Bible Belt
10. Bed Bug

page 11: Trivia—Where Were They Born?

- Germany
- England (United Kingdom, Great Britain)
- Sweden
- Canada

page 12: Rhyming Words and Phrases

1. Hocus pocus (Abracadabra *is also correct.*)
2. Prime time
3. Cookbook
4. Backpack
5. Walkie-talkie
6. Big wig
7. Fender bender
8. Brain drain
9. Back track
10. Tepee
11. Blackjack
12. Wonton
13. Mayday
14. Downtown
15. Night-light

page 13: Who the What?

1. Bozo the Clown
2. Attila the Hun
3. Dennis the Menace
4. Kermit the Frog
5. Frosty the Snowman
6. Popeye the Sailor Man
7. Billy the Kid
8. Mack the Knife
9. Blackbeard the Pirate
10. Stan the Man
11. Alexander the Great

page 13: Word Parts

1. Confront
2. Office
3. Donkey
4. Palace
5. Tango
6. Oxford
7. Cotton
8. Person
9. Random
10. Profit

page 14: It's Charming

1. Chicken
2. Cherry
3. Charity
4. Children
5. Cheap
6. Cheese
7. Church
8. Cheetah
9. Chariot
10. Checkers
11. Chihuahua
12. Chauffeur
13. Chess
14. Chest

page 14: Classic Riddle—Emergency

The surgeon was James's mother.

page 15: Word Finder—Fashion Forward (see right)

page 16: Compound Word Search

Armchair
Bagpipe
Bedrock
Bullpen
Buttercup
Catfish
Corkscrew
Crabgrass
Doormat
Drumstick
Earthworm
Housecoat

page 18: Replace the SWAMP

1. *The Bridge Over the RIVER Kwai*
2. *Go Tell It on the MOUNTAIN*
3. *Treasure ISLAND*
4. *20,000 Leagues Under the SEA*
5. *Little House on the PRAIRIE*
6. *On Golden POND*
7. *Brighton BEACH Memoirs*
8. *Swan LAKE*
9. *How Green Was My VALLEY*
10. *The Old Man and the SEA*

page 15: Word Finder—Fashion Forward

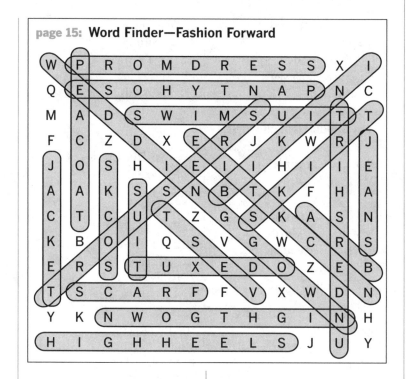

page 18: What's the Missing Number?

1. 12
2. 13
3. 3
4. 10
5. 3
6. 50
7. 99
8. 50
9. 365
10. 7
11. 21

page 19: Just J's

1. Jack
2. Jigsaw
3. Jalopy
4. Japan
5. Jackpot
6. Javelin
7. Jazz
8. Jealousy
9. Jade
10. Johnny
11. Jib
12. Jinx
13. Jamboree
14. Jeep

page 20: What Do They Have in Common?

1. They are all types of dolls.
2. They all have pockets.
3. They are all presidential pets.
4. They all have tails.
5. They are all dances.
6. They all have crowns.
7. They all have pins.
8. They are all types of fish.
9. They all contain ink.
10. They are all slang terms for money.

11. They are all famous Olivers.
12. They are all maiden names of First Ladies (Hillary Rodham Clinton, Laura Welch Bush, and Michelle Robinson Obama).
13. They are all cars made by Chevrolet.
14. They all use brushes.

page 21: Finish the Food Idiom
1. Couch *potato*
2. Flat as a *pancake*
3. Bring home the *bacon*
4. Proof is in the *pudding*
5. Sour *grapes*
6. Spill the *beans*
7. Packed in like *sardines*
8. Nutty as a *fruitcake*
9. The big *cheese* (The Big Apple *is also correct.*)
10. The best thing since *sliced bread*
11. Cut the *mustard*
12. Slower than *molasses*
13. Walk on *eggshells*
14. Sell like *hotcakes*
15. Tough *cookie*

page 21: Trivia—Wood You Know?
• Cedar
• Oak
• Birch
• Cork

page 22: Patchwork
1. Paté
2. Patio
3. Patty
4. Patent
5. Patella
6. Patients
7. Patriot
8. Pattern
9. Patisserie
10. Patricide
11. Patrol
12. Pathetic
13. Patience

page 23: Famous Critters
1. Deer
2. Horse
3. Duck
4. Dinosaur
5. Dolphin
6. Cat
7. Rabbit
8. Whale
9. Horse
10. Dog (German Shepherd)
11. Reindeer
12. Dog (Beagle)

page 23: One-Minute Madness: The Ten Commandments
(*Note: From the Revised Standard Version of the Bible, an authorized revision of the American Standard Version, published in 1901, which was a revision of the King James Version, published in 1611.*)
1. You shall have no other gods before me.
2. You shall not make for yourself a graven image.
3. You shall not take the name of the Lord your God in vain.
4. Remember the Sabbath day, to keep it holy.
5. Honor your father and your mother.
6. You shall not kill.
7. You shall not commit adultery.
8. You shall not steal.
9. You shall not bear false witness against your neighbor.
10. You shall not covet your neighbor's house, . . . wife, . . . nor anything that is your neighbor's.

page 24: Find the Words— The Wedding Party
(see pages 338–339)

page 26: Brrrr!
1. Brazil
2. Bruise
3. Breadwinner
4. Brew
5. Brain
6. Braille
7. Bracelet
8. Breeches
9. Bronze (*Note: Brass is made of copper and zinc.*)
10. Brink
11. Brimstone
12. Brittle
13. Brontosaurus
14. Bribe
15. Brother

Parachute

Plane

Palm tree

Priest/pastor

Piano

Picket fence

Party

Photographer

Pants

Ponytail

Pillow

Pinstripes

Parasol

Plants

Poodle

People

Pocketbook

Pews

Pen

Peacock

Pail

Potted plant (or plant)

Panda

Piñata

Pinwheel

Pom-poms

Policeman

Pole

Pipe

Pineapple

Plates

Plaid

Pie

Pitcher

Pacifier

Pearl necklace

Parrot
(on perch)

Pumpkin

Polka dots

Pendulum

Punchbowl
(or punch)

Presents

Percent sign

Piggybank

Puzzle

page 27: **Anagrams**
1. Inks, Sink, Skin
2. Evil, Live, Veil, Vile
3. Gnus, Guns, Snug, Sung
4. Leap, Pale, Peal, Plea
5. Acres, Cares, Races, Scare
6. Caret, Cater, Crate, Trace
7. Emits, Smite, Mites, Items, Times
8. Teaks, Skate, Steak, Stake, Takes

page 27: **Three-Way Order the List**
(*The national rankings follow in parentheses.*)
Size
Alaska (#1)
Texas (#2)
California (#3)
New York (#30)
Virginia (#37)
New Jersey (#46)

Population
California (#1)
Texas (#2)
New York (#3)
New Jersey (#11)
Virginia (#12)
Alaska (#47)

Median Income
New Jersey (#2)
Alaska (#4)
Virginia (#8)
California (#9)
New York (#17)
Texas (#27)

page 28: **Echo Echo**
1. Boo Boo
2. John-John
3. BB
4. 20/20 (Twenty-twenty)
5. Choo choo
6. Sirhan Sirhan
7. Can-can
8. Dodo
9. So-so
10. Yo-yo
11. Boola Boola
12. Ta-ta

page 29: **Golly Gee**
1. Golden Gate
2. Good Grief
3. Greta Garbo
4. Gas Guzzler
5. Gibson Girls
6. George Gershwin
7. Great Grandchild (or Great Granddaughter)
8. Gas Gauge
9. Generation Gap
10. Geisha Girl

page 29: **Trivia—On a First Name Basis**
- Charles (Dickens and Schulz)
- Walter (Mondale, Matthau, and Cronkite)
- Sally (Ride, Field, and Struthers)
- Victoria

page 30: **Just One Letter, Please**
1. K
2. U
3. R
4. G
5. T
6. V
7. I
8. B
9. T (Mr. T)
10. K
11. A
12. X

page 30: **CHARTREUSE Titles**
1. "Snow WHITE and the Seven Dwarfs"
2. *Anne of GREEN Gables*
3. *WHITE Christmas* ("BLUE Christmas" *is also correct.*)
4. *The PINK Panther*
5. *On GOLDEN Pond*
6. *Hill Street BLUES*
7. "The YELLOW Rose of Texas"
8. *The Man in the GRAY Flannel Suit*
9. *The SCARLET Letter*
10. *How GREEN Was My Valley*
11. *The Hunt for RED October*
12. *A Clockwork ORANGE*

page 31: **Don't Be an Idiom**
1. On the blink (On the fritz *is also correct.*)
2. On a roll
3. On the ball
4. On the wagon
5. On pins and needles (On tenterhooks *is correct, although it doesn't follow the clue's formatted hint of _____ and _____.*)
6. On the chopping block
7. On the dole
8. On the dot (On the nose *is also correct.*)
9. On the house

10. On the lam (On the run *is also correct.*)
11. On the tip of your tongue
12. On the stump (On the hustings *is also correct.*)
13. On the same wavelength (On the same page *is also correct.*)

page 32: What a Pair
1. Red Sox and Yankees
2. Meat and Potatoes
3. Bed and Breakfast
4. Fish and Chips
5. Apples and Oranges
6. Cat and Mouse
7. Soap and Water
8. Milk and Honey
9. Arm and Hammer
10. Stars and Stripes
11. Bacon and Eggs
12. Night and Day

page 32: Trivia—Fowl Facts
• Chicken
• Peacock
• Duck (Eider)
• Aztec

page 33: WHOOZY
The WHOOZY is Merv Griffin.

page 34: Picture Themes
Column A: Animals (Tiger, Turtles, Mouse)
Column B: Rings (Tree Rings, Boxing Ring, Rings of Saturn)
Column C: Baseball Teams (Tigers, Pirates, White Sox)
Column D: Kings (Martin Luther King Jr., Burger King, Chess Piece King)

page 36: WHATZIT
The WHATZIT is the tomato.

page 37: Palindromes
1. Bib
2. Ewe
3. Pup
4. Madam
5. Eve
6. Bob
7. Dud
8. Gig
9. Tut
10. Gag
11. Kayak
12. Nun

page 37: Down to the Wire
(*Other correct answers are possible.*)
1. A word to the wise
2. Belly up to the bar (Admitted to the bar *is also correct.*)
3. Cut to the chase
4. Dressed to the nines
5. Fight to the finish (Race to the finish *is also correct.*)
6. Filled to the brim
7. "Hail to the Chief"

8. Journey to the center of the earth
9. Nose to the grindstone
10. Off to the races
11. Preaching to the choir
12. Stuffed to the gills (Fed up to the gills *is also correct.*)

page 38: Follow the Rules
(see below)

CHAPTER TWO

page 39: It's a Kick
1. Kidnap
2. Kangaroo
3. Kazoo
4. Kiss
5. Kilt
6. Keg
7. Kelp
8. Kernel
9. Kerry
10. Kosher
11. Kamikaze
12. Kibble
13. Kielbasa
14. Kiln
15. Kickoff
16. Klutz

page 38: Follow the Rules
1. TELLTHETRUTH
2. TELL*N*THET*N*RUTH*N*
3. TE*A*LLNTHETNRUTHN
4. TEALLN*D*THETNRUTHN
5. TEALLNDTHETNRUT_N
6. T_ALLNDTHETNRUTN
7. TA__NDTHETNRUTN
8. _ANDTHE_NRU_N

(TELL THE TRUTH) AND THEN RUN

page 40: Homonyms

1. Ate/eight
2. Scent/cent
3. Flower/flour
4. Sow/sew
5. Peak/peek
6. Loan/lone
7. Role/roll
8. Hoarse/horse
9. Pause/paws
10. Eerie/Erie
11. Knight/night
12. Cell/sell
13. Dough/doe

page 41: Hidden Animals

1. Wh*eel*barrow
2. Video*tape*
3. *Horse*radish
4. Kn*owl*edge
5. *Cat*astrophe
6. *Bat*htub
7. G*iant*
8. S*crab*ble
9. Fris*bee*

page 41: Presidential Nicknames

1. Bill Clinton
2. George W. Bush
3. Ronald Reagan
4. Harry Truman
5. Abraham Lincoln
6. Dwight Eisenhower
7. Calvin Coolidge
8. Barack Obama
9. Richard Nixon

page 42: Daily Double

1. Deadbeat Dad
2. Deep Dish
3. Double Deckers
4. Doris Day
5. Designated Driver
6. Donald Duck
7. Danny DeVito
8. Double Dutch
9. Dishonorable Discharge
10. Dish Detergent
11. Dog Days
12. Demolition Derby

page 43: Endings and Beginnings

1. Man (superman; manpower)
2. Store (drugstore; storefront)
3. Shop (pawnshop; shopkeeper)
4. Tooth (bucktooth; toothpaste)
5. Table (turntable; tablecloth)
6. Book (pocketbook; bookkeeper)
7. Pipe (stovepipe; pipeline)
8. Flower (wallflower; flowerpot)
9. Hop (bellhop; hopscotch)
10. Wash (mouthwash; washtub)
11. Ring (earring; ringleader)
12. Arm (firearm; armpit)
13. Bath (birdbath; bathrobe)
14. Horse (hobbyhorse; horseradish)

page 43: Trivia—Just Johns

- John McCain
- John Ritter
- John F. Kennedy Jr.
- John Foster Dulles

page 44: It Starts with a Letter

1. Kmart
2. Q-Tip
3. C-Section
4. T-Bone
5. D-Day
6. J. Crew
7. O-Ring
8. U-Haul
9. E. Coli
10. A List
11. H-Bomb
12. Y Chromosome

page 44: Trivia—Finish the Song Line

- "…in its spell."
- "…come rain or come shine."
- "B, you're so beautiful …"
- "…a kitten up a tree."

page 45: Rhymin' Geography

1. Maine and Spain
2. Nebraska and Alaska
3. Austin and Boston
4. Albuquerque and Turkey
5. Waterloo and Kalamazoo
6. Tacoma and Oklahoma
7. Aruba and Cuba
8. Siberia and Liberia
9. Rome and Nome
10. Minnesota and Sarasota
11. Nice and Greece

page 46: The Eyes Have It—Animals

1. Lion

2. Elephant

3. Panda

4. Owl

5. Zebra

6. Giraffe

7. Tiger

8. Fish

page 47: **Finish the Saying**

1. Beauty is only *skin deep*.
2. Birds of a feather *flock together*.
3. Actions speak *louder than words*.
4. Opportunity seldom *knocks twice*.
5. Blood is *thicker than water*.
6. Dead men *tell no tales*.
7. Two heads are *better than one*.
8. Good fences *make good neighbors*.
9. It takes two *to tango*.
10. A man's home *is his castle*.
11. Give credit where *credit is due*.
12. Honesty is *the best policy*.
13. Money is *the root of all evil*.
14. All is fair *in love and war*.

page 47: **Trivia—Two Out of Three**

- Larry, Moe, and Curly
- Sugar, spice, and everything nice
- Legislative, judicial, and executive
- The Kentucky Derby, the Preakness Stakes, and the Belmont Stakes

page 48: **Put the List in Order**

1. Great Dane
   German Shepherd
   Cocker Spaniel
   Chihuahua
2. Africa (11.7 million square miles)
   North America (9.4 million square miles)
   South America (6.8 million square miles)
   Antarctica (5.3 million square miles)
   Europe (3.9 million square miles)
3. *What's My Line?* (1950)
   Perry Mason (1957)
   Bonanza (1959)
   Dr. Kildare (1961)
   Jeopardy! (1964)
4. J (8 points)
   K (5 points)
   F (4 points)
   G (2 points)
   L (1 point)

5. Katie Couric (born in 1957)
   Meryl Streep (born in 1949)
   Goldie Hawn (born in 1945)
   Barbra Streisand (born in 1942)
   Mary Tyler Moore (born in 1936)
6. *The Wall Street Journal* (2.1 million)
   USA Today (1.8 million)
   The New York Times (916,000)
   The Washington Post (550,000)
7. New York (Albany)
   Louisiana (Baton Rouge)
   Michigan (Lansing)
   New Jersey (Trenton)
8. The Woodstock music festival (1969)
   Gerald Ford becomes the thirty-eighth president (1974)
   The U.S. celebrates its bicentennial (1976)
   The Iran hostage crisis (1979)
9. Everglades (Florida)
   Great Smoky Mountains (North Carolina/Tennessee)
   Yellowstone (Idaho/Montana/Wyoming)
   Mt. Rainier (Washington)
10. *The Lord of the Rings* (150 million)
    The Da Vinci Code (80 million)
    The Diary of a Young Girl (30 million)
    The Godfather (21 million)
    The Cat in the Hat (10 million)

page 49: Trivia—Guess the Gas
- Helium
- Carbon Dioxide
- Neon
- Nitrous Oxide

page 49: One-Minute Madness—South America
1. Argentina
2. Bolivia
3. Brazil
4. Chile
5. Colombia
6. Ecuador
7. French Guiana
8. Guyana
9. Paraguay
10. Peru
11. Suriname
12. Uruguay
13. Venezuela
14. Falkland Islands (Territory of the United Kingdom)

page 50: Mark My Words
1. Marathon
2. Marble
3. Marijuana
4. Marmalade
5. Marsupials
6. Marrow
7. Marzipan
8. Mariachi
9. Marionette
10. Martini
11. Martyr
12. Marquee
13. Marlin

page 51: Run the Alphabet—Fruits and Veggies
(*Other correct answers are possible.*)
A: Apple, Asparagus
B: Blueberry, Beet
C: Cherry, Celery
D: Date, Dragon Fruit
E: Eggplant, Endive
F: Fig, Fava Beans
G: Grapes, Garlic
H: Huckleberry, Honeydew Melon
I: Iceberg Lettuce
J: Jicama, Jerusalem Artichoke
K: Kale, Kumquat
L: Lemon, Lettuce
M: Mango, Mandarin Orange, Melon
N: Nectarine, Navy Beans
O: Onion, Okra, Orange
P: Plum, Pumpkin
Q: Quince
R: Raspberry, Radish
S: Strawberry, Spinach
T: Tangerine, Turnip
U: Ugli Fruit
V: *We didn't know any. Did you?*
W: Watermelon, Watercress
X: *We didn't know any. Did you?*
Y: Yam, Yarrow
Z: Zucchini

page 52 February in History
1692 Salem
1848 Karl Marx and Friedrich Engels
1886 Groundhog Day
1896 The Tootsie Roll
1909 The NAACP (The National Association for the Advancement of Colored People)
1935 Nylon
1954 Dr. Jonas Salk
1959 Fidel Castro
1960 Woolworth's
1964 The Beatles
1964 Muhammad Ali, who was born Cassius Clay

1965 A maple leaf
1972 China
1974 *People*
1983 *M*A*S*H*
1990 South Africa
1992 Ross Perot
1993 Arthur Ashe
1998 Ronald Reagan
    Washington National
    Airport
2000 Charles Schulz

page 53: Letter Speller
1. D (Dee)
2. Y (why)
3. J (jay)
4. M, E (Emmy)
5. M, T (empty)
6. N, V (envy)
7. O, P (Opie)
8. S, O (Esso)
9. X, L (excel)
10. Z, T (ziti)—or Z, D
    depending on your accent!

page 54: M & M's
1. Mad Money
2. Magic Marker
3. Marcel Marceau
4. Mince Meat
5. Moral Majority
6. Medicine Man
7. Margaret Mitchell
8. Meter Maid
9. Mary Magdalene
10. Merchant Marine
11. Mild-Mannered
12. Mt. McKinley

page 54: Trivia—Fictional Doctors
- Dr. Dolittle
- Dr. Benjamin Franklin
  "Hawkeye" Pierce
- Dr. Hannibal Lecter
- Doctor Zhivago

page 55: Geographical Double Entendres
1. China
2. Buffalo
3. Queens
4. Brazil
5. Jupiter
6. Bath
7. Hamburg
8. Canary
9. Yellow
10. Amazon
11. Orange

page 56: X, Y, or Z
1. Zebra
2. Xylophone
3. Yacht
4. Yeast
5. Xerox
6. Zenith
7. Yak
8. Zero
9. Zoot suit
10. Yardstick
11. Zurich
12. Yen
13. Zany
14. Xenophobic
15. Zamboni

page 56: Trivia—1939
- Amelia Earhart
- *Gone with the Wind*
- John Steinbeck
- Poland

page 57: What's Your Movie Song IQ?
1. "As Time Goes By" from *Casablanca* (1942)
2. "Mrs. Robinson" from *The Graduate* (1967)
3. "The Way We Were" from *The Way We Were* (1973)
4. "The Sound of Music" from *The Sound of Music* (1965)
5. "Cabaret" from *Cabaret* (1972)
6. "Everybody's Talkin'" from *Midnight Cowboy* (1969)
7. "Raindrops Keep Fallin' on My Head" from *Butch Cassidy and the Sundance Kid* (1969)
8. "America" from *West Side Story* (1961)
9. "Aquarius" from *Hair* (1979)
10. "Supercalifragilistic-expialidocious" from *Mary Poppins* (1964)
11. "One Last Kiss" from *Bye, Bye, Birdie* (1963)
12. "I Don't Know How to Love Him" from *Jesus Christ Superstar* (1973)
13. "Don't Rain on My Parade" from *Funny Girl* (1968)

page 58: Double Trouble
1. Blood (bloodhound, bloodthirsty, bloodstream)
2. Dog (dogcatcher, dogfight, dogwood, doghouse)
3. Grand (grandmother, grandfather, grandparent, grandstand)

4. Home (homesick, homework, homeland, homeroom)
5. Ice (Iceland, iceberg, icebox, icebreaker)
6. Jack (jackhammer, jackass, jackknife, jackpot)
7. Moon (moonbeam, moonshine, moonwalk, moonlight)
8. Rain (rainbow, raincoat, raindrop, rainforest)
9. Water (waterproof, watermelon, waterfall, watercolor)
10. Green (greenback, greenhouse, Greenland, greengrocer)
11. Earth (earthquake, earthshaking, earthworm)
12. Match (matchmaker, matchstick, matchbox, matchbook)
13. Under (understudy, underwear, underprivileged)
14. Pin (pincushion, pinstripe, pinwheel, pinpoint, pinball)

page 59: Under the Weather

(*Other correct answers are possible.*)
Weather, bed, boardwalk, circumstances, counter, covers, gun, influence, knife, mat, microscope, radar, stars, sun, table, wire

page 59: Over the Hill

(*Other correct answers are possible.*)
Hill, air, barrel, border, counter, edge, head, hump, limit, line, ocean, rainbow, top

page 60: Add It Up

1. 10 + 13 = 23
2. 9 + 3 = 12
3. 1963 + 20 = 1983
4. 13 + 7 = 20
5. 2 (February) + 9 (September) = 11
6. 24 + 4 = 28
7. 1600 + 3 = 1603
8. 5 (*cinco*) + 5 (*cinco*) + 8 (*ocho*) = 18

page 60: Trivia—Steve, Stephen, or Steven

- Stephen King
- Steven Spielberg
- Steve McQueen
- Steve (Stephen) Wozniak

Page 61: Hidden Anatomy

1. H*arm*ony
2. Ob*eye*d
3. Ghet*toes*
4. Th*ankle*ss
5. C*hip*munk
6. P*ear*l
7. Diag*nose*d
8. Zuc*chin*i
9. Hor*rible*
10. Pan*hand*le
11. P*lung*er
12. Paper*back*
13. Or*chest*ra
14. Paci*fist*
15. De*liver*y
16. *Colon*ial
17. *Skin*ny
18. *Foot*age

Page 62: Backwords

(*Semordnilap is "palindromes" spelled backward!*)
1. War/Raw

2. Tops/Spot
3. Nuts/Stun
4. Pets/Step
5. Golf/Flog
6. Tide/Edit
7. Tool/Loot
8. Smart/Trams
9. Tort/Trot

page 62: Trivia—Fictional Last Words

- The Wicked Witch of the West, *The Wizard of Oz*
- Captain Hook, *Peter Pan*
- Charles Foster Kane, *Citizen Kane*
- Captain Ahab, *Moby Dick*

page 63: Name Merge

1. Danny Thomas Alva Edison
2. Jack Benny Goodman
3. Benedict Arnold Schwarzenegger
4. John Wayne Gretsky
5. Rex Harrison Ford
6. Bob Dylan Thomas
7. James Dean Martin
8. Peggy Lee Harvey Oswald
9. Ray Charles Darwin
10. Jackie Robinson Crusoe
11. Marcia Clark Kent

page 64: Wacky Wordies

1. *The Catcher in the Rye*
2. *Sixteen Candles*
3. Undersea diver
4. Walking backward
5. Drink up
6. Feeling under the weather
7. Two peas in a pod
8. *Little House on the Prairie*

page 66: **Sheesh**

1. Shoehorn
2. Shrimp
3. Shuffleboard
4. Goulash
5. Parish
6. Shoplifting
7. Sheriff
8. Succotash
9. Shadow
10. Shrew
11. Radish
12. Skittish
13. Shamrock
14. Macintosh

page 67: **Thirty-Second Madness—Roman Numerals**

1. I (One)
2. V (Five)
3. X (Ten)
4. L (Fifty)
5. C (One hundred)
6. D (Five hundred)
7. M (One thousand)

page 67: **Replace the ELBOW**

1. *A Farewell to ARMS*
2. *Adam's RIB*
3. *EYE of the Needle*
4. *GoldFINGER*
5. *ScarFACE*
6. *"Tom THUMB"*
7. *"The Telltale HEART"*
8. *The Three FACES of Eve*

page 68: **March in History**

1457 The Bible
1857 The elevator
1876 Alexander Graham Bell
1887 Hellen Keller
1889 The Eiffel Tower
1894 The Stanley Cup
1905 Fingerprints
1911 New York City
1916 Albert Einstein
1931 Gambling
1935 Persia
1938 Saudi Arabia
1943 Oskar Schindler
1946 The Iron Curtain
1947 The Domino Theory
1961 The residents of Washington, DC
1964 Jack Ruby
1968 President Johnson announced that he would not seek a second term as president.
1969 Yoko Ono
1981 Dan Rather

page 69: **One-Minute Madness—Smallest U.S. States**

State	Square Miles
West Virginia	24,087
Maryland	9,775
Vermont	9,249
New Hampshire	8,969
Massachusetts	7,838
New Jersey	7,418
Hawaii	6,423
Connecticut	4,845
Delaware	1,955
Rhode Island	1,045

page 70: **Kangaroo Words**

1. Me
2. Ban
3. Bust
4. Sock
5. Arc
6. Joy
7. Cold (or cool)
8. Lit
9. Bloom
10. Story
11. Last
12. One
13. Rage
14. Male (or man)
15. Save

page 71: **What a Pair**

1. Pen and Ink
2. Fair and Square
3. Kiss and Tell
4. Rock and Roll
5. Safe and Sound
6. Cats and Dogs
7. Shoes and Socks
8. Duck and Cover
9. Hook and Eye
10. Bread and Butter
11. Ham and Cheese
12. Body and Soul
13. Trial and Error
14. Down and Out

page 72: **What Do They Have in Common?**

1. They all have stars.
2. They are all characters in the television program *Cheers*.
3. They are all types of golf clubs.
4. They all have buttons.
5. They are all purple.
6. They all have horns.
7. They all lived past the age of one hundred.
8. They all have letters.
9. They all have rings.

10. They are all Beatles songs.
11. They all have eyes.
12. They are all beans.
13. They are all types of sugar.

page 72: Trivia—England
- Heathrow
- Northern Ireland, Scotland, and Wales
- Sausages and mashed potatoes
- Birmingham

page 73: Red, White, or Blue
1. Redcoats
2. Whitewalls
3. Blueprint
4. Redeye
5. Blueberry
6. White cap
7. Blue fin
8. Whiteout
9. Redwood
10. Bluebonnet
11. Blue jay
12. Blue blood
13. Whitewash
14. Bluebeard

page 74: Homonyms
1. Urn/earn
2. Idle/idol
3. Mussels/muscles
4. Corps/core
5. Need/knead
6. Wait/weight
7. Reign/rain
8. Boarder/border
9. Meddle/medal
10. Stares/stairs
11. Pole/poll
12. Right/write
13. Choose/chews
14. Higher/hire

page 75: Where's Grandma?
1. California
2. New York
3. Texas
4. Tennessee
5. Connecticut
6. Florida
7. New Jersey
8. Georgia
9. Colorado
10. Virginia

page 76: Endings and Beginnings
1. Fire (gunfire; firecracker)
2. Pit (snakepit; pitbull)
3. Chair (wheelchair; chairman)
4. Sucker (blooksucker; suckerpunch)
5. Pot (flowerpot; potbelly)
6. Hand (shorthand; handshake)
7. Handle (panhandle; handlebars)
8. Land (homeland; landfill)
9. Line (deadline; linebacker)
10. Friend (boyfriend; friendship)
11. Skin (sheepskin; skinhead)
12. Ground (playground; groundhog)
13. Kick (sidekick; kickstand)
14. Light (flashlight; lightbulb)

page 77: One-Minute Madness—Monopoly Streets
1. Atlantic Avenue
2. Baltic Avenue
3. Boardwalk
4. Connecticut Avenue
5. Illinois Avenue
6. Indiana Avenue
7. Kentucky Avenue
8. Marvin Gardens
9. Mediterranean Avenue
10. New York Avenue
11. North Carolina Avenue
12. Oriental Avenue
13. Pacific Avenue
14. Park Place
15. Pennsylvania Avenue
16. St. Charles Place
17. St. James Place
18. States Avenue
19. Tennessee Avenue
20. Ventnor Avenue
21. Vermont Avenue
22. Virginia Avenue

page 77: Trivia—Famous Freds
- Fred Flintstone
- Fred Allen
- Fred Astaire
- Fred Rogers (of *Mr. Rogers' Neighborhood* on PBS)

page 78: Out of Bounds
(*Other correct answers are possible.*)
Body, bounds, breath, character, commission, control, date, fashion, favor, focus, hand, it, joint, line, luck, mind, nowhere, order, place, pocket, practice, print, reach, sight, sorts, step, town, tune, wedlock, work

page 78: Trivia—Food History
- Lollipops
- Oreo cookies

- Campbell's
- Fortune cookies

page 79: **Up and Down**
1. Touch (touch up; touchdown)
2. Shut (shut up; shut down)
3. Break (break up; breakdown)
4. Back (back up; back down)
5. Crack (crack up; crack down)
6. Cut (cutup; cut down)
7. Let (let up; let down)
8. Shake (shake up; shake down)
9. Wind (windup; wind down)
10. Turn (turn up; turn down)

page 80: Follow the Rules
(see below)

page 81: Trivia—Who, What, and Where?
Who
- Groucho Marx
- Thomas Alva Edison
- Paul McCartney and Ringo Starr
- British Prime Minister Tony Blair

What
- The children listen "to hear sleigh bells in the snow."
- Kwanzaa
- Menorah
- Caspar, Melchior, and Balthazar

Where
- Cooperstown, New York
- Pennsylvania (near Harrisburg)
- Kennebunkport, Maine
- San Francisco, California

CHAPTER THREE

page 82: Backwords
1. Flow/Wolf
2. Maps/Spam
3. Buns/Snub
4. Straw/Warts
5. Drawer/Reward
6. Diaper/Repaid
7. Desserts/Stressed
8. Deliver/Reviled

page 83: Word Parts
1. Injury (in + jury)
2. Restart (rest + art)
3. Poetry (poe + try)

4. Wardrobe (ward + robe)
5. Massage (mass + age)
6. Dampen (dam + pen)
7. Margin (mar + gin)
8. Sundry (sun + dry)
9. Manhattan (man + hat + tan)
10. Endear (end + ear)

page 83: Trivia—The Golden Age of Radio
- Jimmy Durante
- Red Skelton
- Fibber McGee and Molly
- Eve Arden

page 84: Hurrah!
1. Hopscotch
2. Hash
3. Halvah
4. Hitch
5. Hogwash
6. Hallelujah
7. Hunch
8. Hookah
9. Hatch
10. Harsh
11. Hutch

page 84: Classic Riddle— Just One Answer
Nothing.

page 85: Run the Alphabet—Colors
(*Other correct answers are possible.*)
A: Amethyst, Auburn
B: Black, Blue
C: Coral, Cobalt
D: Dark Green, Denim
E: Ecru, Emerald
F: Forest Green, Fuschia
G: Gold, Gray
H: Hot Pink, Harvest Gold

___

page 80: Follow the Rules
1. W H A T D O W O M E N W A N T
2. W H A T D O W O M _ N W A N T E
3. W H A T D O W O M N L W A N T E
4. W H A T D O _ C C O M N L W A N T E
5. C H A T D O C W O M N L W A N T E
6. C H A T _ O C W O _ N L W A N T E
7. C H _ _ O C W O N L W A N T E
8. C H O C _ O _ L _ A _ T E

(WHAT DO WOMEN WANT) CHOCOLATE

I: Indigo, Ivory
J: Jade, Jasmine
K: Kelly Green, Khaki
L: Lavender, Light Brown
M: Magenta, Mustard
N: Navy Blue, Navajo White
O: Olive, Orange
P: Peach, Purple
Q: Quartz
R: Red, Rose
S: Salmon, Silver
T: Tangerine, Taupe
U: Ultramarine, Umber
V: Vermillion, Violet
W: White, Wisteria
X: Xanadu
Y: Yellow
Z: Zaffre

page 86: **Find the Words—
Concert Time** (see pages
352–353)

page 88: **Rhyme Time**
1. Jack; and black
2. Bait; and eight
3. Skirt; and Burt
4. Bored; and Ford
5. Punch; and lunch
6. Flirt; and shirt
7. Pelt; and melt
8. Hate; and skate
9. Throne; and bone
10. Twist; and wrist
11. Chickens; and Dickens
12. Staples; and Naples
13. Shiver; and river
14. Bowling; and strolling

page 88: **Thirty-Second
Madness—The Seven
Deadly Sins**
1. Anger
2. Greed (Avarice)
3. Sloth (Laziness)
4. Pride
5. Lust
6. Envy
7. Gluttony

page 89: **Trimble**
1. Milk
2. Lemonade
3. Cranberry
4. Coffee
5. Water
6. Root Beer
7. Gatorade
Jumble Answer: Iced Tea

Page 90: **Replace the
ARMADILLO**
1. *The Maltese FALCON*
2. *One Flew Over the
   CUCKOO's Nest*
3. *Dances with WOLVES*
4. *The Velveteen RABBIT*
5. *CHICKEN Soup for the Soul*
6. *The Silence of the LAMBS*
7. *To Kill a MOCKINGBIRD*
8. *Lonesome DOVE*
9. *Raging BULL*
10. *GORILLAS in the Mist*
11. *Of MICE and Men*
12. *The HOUND of the
    Baskervilles*
13. *They Shoot HORSES,
    Don't They?*
14. *Six Days of the CONDOR*
15. *RABBIT, Run*
16. *The MOUSE That Roared*

page 91: **Portmanteaus**
1. Alpha and beta (the first
   two letters of the Greek
   alphabet)
2. Motor and town (a
   nickname for Detroit)
3. Breakfast and lunch
4. Glamour and ritz
5. International and police
6. Partner and alimony
7. Monica Lewinsky and
   Watergate (The suffix *–gate*
   is now attached to many
   words to indicate a scandal.)
8. Beef and buffalo (a cross-
   breed of domestic cattle
   and the American bison)
9. Biography and picture (as in
   motion picture)
10. Spanish and English
11. Bombay and Hollywood
    (Bombay, now called
    Mumbai, is the center of
    India's film industry.)
12. Motor and hotel
13. Chuckle and snort (coined
    by Lewis Carroll)
14. Internal and
    communication
15. Cocker spaniel and poodle
    (a popular crossbreed
    of dog)

page 92: **Odd Man Out**
1. France is the odd man out.
   All of the other countries'
   names have four letters.
2. Rather is the odd man out.
   His first name is Dan.
   All of the others are
   named Walter.

3. Postcard is the odd man out. All of the other words have two consecutive double letters.

4. Audrey Hepburn is the odd (wo)man out. The other actresses are all famous redheads.

5. Melbourne is the odd man out. The others are well-known European cities. Melbourne is a city in Australia.

6. Grapefruit is the odd man out. It is the only fruit in the list that does not have a single stone or pit.

7. Haydn is the odd man out. Joseph Haydn was an eighteenth-century composer. The others are all American jazz musicians: Miles Davis, Duke Ellington, Louis Armstrong.

8. The odd man out is tempura. All of the other dishes are cheese-based. Tempura is a Japanese dish of deep fried shrimp or vegetables.

9. "Please, Please Me" is the odd man out. It was recorded by the Beatles. All of the other songs were recorded by Elvis Presley.

10. Zyrtec is the odd man out. It is the only medication in the list that is for allergy symptoms. The rest are painkillers.

11. Wapiti is the odd man out. It is the Shawnee word for the American elk. The rest are names of pasta.

page 93: **Eponyms**
1. Braille (Louis Braille)
2. Scrooge (Ebenezer Scrooge)
3. Caesar salad (Cesare Cardini)
4. Doily (Robert d'Oilly)
5. Guppy (Robert John Lechmere Guppy)
6. Leotard (Jules Léotard) (Léotard was also the inspiration for the 1867 song "The Daring Young Man on the Flying Trapeze.")
7. Nicotine (Jean Nicot)
8. Ferris Wheel (George Washington Gale Ferris Jr.)
9. Pasteurization (Louis Pasteur)
10. Murphy bed (William Lawrence Murphy)

page 94: **Put the List in Order**
1. Donald Trump (born 1946)
   Harrison Ford (born 1942)
   Warren Beatty (born 1937)
   Woody Allen (born 1935)
2. African Elephant (15,000 lbs.)
   Hippopotamus (8,500 lbs.)
   Giraffe (3,600 lbs.)
   Polar Bear (1,200 lbs.)
   Gorilla (600 lbs.)
3. Lake Champlain
   Lake Erie
   Great Salt Lake
   Lake Tahoe
4. George W. Bush (New Haven, CT)
   Ronald Reagan (Tampico, IL)
   Bill Clinton (Hope, AR)
   Barack Obama (Honolulu, HI)
5. Brazil (203.4 million)
   Russia (138.7 million)
   Mexico (113.7 million)
   Germany (81.4 million)
   United Kingdom (62.6 million)
6. Nile (Africa—4,180 miles)
   Amazon (South America—3,912 miles)
   Mississippi (United States—3,710 miles)
   Yangtze (China—3,602 miles)
7. Scissors (circa 1500)
   Bicycle (1818)
   Sewing Machine (1876)
   Cash Register (1879)
   Helicopter (1939)
8. Mandarin Chinese (1+ billion)
   English (500 million)
   Hindi (450 million)
   Spanish (390 million)
   Russian (275 million)
9. *Meet the Press* (premiered in 1947)
   The Tonight Show (premiered in 1954)
   General Hospital (premiered in 1963)
   Masterpiece Theater (premiered in 1971)
10. Caroline Kennedy (1957)
    Ron Reagan (1958)
    John F. Kennedy Jr. (1960)
    Amy Carter (1967)

Church (or cathedral)

Chimney

Candy

Canopy

Cabinets

Chef

Curtains

Customers

Coffee/ coffeepot

Cactus

Cake

Café

Cabbage

Coconuts

Chair

Corn

Carrots

Curls (hair)

Cobblestones

Cans

Collar

Coat

Cheetah

Chimpanzee

Children

Crosswalk

Cap

Clothes

Cabdriver

Checks

Caboose

Crab

Cab

Chains

Crane

Clouds
Cabin
Cap
Canoe
Cave
Camera
Cap
Caddy
Cars
Chandelier
Calendar
Curtain
Clarinet
Candles
Cube
Conductor
Cobweb
Candelabra
Cello
Circles
Clock
Carnations
Circus
Cobra
Computer
Chicken
Checks
Cheerleader
Clown
Chair
Camel
Cane
Crocodile
Calculator
Cat
Cage
Carousel

page 95: **Stinky Pinky**
1. Young lung
2. Ewe's shoes
3. Crook book
4. Cruel school
5. Bland gland
6. French wrench
7. Broke yolk
8. Middle fiddle
9. Awful waffle
10. Cold gold
11. Creepy tepee
12. Beef thief
13. Sinister minister
14. Fake flake

page 95: **Trivia— Elementary Science**
- Diamond
- Talc
- Caffeine
- Gold and Copper

page 96: **What a Pair**
1. Tom and Jerry
2. Punch and Judy
3. Fred and Ginger
4. Betty and Veronica
5. Ben and Jerry
6. Mutt and Jeff
7. Dick and Jane
8. Jack and Jill
9. Penn and Teller
10. Charles and Diana
11. Barnes and Noble

page 96: **Trivia—Islands**
- Hawaii
- Australia
- Venice
- Hilton Head

page 97: **Double Trouble**
1. Bath (bathhouse, bathrobe, bathwater, bathtub)
2. Day (daydream, daybreak, daylight, daytime)
3. Hair (haircut, hairbrush, hairdresser, hairspray)
4. Land (landlord, landmark, landslide, landlocked)
5. Black (blackmail, blacksmith, blackberries, blackjack)
6. Moon (moonbeam, moonshine, moonwalk, moonlight)
7. Pot (potholder, potluck, potbelly, pothole)
8. Wind (windshield, windfall, windpipe, windswept)
9. Door (doorbell, doorknob, doormat, doorway)
10. Honey (honeybee, honeycomb, honeydew, honeymoon)
11. Paper (paperback, paperboy, paperhanger, paperweight)
12. Pig (pigsty, pigpen, pigtail, pigskin)

page 98: **Oops!**
1. Blooper
2. Troop
3. Stoop
4. Coop
5. Scoop
6. Droop
7. Hoop
8. Snoop
9. Cooperate
10. Loophole
11. Sloop
12. Cooper

page 99: **Finish the Saying**
1. Experience is the *best teacher.*
2. Discretion is the *better part of valor.*
3. Bad news *travels fast.*
4. Jack of all trades, *master of none.*
5. Necessity is the *mother of invention.*
6. Nothing is certain but *death and taxes.*
7. Nothing ventured, *nothing gained.*
8. Once bitten, *twice shy.*
9. Still waters *run deep.*
10. Practice *makes perfect.*
11. Home is where *the heart is.*

page 99: **Body Expressions**
1. Spine
2. Eye
3. Blood
4. Toe
5. Bone
6. Hair
7. Heart
8. Jaw
9. Mind
10. Mouth

page 100: **Wacky Wordies**
1. A shot in the dark
2. Go under the knife
3. Earrings
4. Cat in the Hat
5. A pair of jacks
6. The United States
7. Read between the lines
8. Seven year itch

page 102: **Finish the Quote**
1. "... ask what you can do for your country."
2. "... tear down this wall!"

3. "'... no new taxes.'"
4. "... is fear itself."
5. "... it's black."
6. "... sting like a bee."
7. "... get out of the kitchen."
8. "... to lose for my country."
9. "... on the face of the earth."
10. "'... carry a big stick.'"

page 103: World of Music
1. Dover
2. Paree (Paris)
3. Georgia
4. San Jose
5. St. Louis
6. Bethlehem
7. Wichita
8. San Francisco
9. Kentucky
10. Tennessee

page 103: Famous Critters
1. Chimpanzee
2. Mouse
3. Monkey
4. Horse
5. Bear
6. Frog
7. Horse
8. Skunk
9. Groundhog
10. Squirrel and Moose
11. Horse
12. Mouse
13. Bear

page 104: Anagrams
1. Loop, Polo, Pool
2. Mesa, Same, Seam
3. Abets, Baste, Betas, Beast, Beats

4. Taser, Aster, Rates, Stare, Tears
5. Leapt, Petal, Plate, Pleat
6. Bleary, Barely, Barley
7. Stable, Bleats, Tables
8. Starer, Arrest, Rarest, Raters

page 104: Replace POTTERSVILLE
1. *A Tree Grows in BROOKLYN*
2. *April in PARIS*
3. *Blue HAWAII*
4. "GEORGIA on My Mind"
5. "CHATTANOOGA Choo Choo"
6. "I Left My Heart in SAN FRANCISCO"
7. *Lost in YONKERS*
8. "CALIFORNIA, Here I Come"
9. *WKRP in CINCINNATI*

page 105: Word Finder— A Lot of Cats (see left)

page 106: Follow the Rules (see page 356)

page 107: Fiddle Faddle
1. Fannie Farmer
2. Fast Food
3. Fat Free
4. Forest Fire
5. Flat Feet
6. Flip Flops
7. Fly Fishing
8. Football Field
9. Francisco Franco
10. Forbidden Fruit
11. Fossil Fuels
12. Founding Father
13. Free Fall
14. Frequent Flyer

page 105: Word Finder—A Lot of Cats

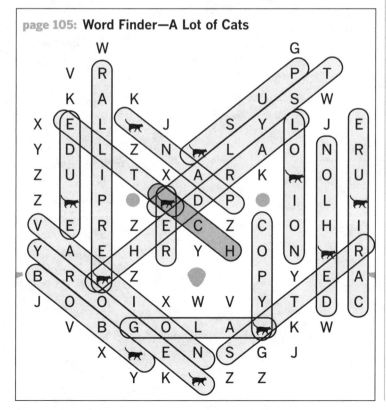

15. Frozen Food
16. Femme Fatale

page 108: **Picture Themes**
1. Column A: Sun (Sundial, Sunflowers, Sunglasses)
2. Column B: Movies (*Tootsie, Ghost, The Birds*)
3. Column C: Games (Checkers, Gin, Twister)
4. Column D: Presidents (Wilson, Hoover, Ford)

page 110: **One-Minute Madness—Major League Baseball Teams**
1. Arizona Diamondbacks
2. Atlanta Braves
3. Baltimore Orioles
4. Boston Red Sox
5. Chicago Cubs
6. Chicago White Sox
7. Cincinnati Reds
8. Cleveland Indians
9. Colorado Rockies
10. Detroit Tigers
11. Florida Marlins
12. Houston Astros
13. Kansas City Royals
14. Los Angeles Angels
15. Los Angeles Dodgers
16. Milwaukee Brewers
17. Minnesota Twins
18. New York Mets
19. New York Yankees
20. Oakland Athletics
21. Philadelphia Phillies
22. Pittsburgh Pirates
23. San Diego Padres
24. San Francisco Giants
25. Seattle Mariners
26. St. Louis Cardinals
27. Tampa Bay Rays
28. Texas Rangers
29. Toronto Blue Jays
30. Washington Nationals

page 111: **What's Your Movie Song IQ?**
1. "Diamonds Are a Girl's Best Friend" from *Gentlemen Prefer Blondes* (1953)
2. "Moon River" from *Breakfast at Tiffany's* (1961)
3. "Summertime" from *Porgy and Bess* (1959)
4. "Gonna Fly Now" from *Rocky* (1976)
5. "My Favorite Things" from *The Sound of Music* (1965)
6. "I Could Have Danced All Night" from *My Fair Lady* (1964)
7. "Some Enchanted Evening" from *South Pacific* (1958)
8. "Shall We Dance?" from *The King and I* (1956)
9. "Fame" from *Fame* (1980)
10. "Stayin' Alive" from *Saturday Night Fever* (1977)
11. "My Heart Will Go On" from *Titanic* (1997)
12. "Ol' Man River" from *Show Boat* (1936)

page 111: **Trivia—Unique States**
• Maine
• Iowa
• Wyoming
• Michigan

page 106: **Follow the Rules**
1. O L D A G E I S N O T
2. O L _ A G E I S N O T *D*
3. O L A G E *T* S N O *I* D
4. O L A G E T S N *T M* O I D
5. *F* O L A G E T S N T M O I D
6. F O L A G E T *H* N T M O I D
7. F O L A G *R* E T H N T M O I D
8. F O L A G R _ T H N E *T* M O I D
9. F O L A G R T H N E T *I* M O I D
10. F O L _ G R T H N E T I M _ I D
11. F O _ _ R T H _ E T I M I D

(OLD AGE IS NOT) FOR THE TIMID

page 112: **April in History**
753 B.C. Romulus and Remus
1492 King Ferdinand and Queen Isabella of Spain
1775 Lexington, Massachusetts (*Note: The American Revolutionary War began the next day with the Battle of Concord.*)
1861 Fort Sumter
1865 Ford's Theater
1896 Athens, Greece
1912 Southampton
1913 The zipper

1936 The kidnap and murder of the twenty-month-old son of aviator Charles Lindbergh
1945 Eva Braun
1945 Cerebral hemorrhage (stroke)
1947 Jackie Robinson
1953 DNA (deoxyribonucleic acid)
1961 Yuri Gagarin
1964 Tanzania
1968 Memphis, Tennessee
1975 Saigon
1986 The Soviet Union (now Ukraine)
1993 Waco, Texas
1995 Oklahoma City
1999 Columbine High School

page 113: Trivia—Famous Disasters
- The Great Chicago Fire
- The explosion of the *Hindenburg*
- A massive undersea earthquake
- Pompeii and Herculaneum

page 114: WHATZIT
The WHATZIT is the peanut.

page 115: WHOOZY
The WHOOZY is Eleanor Roosevelt.

page 116: Name Merge
1. Willie Nelson Mandela
2. Gene Kelly Ripa
3. Pete Rose Kennedy
4. Paul Simon Cowell
5. Betsy Ross Geller
6. Meg Ryan O'Neal
7. Anne Frank Lloyd Wright
8. Babe Ruth Bader Ginsburg
9. Ron Howard Cosell
10. Kirk Douglas MacArthur

page 117: Geographical Double Entendres
1. Plains
2. Cork
3. Needles
4. Sisters
5. Limerick
6. Sandwich
7. Snake
8. Easter
9. Truth or Consequences
10. Bologna

page 117: Trivia—Ohio Born
- Gloria Steinem
- George Steinbrenner
- Paul Lynde
- Don King

page 118: Cotton Candy
1. Credit Card
2. *Candid Camera*
3. Cape Canaveral
4. Crew Cut
5. Cable Car
6. Chicago Cubs
7. Cat's Cradle
8. Cold Cuts
9. Charlie Chaplin
10. Cheshire Cat
11. Chinese Checkers (Contrary to its name, this game was actually invented in nineteeth-century Germany.)
12. Coin Collector

page 119: What Do They Have in Common?
1. They are all types of drums.
2. They are all characters in *The Mary Tyler Moore Show*.
3. They are all types of bread.
4. They are all brands of soap.
5. They are all shades of blue.
6. They are all breeds of horses.
7. They are all U.S. Olympic swimmers who won multiple gold medals.
8. They are all breeds of cats.
9. They are all famous horses. (Champion belonged to Gene Autry; Silver to the Lone Ranger; and Trigger to Roy Rogers.)
10. They are all types of knots.
11. They are all TV doctors.
12. They are three types of jumps in figure skating.
13. They are all islands in the Caribbean.

page 120: Wowie!
1. Downtown
2. Wheelbarrow
3. Whistleblower
4. Powwow
5. Stowaway
6. Wallflower
7. Lawnmower
8. *(The) Watchtower*
9. Waterfowl
10. Welterweight
11. Wigwams (Wigwams were different from tepees and more permanent.)
12. Willpower
13. Awkward
14. Swallow

page 121: Just One Letter

1. Z
2. W
3. L
4. Y
5. C
6. H
7. S
8. Q
9. O
10. M or N
11. Y

page 121: Alma's Shopping List

1. Pepper
2. Beans
3. Peach
4. Candy
5. Bacon
6. Brawny
7. Honey
8. Soup
9. Plum
10. Beer
11. Wisk
12. Sprite
13. Grapes
14. Cloves

page 122: Compound Word Search

Butterfingers
Chestnut
Eyeglasses
Fishhook
Hairbrush
Headquarters
Honeymoon
Horseshoe
Jackknife
Panhandle
Rainbow
Wheelchair

page 124: Va-Va-Voom!

1. Vacancy
2. Vault
3. Vaccination
4. Vaudeville
5. Valley
6. Vampires
7. Vacuum
8. Vagabond
9. Valance
10. Valedictorian
11. Valuable
12. Van Dyke
13. Vaseline
14. Vandalize

CHAPTER FOUR

page 125: Homonyms

1. Hole/whole
2. Maul/mall
3. Pried/pride
4. Cheep/cheap
5. Mousse/moose
6. Links/lynx
7. Berth/birth
8. Route/root
9. Board/bored
10. Seize/seas

page 126: One-Minute Madness—U.S. Currency

Paper Currency
1. $1   George Washington
2. $2   Thomas Jefferson
3. $5   Abraham Lincoln
4. $10   Alexander Hamilton
5. $20   Andrew Jackson
6. $50   Ulysses Grant
7. $100   Benjamin Franklin
Coins
8. 1¢   Abraham Lincoln
9. 5¢   Thomas Jefferson
10. 10¢   Franklin Roosevelt
11. 25¢   George Washington
12. 50¢   John F. Kennedy
(*Note: Minting of the one-dollar Presidential series and the Native American series were suspended in December 2011. Currently, no one-dollar coins are being minted.*)

page 126: What's the Missing Number?

1. 60
2. 15
3. 1600
4. 77
5. 4
6. 64,000
7. 57
8. 5
9. 88
10. 1,001
11. 18
12. 39
13. 6

page 127: Where's the Landmark?

1. France (The Eiffel Tower)
2. Russia (St. Basil's Cathedral)
3. Australia (The Sydney Opera House)
4. Italy (The Colosseum)
5. United Kingdom (Stonehenge)
6. India (The Taj Majal)
7. Peru (Machu Picchu)
8. Greece (The Parthenon)

page 128: Mum's the Word

1. Mushroom
2. Museum
3. Monogram
4. Millennium

5. Mammogram
6. Malapropism
7. Mausoleum
8. Mayhem
9. Meerschaum
10. Metabolism
11. Memorandum
12. Microorganism
13. Macadam
14. Maim

page 129: aka Acronyms

1. Missing in action; absent without leave
2. *Répondez s'il vous plaît*; as soon as possible
3. Breaking and entering; driving under the influence
4. Disk jockey; long-playing (record)
5. Thank God it's Friday; bring your own booze
6. Chief financial officer; trademark
7. Grade point average; big man on campus
8. Social security; individual retirement account
9. High-definition television; liquid crystal display
10. Registered nurse; emergency medical technicians; cardiopulmonary resuscitation
11. Home Box Office; Public Broadcasting Service
12. Adjustable rate mortgage; private mortgage insurance
13. Volkswagen; all-wheel drive
14. Gross national product; United Kingdom

page 130: What's the Question?

1. "What's up, doc?"
2. "How Much Is That Doggie in the Window?"
3. "Who's on first?"
4. *My Fair Lady*
5. *The Lone Ranger*
6. "Is That All There Is?"
7. "...where your children are?"
8. *Guess Who's Coming to Dinner*
9. "Are you ready for some football?"
10. "To be, or not to be..." ("...that is the question.")
11. "You talkin' to me?"
12. Lauren Bacall in *To Have and Have Not*
13. "Who loves ya', baby?"

page 131: Hidden Colors

1. Ch*amber*maid
2. P*rose*cutor
3. *Aqua*rium
4. *Cream*puff
5. C*red*its
6. Comp*liment*
7. Bo*tany*
8. T*rust*worthy
9. S*teal*th
10. Stin*gray*
11. *Gold*fish
12. Pi*ecru*st
13. Im*peach*

page 131: Trivia—First Ladies

• Jacqueline Kennedy
• Pat Nixon
• Bess Truman (Margaret) and Hillary Clinton (Chelsea)
• Edith Wilson

page 132: Knot Too Hard

1. Knowledge
2. Knapsack
3. Knockwurst
4. Knickknacks
5. Knuckles
6. Knickerbockers
7. Knife
8. Knob
9. Knockout
10. Knesset

page 132: Trivia—Inventions

• Jacques Cousteau
• Volvo
• The passenger elevator
• Dynamite

page 133: Odd Man Out

1. *A Study in Scarlet* is the odd man out. It is a Sherlock Holmes novel written by Sir Arthur Conan Doyle. The others are James Bond books written by Ian Fleming.
2. Tom Brady is the odd man out because he is the only person in the list who doesn't play baseball. Brady plays football.
3. Snowflake is the odd man out. The others all have trunks.
4. Z is the odd man out. All of the other letters are Roman numerals.
5. Flounder is the odd man out. It is the only fish. The other three are crustaceans.
6. Mary is the odd (wo)man out. The others are the four sisters in *Little Women* by Louisa May Alcott.

7. ESP is the odd man out. ESP stands for extra-sensory perception. All of the others are acronyms related to computers, the Internet, and/or e-mail.

8. Brussels is the odd man out. Is it the only city that is not in Germany. Brussels is in Belgium.

9. *On Golden Pond* is the odd man out. It is the only movie that did not star Meryl Streep.

10. Trenton is the odd man out. It is the only city on the list that is north of the Mason-Dixon line.

page 134: May in History
1792 The New York Stock Exchange

1844 Samuel F. B. Morse. The message was sent instantly from the Supreme Court chamber in the Capitol Building in Washington, DC, to the B&O Railroad Depot in Baltimore, Maryland.

1859 The chiming of Big Ben, the clock that towers over the Houses of Parliament in London

1869 The transcontinental railroad, which linked the United States from coast to coast by rail

1915 The *Lusitania*

1916 Norman Rockwell

1925 Darwin's theory of evolution

1927 Paris, France

1934 Bonnie Parker and Clyde Barrow

1934 Dionne

1953 Hillary and Norgay were the first people to climb to the top of Mt. Everest.

1954 Brown v. the Board of Education knocked down the doctrine of "separate but equal" by ruling that racial segregation in public educational facilities is inherently unequal and therefore unconstitutional.

1960 Birth control. Birth control pills weren't legally available to all women, married or not, until 1972.

1961 Alan B. Shepard

1970 Ohio

1972 George Wallace

1980 Smallpox

1994 Nelson Mandela

1994 England and France

2005 Felt revealed that he was "Deep Throat," the Watergate whistleblower who had given crucial information to *Washington Post* reporters Carl Bernstein and Bob Woodward.

2011 The Navy SEALS

page 135: One-Minute Madness: Three-Letter Anatomy
1. Arm
2. Ear
3. Eye
4. Gum
5. Hip
6. Jaw
7. Leg
8. Lip
9. Rib
10. Toe

page 136: Word Finder—In the Kitchen (see page 361)

page 137: Rhyme Time
1. Rage; and stage
2. Scold; and old
3. Plot; and yacht
4. Plum; and slum
5. Deuce; and goose
6. Ghost; and toast
7. Canteen; and caffeine
8. Little Rock; and alarm clock
9. Truth; and youth
10. Science; and appliance
11. Bahamas; and pajamas
12. Curse; and nurse

page 137: Trivia—Don't Be Blue
- Blue collar
- Blue blood
- Once in a blue moon
- Out of the blue
- Blueprints
- Blue laws
- Big Blue
- Blue dog

page 138: Replace the SPINACH
1. *Charlie and the CHOCOLATE Factory*
2. *The GRAPES of Wrath*
3. *Green EGGS and HAM*
4. *Fried Green TOMATOES at the Whistle Stop Café*
5. *Goodbye, Mr. CHIPS*
6. *James and the Giant PEACH*

7. "STRAWBERRY Fields Forever"
8. *Mystic PIZZA*
9. *A FISH Called Wanda*

page 138: Down to the Wire

1. *Tell* it to the Marines
2. *Up* to the minute
3. *Rotten* to the core
4. *Power* to the people
5. *Gone* to the dogs
6. *Fuel* to the fire (*Feet* to the fire *is also correct.*)
7. *Rise* to the occasion
8. *Joy* to the world
9. *Exception* to the rule
10. *Key* to the city
11. *Married* to the mob

page 139: Something Old, Something New

1. Newt
2. Mold
3. Solder
4. Newton
5. Newborn
6. Goldfish
7. Scaffold
8. Blindfold
9. Newspaper
10. Potholder
11. Threshold
12. Cold
13. Billfold
14. Sinew

page 140: Double Trouble

1. Eye (eyeball, eyeglasses, eyelashes, eyewitness)
2. Hand (handshake, handcuff, handwriting, handsome)
3. Tooth (toothpaste, toothpick, toothbrush)
4. Finger (fingernail, fingerprint, fingertip)

5. Hair (haircut, hairdo, hairdresser)
6. Foot (football, footstool, footnote, footlocker)
7. Heart (heartache, heartbeat, heartburn)
8. Brain (brainstorm, brainwash, brainteaser, brainchild)
9. Head (headlights, headquarters, headlock, headphones)
10. Back (background, backstroke, backfire, backdrop)
11. Arm (armpit, armchair, armrest)
12. Neck (neckline, necktie, necklace)
13. Thumb (thumbscrew, thumbtack, thumbnail)

page 141: Political Quotes

1. Barack Obama, 2008 presidential campaign slogan.
2. George W. Bush, banner displayed on the USS *Abraham Lincoln* during a speech by George W. Bush on May 1, 2003. (Official fighting continued in Iraq for another seven years.)
3. Bill Clinton, when asked if he ever smoked marijuana.
4. George H. W. Bush, responding to concerns that his campaign lacked a unifying theme.
5. Al Gore, during a 1999 CNN interview, often misquoted as "I invented the Internet."

page 136: Word Finder—In the Kitchen

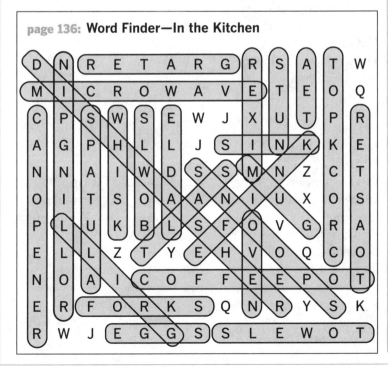

6. Richard Nixon, defending himself in 1973 from accusations of having profited through his government service.

7. Ronald Reagan, about and to Jimmy Carter during their 1980 presidential debate. It was (reluctantly) used by Reagan again about Walter Mondale in their 1984 presidential debate. (*Note: This quotation was also borrowed by Sarah Palin during the 2008 vice presidential debate with Joe Biden.*)

8. Franklin D. Roosevelt, in his first inaugural address.

9. John McCain, as the economy plummeted in 2008. (Herbert Hoover said something similar in 1929, four days before the stock market crashed and the Great Depression followed.)

10. Jimmy Carter, in a 1976 interview with *Playboy Magazine*.

page 141: Trivia—Name the Condiment
- Ketchup
- Mayonnaise
- Worcestershire Sauce
- Duck Sauce

page 142: Laundry List
1. Lucky Lindy
2. Leash Law
3. Little League
4. Liquor License
5. Lois Lane
6. Land Line
7. Labor Leaders
8. Leading Lady
9. Lemon Law
10. Loose Leaf
11. Laugh Lines

page 142: Trivia—It's a Job
- Attorney
- Physician
- Architect
- Astronaut

page 143: Run the Alphabet—Foreign Cities
(*Other correct answers are possible.*)
A: Alexandria, Athens
B: Beijing, Beirut
C: Cairo, Copenhagen
D: Damascus, Dublin
E: Edinburgh, Edmonton
F: Florence, Freeport
G: Glasgow, Gdansk
H: Hong Kong, Hamburg
I: Istanbul, Inverness
J: Jerusalem, Jakarta
K: Krakow, Kyoto
L: London, Lima
M: Madrid, Moscow
N: Naples, Nuremburg
O: Oslo, Orleans
P: Panama City, Paris
Q: Quito, Quebec City
R: Rio de Janeiro, Reykjavik
S: Sydney, Stockholm
T: Tehran, Toronto
U: Ulan Bator (Mongolia), Uppsala (Sweden)
V: Vancouver, Valparaiso
W: Winnipeg, Warsaw
X: Xiamen (China), Xavantina (Brazil)
Y: York, Yokohama
Z: Zurich, Zagreb

page 144: A Bag of Tricks
1. Bagpipe
2. Baghdad
3. Fleabag
4. Windbag (Gasbag *is also correct.*)
5. Baguette
6. Moneybags
7. Airbag
8. Bagel
9. Carpetbaggers
10. Rutabaga
11. Lumbago
12. Zabaglione

page 145: Trimble
1. Silver
2. Ruby
3. Yellow
4. Bronze
5. Green
6. Brown
7. Blue
8. Orange
9. Gold
10. White
Jumble Answer: Lavender

page 146: Add It Up
1. 5 (sides in a pentagon) + 202 (area code for Washington, DC) = 207
2. 1941 + 1962 = 3903
3. 50 (U.S. states) + 4 (U.K. countries—England, Northern Ireland, Scotland, and Wales) = 54
4. 88 + 8 = 96

5. $9 + 6 = 15$
6. $14 + 20 = 34$
7. $10 (X) + 100 (C) + 5 (V) = 115$
8. 212 degrees + 98.6 degrees = 310.6

page 146: Trivia—History of Medicine

- Penicillin
- Louis Pasteur
- Heroin and Aspirin
- Thalidomide

page 147: By Land and Sea

1. Landlord
2. Season
3. Seafood
4. Landfill
5. Slander
6. Back seat
7. Seagull
8. Island
9. Seam
10. Seatbelt
11. Bland
12. Garland
13. Landmark
14. Landslides

page 148: Wacky Wordies

1. Torn between two lovers
2. Eyewitness
3. Everything under the sun
4. Wet behind the ears
5. Shrinking violet
6. First Lady
7. Safety in numbers
8. Square dancing

page 150: Follow the Rules

(see right)

page 151: Initial Reaction

1. J. P. Morgan
2. P. T. Barnum
3. H. G. Wells
4. W. C. Fields
5. e. e. cummings
6. J. R. R. Tolkien
7. S. I. Hayakawa
8. E. F. Hutton
9. A. A. Milne
10. I. M. Pei
11. J. C. Penney
12. J. D. Salinger
13. B. F. Skinner
14. T. S. Eliot
15. M. C. Escher

page 151: Trivia—It's Spring!

- Tulip
- Daffodil
- Forsythia
- Abraham Lincoln

page 152: Catch Some ZZ's

1. Dizzy
2. Puzzle
3. Blizzard
4. Jazz
5. Buzzard

6. Embezzle
7. Sizzle
8. Guzzle
9. Mezzanine
10. Buzz
11. Paparazzi
12. Schnozzola, (or just "The Schnozz")
13. Mozzarella
14. Muzzle
15. Nozzle
16. Gizzard

page 152: Classic Riddle— A Windy Day

Mike and Ike are goldfish. A high wind blew the fishbowl off the table, shattering the glass and throwing Mike and Ike onto the floor.

page 153: Odd Man Out

1. Goulash is the odd man out. It is the only word on the list that is not a type of bread.
2. Borzoi is the odd man out. A Borzoi is a type of dog. All of the others are breeds of cats.

page 150: Follow the Rules

1. A L I G H T P U R S E
2. *I* L *A* G H T P U R S E
3. I L *S* A G H T P U R S E
4. I L S A G H T *E* P U R S E
5. I L S A G H T E *V* P U R S E
6. I L S A G H T E V *Y* P U R S E
7. I L S A G H T E *A* V Y P U R S E
8. I L S A G H T E A V Y *C* U R S E
9. I _ S A _ H _ E A V Y C U R S E

(A LIGHT PURSE) IS A HEAVY CURSE

3. July 4, 1976 is the odd man out. It was the day the U.S. celebrated the country's bicentennial anniversary. The other dates are when disasters occurred: December 7, 1941—Pearl Harbor was attacked; August 29, 2005—Hurricane Katrina made landfall near New Orleans; September 11, 2001—the World Trade Center and other U.S. sites were attacked.
4. The Great Communicator is the odd man out. It is a nickname for Ronald Reagan. The others are all nicknames for Abraham Lincoln.
5. *What Ever Happened to Baby Jane?* is the odd man out. It is the only movie in the list that did not star Elizabeth Taylor.
6. Mickey Mouse is the odd man out. He is an animated character; the others are puppets.
7. Zenith is the odd man out. It is not one of the names of the NASA space shuttle missions.
8. Richard is the odd man out. All of the others are famous people who share the last name of Jackson.
9. Columbia University is the odd man out because it is the only college on the list that is not located in Massachusetts. Columbia is in New York City.
10. Cauliflower is the odd man out because it is the only food on the list that is not yellow.

Page 154: Double Trouble

1. Bird (mockingbird, jailbird, hummingbird, bluebird)
2. Cloth (cheesecloth, washcloth, tablecloth, facecloth)
3. Stone (birthstone, cobblestone, milestone, tombstone)
4. Car (streetcar, boxcar, sidecar, motorcar)
5. Wood (dogwood, driftwood, firewood, Hollywood)
6. Nut (doughnut, hazelnut, peanut, chestnut)
7. Glass (eyeglass, fiberglass, hourglass, wineglass)
8. Bug (ladybug, bedbug, litterbug, shutterbug)
9. Lift (facelift, forklift, chairlift, shoplift, uplift)
10. Maker (troublemaker, pacemaker, matchmaker
11. Stick (breadstick, chopstick, lipstick, matchstick, slapstick)
12. Yard (backyard, junkyard, lumberyard, schoolyard)
13. Hole (cubbyhole, foxhole, manhole, pigeonhole)
14. Town (boomtown, hometown, shantytown, downtown)
15. Fish (jellyfish, shellfish, goldfish, catfish)

page 155: One-Minute Madness: U.S. Surnames

1.	Johnson	1.8 million
2.	Williams	1.5 million
3.	Brown	1.38 million
4.	Jones	1.36 million
5.	Miller	1.1 million
6.	Davis	1 million
7.	Garcia	858,000
8.	Rodriguez	804,000
9.	Wilson	783,000
10.	Martinez	775,000
11.	Anderson	762,000
12.	Taylor	720,000
13.	Thomas	710,000
14.	Hernandez	706,000
15.	Moore	698,000
16.	Martin	672,000
17.	Jackson	666,000
18.	Thompson	644,000
19.	White	639,000

page 155: Trivia—In the Middle

- Scott
- Waldo
- Lloyd
- Wilkes

page 156: Word Play

1. Envelope
2. Mushroom
3. An X
4. The letter "t"
5. "e" (alphabEt)
6. An electrician

page 156: Replace the ELBOW

1. *The Man with the Golden ARM*
2. *The Lovely BONES*
3. *Their EYES Were Watching God*

4. *The HEART Is a Lonely Hunter*
5. *The HANDmaid's Tale*
6. *HAIRspray*
7. *BraveHEART*
8. *Bury My HEART at Wounded KNEE*
9. *The SKIN of Our TEETH*

page 157: The Eyes Have It

1. Pat Nixon

2. Nancy Reagan

3. Laura Bush

4. Michelle Obama

5. Mamie Eisenhower

6. Betty Ford

7. Hillary Clinton

8. Eleanor Roosevelt

page 158: June in History

622   Saudi Arabia
1692 Witchcraft
1779 Benedict Arnold, whose name quickly became synonymous with treason
1876 The Battle of the Little Big Horn
1885 The Statue of Liberty. It traveled in pieces packed into 214 crates and took four months to reassemble.
1903 Henry Ford (The Ford Motor Company)
1935 Alcoholics Anonymous
1944 Normandy
1950 Korea. This marked the beginning of the three-year-long Korean Conflict.
1953 Julius and Ethel Rosenberg
1963 Governor George Wallace
1966 The Miranda case required that the police inform a suspect of his constitutional rights to remain silent and to have a lawyer represent him and protect him against self-incrimination.
1967 Thurgood Marshall
1968 Andy Warhol
1968 The Ambassador Hotel
1973 John Dean
1974 The Heimlich Maneuver
1974 Mikhail Baryshnikov
1997 Tyson bit off a portion of the ear of his opponent, Evander Holyfield.
1997 Hong Kong

page 159: Trivia—Before They Were President

• Jimmy Carter
• Harry Truman
• Theodore Roosevelt
• Woodrow Wilson

CHAPTER FIVE

8. Sasquatch
9. Snitch
10. Hopscotch
11. Smooch
12. Quench
13. Scorch

page 166: Trivia—Extreme Geography

- Mt. Everest
- Russia (Canada is the second largest.)
- Antarctica
- Libya (136° in El Azizia, Libya in 1922)

page 167: TV Theme Songs

1. *The Brady Bunch*
2. *Mr. Ed*
3. *The Jeffersons*
4. *The Beverly Hillbillies*
5. *All in the Family*
6. *Golden Girls*
7. *Cheers*
8. *Car 54, Where Are You?*
9. *Welcome Back, Kotter*
10. *WKRP in Cincinnati*
11. *Family Ties*
12. *Laverne & Shirley*
13. *F Troop*
14. *The Nanny*

page 168: Borrowed from India

1. Pajamas
2. Bangle
3. Candy
4. Cash
5. Cot
6. Pal
7. Dungaree
8. Orange

9. Shampoo
10. Dinghy
11. Jungle
12. Cummerbund
13. Sugar
14. Veranda

page 169: WHOOZY

The WHOOZY is Edgar Allan Poe.

page 169: Trivia—Guess the Category (Birds)

- *The Partridge Family*
- *One Flew Over the Cuckoo's Nest*
- Steven Crane
- Christopher Wren

page 170: Numerical Titles

1. "Fifty Ways to Leave Your Lover"
2. *The House of the Seven Gables*
3. *A Tale of Two Cities*
4. *Around the World in Eighty Days*
5. *Three Men and a Baby*
6. *Fahrenheit 451*
7. *Eight Is Enough*
8. "Seventy-Six Trombones"
9. *Ocean's Eleven* (*Note:* Twelve *or* Thirteen *would also be correct.*)
10. *Sixteen Candles*
11. *Catch-22*
12. *Four Weddings and a Funeral*
13. *The 39 Steps*
14. *Six Days of the Condor* (*Three Days of the Condor,* a 1975 movie, *is also correct.*)

15. *North Dallas Forty*
16. *The Crying of Lot 49*
17. *One Hundred Years of Solitude*
18. *Three Coins in the Fountain*
19. *Slaughterhouse Five*
20. *101 Dalmatians*

page 170: Thirty-Second Madness—States with Two-Word Names

1. New Hampshire
2. New Jersey
3. New Mexico
4. New York
5. North Carolina
6. North Dakota
7. Rhode Island
8. South Carolina
9. South Dakota
10. West Virginia

page 171: What a Pair

1. Cut and Dry
2. Rod and Reel
3. Law and Order
4. Smoke and Mirrors
5. Mover and Shaker
6. Trial and Error
7. Fair and Square
8. Coat and Tie
9. Divide and Conquer
10. Assault and Battery
11. Bow and Arrow
12. Song and Dance
13. Nuts and Bolts
14. Tar and Feathers
15. Fine and Dandy

page 172: July in History

1789 A prison

1799 The Rosetta Stone

1804 Alexander Hamilton

1826 John Adams died at age ninety in Braintree, Massachusetts, and Thomas Jefferson died at age eighty-three at Monticello, his home near Charlottesville, Virginia.

1897 Guglielmo Marconi

1925 *Mein Kampf*

1925 Clarence Darrow and William Jennings Bryan

1946 Dr. Benjamin Spock (author of *The Common Sense Book of Baby and Child Care*)

1948 Idlewild

1950 Vietnam

1954 *The Fugitive,* which debuted in 1963 and ran for four seasons

1961 Ernest Hemingway

1966 Medicare. Before Medicare, fewer than half of America's seniors had health insurance.

1969 "That's one small step for man, one giant leap for mankind."

1969 Mary Jo Kopechne

1976 Nadia Comaneci

1978 Louise Brown was the first baby conceived outside the womb through *in vitro* fertilization (IVF). (Today, more than three million IVF babies have been born around the world.)

1984 Geraldine Ferraro

1985 Rock Hudson

2008 Frozen water

page 173: Trivia—Russia

- Google
- The Kremlin
- Vladimir Putin
- Golda Meir

page 174: Endings and Beginnings

1. House (slaughterhouse; housekeeper)
2. Milk (buttermilk; milkshake)
3. Time (bedtime; timetable)
4. Hood (childhood; hoodwink)
5. Fire (ceasefire; firefighter)
6. Finger (ladyfinger; fingernail)
7. Wind (whirlwind; windbreaker)
8. Stock (laughingstock; stockbroker)
9. Place (birthplace; placekicker)
10. Board (cardboard; boardwalk)

page 174: Who the What?

1. Dora the Explorer
2. Jimmy the Greek
3. Catherine the Great
4. Conan the Barbarian (*Destroyer* is also correct.)
5. Oscar the Grouch
6. Ivan the Terrible
7. Joe the Plumber (*Bartender* is also correct.)
8. Jack the Ripper (Jack the Giant Killer *is also correct.*)
9. John the Baptist
10. André the Giant

page 175: Name Merge

1. John Glenn Miller
2. O. Henry Kissinger
3. Barney Frank Sinatra
4. Thomas Jefferson Davis
5. Washington Irving Berlin
6. Harry Morgan Freeman
7. Edmund Hillary Rodham Clinton
8. Jason Alexander Graham Bell
9. George C. Scott Joplin
10. Lewis Carroll O'Connor
11. Mary Martin Scorscese

page 176: Picture Themes

Column A: Blue (IBM–Big Blue, Blue Jay, Blue Angels)

Column B: Car Models (Beetle–VW, Rabbit–VW, Jaguar)

Column C: Military Ranks (Private, General, Colonel)

Column D: Rock Bands (Kiss, The Doors, The Monkees)

page 178: Hidden Animals

1. *Cow*ardly
2. *Gram*mar
3. T*ox*ic
4. Un*bear*able
5. Mi*crow*ave
6. *Dog*matic
7. Int*raven*ous
8. S*hare*holders

page 178: Alma's Shopping List

1. Cake
2. Onion
3. Cream
4. Broth
5. Lime
6. Cheer

7. Chips
8. Soda
9. Crest
10. Folgers
11. Ginger
12. Ham
13. Bread
14. Water

page 179: Odd Man Out

1. Truman is the odd man out. All of the other presidents were Republicans. Truman was a Democrat.
2. Clog is the odd man out. Clogs are a type of shoe. All of the others are types of hats.
3. Eyeglasses is the odd man out. All of the other items have buttons.
4. Left Bank is the odd man out. The Left Bank is in Paris. All of the other places are in London.
5. "Folsom Prison Blues" is the odd man out. The others are songs sung by Johnny Mathis. "Folsom Prison Blues" is by Johnny Cash.
6. Canary Islands is the odd man out. It is a set of islands off the coast of northwest Africa. The others are located in the Caribbean.
7. Flatbush is the odd man out. It is a neighborhood in New York City. All of the others are neighborhoods in Los Angeles.
8. *A Star Is Born* is the odd man out. It is the only movie in the list that did not feature Gene Kelly.
9. Cassoulet is the odd man out. It is a slow-cooked French stew. All the others are forms of stuffed dumplings.
10. Volleyball is the odd man out. It is the only sport in the list that does not require a racquet.
11. Stethoscope is the odd man out. All of the other items are surgical instruments. The stethoscope is an acoustic medical device for listening to the heart and lungs.
12. Orkney is the odd man out. While all are place names, Orkney is the only one that is not also a breed of dairy cow.

page 180: Pencil Play

1. Pablo Picasso
2. Pay Phones (or Public Phones)

3. Pedal Pushers
4. Penny Pincher
5. Peppermint Patty
6. Peter Pan
7. Playing Possum
8. Pol Pot
9. Printing Press
10. Pulitzer Prize
11. Pumpkin Pie (or Pecan Pie)
12. Peace Pipe
13. Ping-Pong
14. Pied Piper

page 181: Follow the Rules
(see below)

page 182: Word Parts

1. Begone (beg + one)
2. Automatic (auto + ma + tic)
3. Example (ex + ample)
4. Capability (cap + ability)
5. Summary (sum + mary)
6. Menswear (men + swear)
7. Impair (imp + air)
8. Hatred (hat + red)
9. Curfew (cur + few)
10. Thinking (thin + king)

---

page 181: Follow the Rules

1. ALL*M*OTHERSARE
2. AL*R*MOTHERSA*L*E
3. *W*ALRMOTHERSALE
4. WALRM*IN*OTHERSALE
5. WALRM*K*INOTHERSALE
6. WALRMKINO*O*THERSALE
7. WALRMKINOOTHERS*G*ALE
8. W*O*LRMKINA*A*OTHERSGALE
9. WOLRMKINA_____GALE*OTHERS*
10. WOLR*A*KINAG*M*LEOTHERS
11. WO_R_KIN_GM__OTHERS

(ALL MOTHERS ARE) WORKING MOTHERS

4. Milton Berle
5. Joe Namath
6. Charlie Chaplin
7. Donald Trump
8. O. J. Simpson
9. Jackie Gleason
10. Wayne Gretsky
11. Muhammad Ali
12. Al Capone
13. Karl Rove
14. Mel Tormé
15. Thomas Edison
16. Pete Rose
17. Jerry (Edmund G.) Brown Jr.
18. Jack Kevorkian

page 189: Trivia—Food
- Julienne
- Grass
- Seaweed
- Truffles

page 190: Put on Your Thinking Cap
1. Capillaries
2. Capital
3. Capon
4. Cappuccino
5. Capsized
6. Capsule
7. Captain
8. Capture
9. Capacity
10. Capra
11. Capuchin
12. Captivate
13. Capricorn
14. Capitulate
15. Capitalism

page 191: Colorful People
1. Lorne Greene
2. Molly Brown

3. Zane Grey
4. Shirley Temple Black
5. Murphy Brown
6. Vida Blue
7. Helen Gurley Brown
8. The Red Baron
9. Amy Tan
10. Alan Greenspan
11. Red Auerbach
12. Mr. Greenjeans
13. Dan Brown

page 192: Find the Words—Family Time (see pages 372–373)

page 194: Twy This!
1. Twain
2. Twilight
3. Tweezers
4. Twinkle
5. Tweed
6. Twirl
7. Twerp (Twit *is also acceptable.*)
8. Twiggy
9. Tweak
10. Twine
11. Twinge
12. Twitter

page 194: Trivia—Soup
- Cream of Mushroom, Chicken Noodle, and Tomato
- Tomato
- Okra
- Potatoes and Leeks

page 195: One-Minute Madness—U.S. Presidents
1. George Washington
2. John Adams

3. Thomas Jefferson
4. James Madison
5. James Monroe
6. John Quincy Adams
7. Andrew Jackson
8. Martin Van Buren
9. William Henry Harrison
10. John Tyler
11. James Knox Polk
12. Zachary Taylor
13. Millard Fillmore
14. Franklin Pierce
15. James Buchanan
16. Abraham Lincoln
17. Andrew Johnson
18. Ulysses S. Grant
19. Rutherford B. Hayes
20. James Garfield
21. Chester Arthur
22. Grover Cleveland
23. Benjamin Harrison
24. Grover Cleveland
25. William McKinley
26. Theodore Roosevelt
27. William Howard Taft
28. Woodrow Wilson
29. Warren Harding
30. Calvin Coolidge
31. Herbert Hoover
32. Franklin D. Roosevelt
33. Harry S Truman
34. Dwight D. Eisenhower
35. John F. Kennedy
36. Lyndon Johnson
37. Richard Nixon
38. Gerald Ford
39. Jimmy Carter
40. Ronald Reagan
41. George H. W. Bush
42. William J. Clinton
43. George W. Bush
44. Barack H. Obama

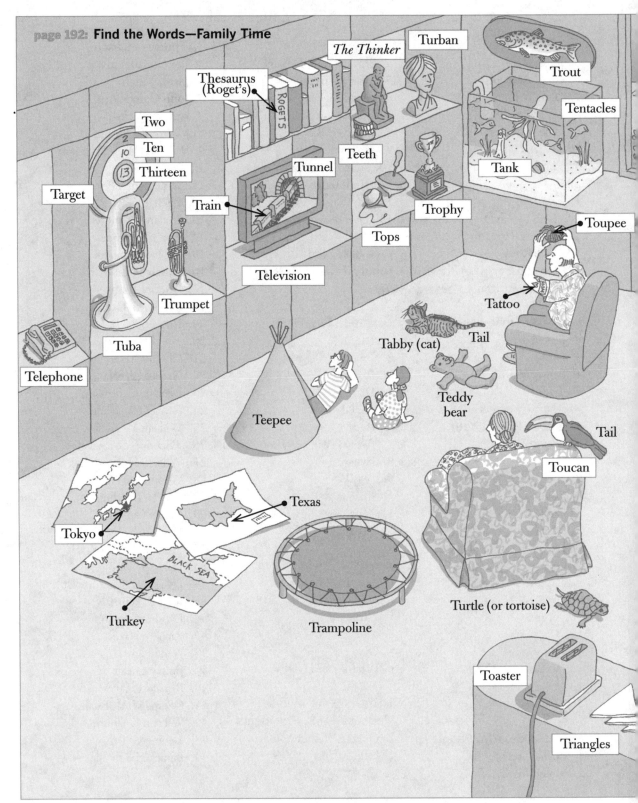

The Thinker
Turban
Trout
Tentacles
Thesaurus (Roget's)
Two
Ten
Thirteen
Teeth
Tank
Target
Tunnel
Train
Trophy
Toupee
Tops
Tattoo
Television
Trumpet
Tuba
Tabby (cat)
Tail
Teddy bear
Telephone
Teepee
Tail
Toucan
Texas
Tokyo
Turtle (or tortoise)
Turkey
Trampoline
Toaster
Triangles

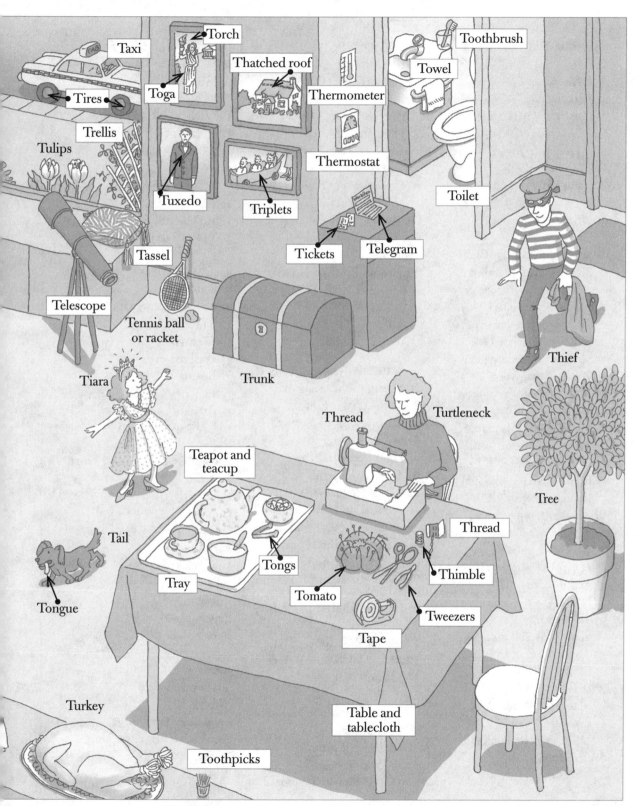

Taxi

Torch

Toga

Tires

Thatched roof

Thermometer

Toothbrush

Towel

Trellis

Tulips

Tuxedo

Thermostat

Triplets

Toilet

Tassel

Telescope

Tickets

Telegram

Thief

Tennis ball or racket

Trunk

Tiara

Thread

Turtleneck

Tree

Teapot and teacup

Tail

Thread

Tongue

Tray

Tongs

Tomato

Thimble

Tweezers

Tape

Turkey

Table and tablecloth

Toothpicks

1. *It Happened One Night* (1934)
   Gone with the Wind (1939)
   Casablanca (1943)
   On the Waterfront (1954)
   Ben-Hur (1959)
2. Giant tortoise (150 years)
   Parrot (75 years)
   Alligator (50 years)
   Horse (30 years)
3. Shakespeare dies (1616)
   Plymouth Rock landing (1620)
   Smallpox vaccine (1796)
   Telephone patented (1876)
4. Days in a fortnight (14)
   Months in a decade (120)
   Weeks in two years (104)
   The number of minutes in four hours (240)
5. Lyndon B. Johnson (6'4")
   Thomas Jefferson (6'2½")
   Ronald Reagan (6'1")
   Richard Nixon (5'11½")
   Jimmy Carter (5'9½")
6. *Truth or Consequences* (1950)
   The Price Is Right (1956)
   Jeopardy! (1964)
   Hollywood Squares (1966)
   Family Feud (1976)
7. Jupiter (88,856 miles in diameter)
   Saturn (74,898 miles in diameter)
   Earth (7,953 miles in diameter)
   Mars (4,225 miles in diameter)
   Mercury (3,044 miles in diameter)
8. Brad Pitt (1963)
   Tom Cruise (1962)
   George Clooney (1961)
   Tom Hanks (1956)
   Meryl Streep (1949)
9. The Battle of Britain (1940)
   Attack on Pearl Harbor (1941)
   The Battle of Midway (1942)
   The Battle of the Bulge (1944)
   The Battle of Iwo Jima (1945)
10. Brooks Brothers (1818)
    Barnes & Noble (1873)
    Sears (1886)
    JCPenney (1902)
    Walmart (1962)

page 197: **Whose Quote Is It?**

1. Martin Luther King Jr.
2. Thomas Alva Edison
3. Anne Frank
4. Samuel Goldwyn
5. Leroy "Satchel" Paige
6. Thomas Jefferson
7. Lillian Hellman (She refused to "name names" during the anti-communist hysteria of the 1950s.)
8. Albert Einstein
9. Louis "Satchmo" Armstrong

page 198: **August in History**

1859 Pennsylvania
1888 Jack the Ripper
1902 "...but liquor is quicker."
1902 Fanny Farmer
1912 Tarzan
1945 Hiroshima and Nagasaki
1947 Pakistan
1954 *Sports Illustrated*
1956 Jackson Pollock
1963 The Lincoln Memorial
1968 Hubert Humphrey
1974 Nixon left Washington the next day.
1977 Memphis, Tennessee
1977 Nelson Rockefeller
1980 Lech Walesa
1981 The Professional Air Traffic Controllers Organization
1984 Truman Capote
1997 The Ritz Hotel in Paris
2005 Ray Nagin

page 199: **Trivia—Mayor of Where?**

- New York City
- San Francisco
- Chicago
- Washington, DC
- Boston
- Philadelphia
- Atlanta
- Los Angeles

page 200: **Compound Word Search**

Bootleg
Courtship
Dishwater
Earphone
Footlocker
Inkwell
Litterbug
Paperweight
Shoelace
Starfish
Streetcar
Tablespoon

page 202: **British vs. American English**

1. Flat
2. Torch

3. Trolley
4. Biscuit
5. Chips
6. Bonnet
7. Suspenders
8. Petrol
9. Pacifier
10. Bangs
11. Amber
12. Band-Aid (adhesive bandage)
13. A run in their stockings
14. Nappy (or napkin)
15. Antenna
16. News anchor
17. Chemist
18. Boot
19. Eggplant
20. Phone booth
21. Coach
22. Spanner
23. Busy signal
24. Sweater

page 203: Trivia—What's the Story?

- "The Legend of Sleepy Hollow" by Washington Irving
- *Of Mice and Men* by John Steinbeck
- *The Great Gatsby* by F. Scott Fitzgerald
- *The House of the Seven Gables* by Nathaniel Hawthorne

page 204: Trivia—Pick Your Poison

- Skull and crossbones
- Lead
- Hemlock
- Cyanide

page 204: Thirty-Second Madness—Ivy League Colleges

1. Brown University, Providence, Rhode Island
2. Columbia University, New York, New York
3. Cornell University, Ithaca, New York
4. Dartmouth College, Hanover, New Hampshire
5. Harvard University, Cambridge, Massachustetts
6. Princeton University, Princeton, New Jersey
7. University of Pennsylvania, Philadelphia, Pennsylvania
8. Yale University, New Haven, Connecticut

page 204: Trivia— Who Said It?

- New York City Mayor Rudy Giuliani (on September 11, 2001)
- President Gerald Ford (after taking the oath of office)
- King Edward VIII (in his abdication speech)
- Richard Nixon (in his White House farewell)

CHAPTER SIX

page 205: Odd Man Out

1. Florida is the odd man out. It is not one of the thirteen original colonies.
2. Flamingo is the odd man out. It is the only animal that is not also the name of a car (Mercury Cougar; Volkswagen Rabbit; Ford Falcon; Chevrolet Impala).
3. Nori is the odd man out. It is the seaweed wrapper used in sushi; the others are types of mushrooms.
4. Orient is the odd man out. It is the only six-letter word in the list that doesn't contain double letters.
5. Beryllium is the odd man out. It is a metallic element; the others are types of flowers.
6. Nordstrom is the odd man out. It is a department store; the others are art museums.
7. Glasgow is the odd man out. It is the only city in the list that is not in Florida.
8. WWW is the odd man out. It is the only item on the list that is not a cable television channel. WWW, which stands for World Wide Web, is the Internet.
9. "Younger Than Springtime" is the odd man out because it is a song from the musical *South Pacific.* The others are songs from *The Sound of Music.*
10. Enigma is the odd man out. It is the only word in the list that is not a letter in the Greek alphabet.
11. Colorado is the odd man out. Colorado is landlocked. All of the other states border an ocean.

12. Fennel is the odd man out.
    While they are all names of
    common herbs and spices,
    fennel is the only one that
    is not also a person's first
    name.

page 206: Replace the SPINACH

1. *The Big Rock CANDY Mountain*
2. *A Clockwork ORANGE*
3. *The CHERRY Orchard*
4. *The ONION Field*
5. *A RAISIN in the Sun*
6. *"The CANDY Man"*
7. *What's Eating Gilbert GRAPE?*
8. *The APPLE Dumpling Gang*
9. *Like Water for CHOCOLATE*

page 206: One-Minute Madness—Land Countries

1. England
2. Finland
3. Greenland
4. Holland (Netherlands)
5. Iceland
6. Ireland (Republic of)
7. New Zealand
8. Poland
9. Scotland
10. Swaziland
11. Switzerland
12. Thailand

page 207: By the Numbers

1. 1976
2. 96 years old
3. 47 minutes
4. 2:00 P.M.

5. $160
6. 500 (911 minus 411)
7. 87 years
8. 180 (212° minus 32°)
9. 24 inches (6" + 18")
10. 11 (13 minus 2)
11. 4 pounds
12. 27 (9 innings x 3 players per inning)
13. 180°

page 208: Slippery Slope

1. Simple Simon
2. Secret Service
3. *Sad Sack*
4. Saddle Shoes
5. Seattle Slew
6. Swizzle Stick
7. Summer Solstice
8. Status Symbol
9. Step Stool
10. Stick Shift
11. Short Stop
12. Side Saddle
13. Sing Sing
14. Stainless Steel

page 209: More or Less?

1. The 2010 Census put the
   U.S. population at roughly
   307 million. While there is
   no exact count of squirrels,
   it is reasonable to assume
   there are 1.5 squirrels per
   acre of land in the U.S.,
   which would result in
   approximately 1.12 billion
   squirrels. That means
   that squirrels outnumber
   humans by three to one.
2. The average human head
   has about 100,000 hairs.
   The average bald eagle

has about 7,200 feathers.
Therefore, the human head
has ten times more hairs
than eagles have feathers.
(*Note: A German scientist
discovered that hair
thickness was related to hair
color. Blonds average about
140,000 hairs, while people
with black hair average
about 90,000 hairs on their
heads.*)

3. In 1900, the average man
   was about 5'7" tall. Today,
   the average woman's height
   is about 5'4". Therefore,
   the men in 1900 were taller
   than women are today.
4. Per 2010 information, the
   average British household
   has about thirty stations
   to watch. The average
   American family has a
   whopping 118 television
   channels.
5. According to Federal
   statistics, roughly 1.3
   million Americans are
   legally blind, while three
   times that number (roughly
   4.5 million Americans)
   have significant hearing
   loss.
6. Where you live might
   influence your answer to
   this question. If you live
   in the U.S. northeast or
   southwest, you might be
   surprised to learn that there
   are about twelve million
   more German Americans
   than Irish Americans.
   According to the 2000

U.S. Census, 42.8 million Americans claim a German heritage, while 30.5 million Americans claim to have an Irish background.

page 209: **Anagrams**

1. Sepal, Pleas, Lapse, Peals, Leaps, Pales
2. Teals, Slate, Tales, Stale, Least, Steal
3. Warder, Redraw, Drawer, Warred, Reward
4. Tinsel, Inlets, Enlist, Listen, Silent
5. Padres, Spared, Rasped, Drapes, Spread, Parsed
6. Lusters, Results, Rustles
7. Rattles, Startle, Starlet
8. Pertains, Painters, Repaints, Pantries

page 210: **What Do They Have in Common?**

1. They are all pumps.
2. They are all mountains in the U. S.
3. They all have shells.
4. They are all stories that feature horses.
5. They are all soups.
6. They are all pieces (or tokens) that move around the board in Monopoly.
7. They all run.
8. They all mean *please*. (German, Spanish, and Italian.)
9. They are all characters played by James Stewart. (Elwood P. Dowd in *Harvey,* Jefferson Smith in *Mr. Smith Goes to Washington,* Roger Hobbs in *Mr. Hobbs Takes a Vacation,* and George Bailey in *It's a Wonderful Life.*)
10. They all have heads.
11. They are all the real names of authors who wrote under pen names. (Eric Blair is George Orwell, Samuel Clemens is Mark Twain, and Charles Dodgson is Lewis Carroll.)
12. They are all brands of typewriters.

page 210: **Trivia—What Happened On . . . ?**

- Pearl Harbor was bombed.
- Martin Luther King Jr. was assassinated.
- The *Titanic* sank.
- Richard Nixon resigned.

page 211: **Boo!**

1. Booze
2. Boomerang
3. Bookie (or Bookmaker)
4. Boomers (i.e., Baby Boomers)
5. Bookworm
6. Boondocks
7. Bootleg
8. Booster
9. Bookmobile
10. Booths
11. Bookkeeper
12. Boomtown
13. Boondoggle
14. Boor
15. Bootlicker

page 212: **Flag Day**

1. Australia
2. Canada
3. Cuba
4. Japan
5. Brazil
6. South Korea
7. Iraq
8. Mexico

page 214: **Are You Decent?**

1. Decaf (decaffeinated)
2. Decanter
3. Deceased
4. Deck
5. Deceive
6. Decapitate
7. Decathlon
8. Decay
9. Decibel
10. Decide
11. Decongestant
12. Decrease
13. Decadent
14. Deciduous

page 215: **Trivia— Alphabetical Geography**

- Mexico, Luxembourg
- Iraq, Iran
- Vanuatu, Venezuela, Vietnam, Virgin Islands (Vatican City *is also acceptable.*)
- Peru

page 215: **One-Minute Madness—Salad Days**

1. Bean (or Three Bean)
2. Caesar
3. Chef
4. Chicken
5. Cobb

6. Egg
7. Fruit
8. Garden
9. Greek
10. Green
11. Macaroni
12. Niçoise
13. Pasta
14. Poke
15. Potato
16. Spinach
17. Tossed
18. Tuna
19. Waldorf

page 216: TV Hometowns
1. Mayberry, North Carolina
2. Minneapolis, Minnesota
3. Seattle, Washington
4. North Caldwell, New Jersey
5. Washington, DC
6. Lynbrook (Long Island), New York
7. Milwaukee, Wisconsin
8. Boulder, Colorado
9. Atlanta, Georgia
10. Miami, Florida
11. Cicely, Alaska
12. Virginia City, Nevada
13. Schooner Bay, Maine
14. Hooterville (no state)
15. Dodge City, Kansas
16. Cocoa Beach, Florida
17. Boston, Massachusetts
18. San Francisco, California
19. Phoenix, Arizona
20. Nantucket, Massachusetts
21. Lanford, Illinois
22. Cabot Cove, Maine

page 217: Political Quotes
1. Vice President Walter Mondale, when attacking Colorado Senator Gary Hart in a 1984 Democratic primary debate. The phrase came from a television ad for Wendy's hamburgers.
2. John McCain, used repeatedly during his 2008 presidential campaign.
3. Ross Perot, in 1992, referring to American jobs going to Mexico if the North American Free Trade Agreement (NAFTA) was ratified.
4. Thomas Jefferson, in his first inaugural address, to unite the competing parties after a particularly contentious campaign.
5. Senator Lloyd Bentsen, to Senator Dan Quayle in the 1988 vice presidential debates.
6. Hillary Clinton, in defense of her husband when the Lewinsky scandal broke.
7. Attorney Joseph N. Welch, to Senator Joseph McCarthy in 1954 on McCarthy's cruel and relentless personal attacks on individuals he suspected (often without an iota of evidence) of having Communist ties.
8. Ronald Reagan, when discussing relations with the Soviet Union.

page 217: Trivia—It's Greek to Me
- Aesop
- George Stephanopoulos
- Michael Dukakis
- Aristotle

page 218: Capitonyms
1. China/china
2. Joey/joey
3. Pound/pound
4. August/august
5. Job/job
6. Polish/polish
7. Cash/cash
8. Crest/crest
9. Apple/apple
10. Sprite/sprite

page 218: Trivia—Hispanic Heritage
- *This Old House*
- Martin Sheen
- Rita Hayworth
- Roberto Clemente

page 219: WHATZIT
The WHATZIT is the cranberry.

page 220: September in History
1846 Ether
1901 William McKinley
1927 Gene Tunney
1939 Poland
1940 Cave paintings of prehistoric animals created seventeen thousand years earlier during the Neolithic era.

1952 Charlie Chaplin (*Note: Chaplin did not return to the United States until 1972, when he was honored with an Academy Award for his lifetime contribution to film. When he stepped on the stage, he received the longest standing ovation in Oscar history.*)

1957 Little Rock, Arkansas

1957 Jack Kerouac

1959 Disneyland

1963 Birmingham, Alabama

1967 George Romney

1969 Ho Chi Minh

1972 Munich, West Germany

1976 Mao Zedong (Tse-tung)

1978 Menachem Begin (Israel), Jimmy Carter (United States), and Anwar El Sadat (Egypt)

1982 Extra-strength Tylenol (The case remains unsolved.)

2001 The World Trade Center in New York City, the Pentagon in Arlington, Virginia, and a field near Shanksville, Pennsylvania

page 221: Trivia—Candy Slogans and Jingles

- Hershey's Chocolate Bar
- Peter Paul Mounds and Almond Joy
- Kit Kat Bar
- York Peppermint Patty

page 222: Rhyme Time

1. Button; and mutton
2. Hover; and cover
3. Smuggle; and juggle
4. Coffee pot; and parking lot
5. Labor; and neighbor
6. Pun; and gun
7. Trance; and dance
8. Squirt gun; and home run
9. Apple pie; and junior high
10. Silhouette; and suffragette
11. Flash; and cash
12. Wizard; and lizard
13. Bamboo; and Peru
14. Racket; and bracket
15. Airbag; and jet lag

page 223: One-Minute Madness—Punctuation Marks

1. Apostrophe   '
2. Brackets   [ ] { }
3. Colon   :
4. Comma   ,
5. Dash   —
6. Ellipsis   . . .
7. Exclamation mark   !
8. Full stop/period   .
9. Guillemets   « »
10. Hyphen   -
11. Parentheses   ( )
12. Question mark   ?
13. Quotation marks   ' ' " "
14. Semicolon   ;
15. Slash/stroke   /
16. Solidus   /

page 223: Presidential Nicknames

1. Gerald Ford
2. John F. Kennedy
3. George H. W. Bush
4. Theodore Roosevelt
5. William Henry Harrison
6. Thomas Jefferson
7. Andrew Jackson
8. Martin Van Buren
9. Zachary Taylor
10. Woodrow Wilson

page 224: CHARTREUSE Titles

1. *The Color PURPLE*
2. *GOLDfinger*
3. *YELLOW Submarine*
4. "GREENsleeves"
5. *A Patch of BLUE*
6. "RED River Valley"
7. *The SCARLET Pimpernel*
8. *The Unsinkable Molly BROWN*
9. *BLACK Hawk Down*
10. *I Am Curious YELLOW*
11. *Island of the BLUE Dolphins*
12. *The LAVENDER Hill Mob*
13. *GREY Gardens*
14. *BLACK Like Me*
15. "BLUE Moon"

page 224: Trivia—Saints

- St. Paul
- Mt. St. Helens
- "When the Saints Go Marching In"
- St. Croix, St. John, and St. Thomas

page 225: Wise Words

1. West Wing
2. White Water
3. Wrist Watch
4. Walla Walla
5. White Whale
6. Weeping Willow
7. Wonder Woman
8. Wailing Wall (Western Wall *is also a correct answer.*)

9. Widow's Walk
10. Wilbur Wright
11. Windshield Wiper
12. Wishy-Washy (Weak-Willed *is also a correct answer.*)
13. Welcome Wagon
14. Wolf Whistles

page 226: **Phun Times**
1. Phobia
2. Philanthropist
3. Phoenix
4. Photosynthesis
5. Pharaoh
6. Philodendron
7. Phantom
8. Phlebitis
9. Philanderer
10. Photography
11. Physics
12. Phooey
13. Pheromones
14. Philatelist

page 227: **Double Trouble**
1. Paper (wastepaper, wallpaper, newspaper, notepaper)
2. Lock (gridlock, hemlock, wedlock, padlock)
3. Neck (bottleneck, redneck, rubberneck, turtleneck)
4. Dog (bulldog, hotdog, sheepdog, watchdog)
5. Hood (brotherhood, falsehood, neighborhood, motherhood)
6. Weed (milkweed, tumbleweed, seaweed, ragweed)
7. Ship (citizenship, flagship, courtship, friendship)

8. Line (breadline, clothesline, frontline, neckline)
9. Cracker (firecracker, nutcracker, safecracker, wisecracker)
10. Cast (broadcast, forecast, outcast, typecast)
11. Proof (bulletproof, waterproof, ovenproof, childproof)
12. Cap (kneecap, snowcap, whitecap, icecap)
13. Pipe (bagpipe, windpipe, drainpipe, stovepipe)
14. Lord (landlord, warlord, slumlord, overlord)

page 228: **Wacky Wordies**
1. Pie in the sky
2. Three Mile Island
3. Split-level house

4. Head over heels in love
5. Sign on the dotted line
6. Five o'clock shadow
7. Half asleep
8. Study overseas

page 230: **Word Finder— By the Letter** (see below)

page 231: **Stinky Pinky**
1. Bare chair
2. Swine wine
3. Snake cake
4. Green queen
5. Sandy candy
6. Lighter fighter
7. Drab cab
8. Waiter hater
9. Proud cloud
10. Spare hare
11. Runny honey

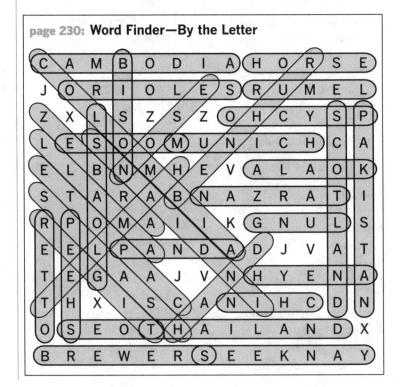

page 230: Word Finder—By the Letter

page 232: **Portmanteaus**
1. Electronic and mail
2. Charcoal and broil
3. Car and hijack
4. Gasoline and alcohol
5. Guess and estimate
6. Parachute and trooper
7. McDonald's and mansion (McMansion is used to describe a large new house which is judged to be pretentious, tasteless, or badly designed for its neighborhood.)
8. Marionette and puppet
9. Smoke and fog
10. Squirm and wiggle
11. Spoon and fork (Patents for sporks date back to the late nineteenth century.)
12. Binary digit
13. Frankenstein and food ("Frankenfood" is a negative reference to genetically modified foods.)
14. Motor and pedal (a bicycle with a small motor)
15. Slovenly language
16. Capsule and tablet (an easier-to-swallow pill)
17. Cybernetic organism

page 233: **Blank of Plank**
1. Abuse of Power
2. Bay of Pigs
3. Bird of Prey (or Paradise)
4. Book of Proverbs (or Psalms)
5. Breach of Promise
6. Burden of Proof
7. Change of Pace
8. Coat of Paint
9. Crime of Passion
10. Cult of Personality
11. Horn of Plenty
12. Invasion of Privacy
13. Laws of Physics
14. Member of Parliament
15. Mother of Pearl
16. Pad of Paper
17. Piece of Pie
18. Plaster of Paris
19. Prince of Peace (or Persia)
20. Proof of Purchase
21. Rites of Passage

page 233: **Trivia—Women Inventors**
• Toll House cookies
• Wite-Out (*Fun Fact: Bette Nesmith Graham's son is Mike Nesmith, a former member of the Monkees.*)
• Windshield wipers
• Scotchgard

page 234: **Borrowed from Irish**
1. Bog
2. Colleen
3. Galore
4. Leprechaun
5. Loch, Lake
6. Baltimore [*Baile an t' mhor* = Baile (town) an t' (the house) mhor (big)]
7. Shanty
8. Slob
9. Brogue
10. Bard
11. Smithereens
12. Whiskey

page 235: **Trivia—Business History**
• Ben Cohen and Jerry Greenfield (Ben & Jerry's)
• Hallmark Cards
• Levittown, New York (In 1947, the houses sold for eight to twelve thousand dollars.)
• Elisha Otis
• Mattel
• Avon
• Motorola
• Snapple
• King Camp Gillette
• Willis Carrier
• Ole Evinrude

page 235: **Classic Riddle—Bottoms Up**
Their ice cubes were poisoned. Jack drank slowly, which gave the ice cubes time to melt and release the poison. But Jesse drank quickly, before the ice cubes melted, and therefore didn't get much of the poison.

page 236: **Color Coded**
1. Pink
2. Green
3. Blue (IBM is nicknamed "Big Blue.")
4. Red
5. Orange and Black
6. Brown
7. Purple ("The Purple People Eater" is a novelty song from 1958.)
8. White and Blue
9. Silver
10. Rose
11. Orange
12. Blue (North) and Gray (South)

page 237: **Homonyms**

1. Adds/Ads
2. Tide/tied
3. Ail/ale
4. Aye/eye
5. Bawled/bald
6. Beach/beech
7. Beat/beet
8. Boulder/bolder
9. Brake/break
10. Buy/bye

page 237: **Trivia—Marine Matters**

- Lobster
- Salmon
- Seahorse
- Clams (Quahog and whelk *are also correct.*)

page 238: **Euphemisms**

1. Naked
2. Go to the bathroom
3. Unemployed
4. Pregnant
5. Bathroom
6. Lie
7. Broke or poor
8. Vomit
9. Taxes
10. Underwear
11. Janitor
12. Drug addiction
13. Torture
14. Wiretapping and bugging
15. A strike or work slowdown

page 239: **Run the Alphabet—Clothing**

(*Other correct answers are possible.*)

A: Ascot, Apron
B: Blazer, Bikini
C: Coat, Camisole
D: Dress, Duster
E: Earmuffs, Espadrilles
F: Fur Coat, Fedora
G: Gloves, Garters
H: Hat, Hosiery
I: Izod Shirt
J: Jacket, Jersey
K: Kimono, Knickers
L: Lingerie, Leggings
M: Miniskirt, Moccasins
N: Negligee, Nightgown
O: Overcoat, Overalls
P: Pants, Parka
R: Raincoat, Robe
S: Scarf, Shirt
T: Tie, Toga
U: Underwear, Uniform
V: Vest, Veil
W: Windbreaker, Wetsuit
X: *We didn't know any. Did you?*
Y: Yarmulke
Z: Zoot Suit

page 240: **Pro and Con**

1. Procrastinate
2. Contest
3. Concierge
4. Propane
5. Prosciutto
6. Protégé
7. Congo (The Democratic Republic of . . .)
8. Conflagration
9. Protractor
10. Conservative
11. Produce
12. Contractions
13. Programmer
14. Contagious
15. Prosecutor
16. Conundrum

page 241: **What Do They Have in Common?**

1. They were all vice presidents of the United States.
2. They are all names of angles.
3. They are all famous paintings. (*Night Watch* by Rembrandt, *Water Lilies* by Monet, *The Starry Night* by Van Gogh, and *American Gothic* by Grant Wood)
4. They are all yo-yo tricks.
5. They all have branches.
6. They are all endangered species. (In fact, they are on the World Wildlife Fund's list of ten most endangered animals.)
7. They all have keys.
8. They are all types of olives.
9. They all have teeth.
10. They are all countries that changed their names. (Kampuchea is now called Cambodia; Ceylon is now Sri Lanka; Siam is now Thailand; and Burma is now called Myanmar.)
11. They all have grades.
12. They are all marsupials (mammals that raise their young in a pouch).
13. They all have titles.

page 241: **Trivia—Take Your Vitamins**

- Vitamin C
- Potassium
- Vitamin D
- Iodine

page 242: **Film Biographies**

1. N. Jake LaMotta (Robert De Niro)
2. E. William Wallace (Mel Gibson)
3. H. Moses (Charlton Heston)
4. M. Charles A. Lindbergh (James Stewart)
5. J. Vincent van Gogh (Kirk Douglas)
6. F. Lou Gehrig (Gary Cooper)
7. C. Michelangelo (Charlton Heston)
8. K. Joan Crawford (Faye Dunaway)
9. L. Ludwig van Beethoven (Gary Oldman)
10. Q. Ray Charles (Jamie Foxx)
11. B. Dian Fossey (Sigourney Weaver)
12. O. Edward R. Murrow (David Strathairn)
13. G. George M. Cohan (James Cagney)
14. I. Tina Turner (Angela Bassett)
15. A. Johnny Cash (Joaquin Phoenix)
16. D. Billie Holiday (Diana Ross)
17. P. Woody Guthrie (David Carradine)

Page 242: **Trivia—High School Reading List**

- *Uncle Tom's Cabin*
- *Robin Hood*
- *The Prince and the Pauper*
- *Pygmalion*

page 243: **U.S. Citizen Test**

1. "We the people . . ."
2. Life, liberty, and the pursuit of happiness
3. Nine
4. Connecticut, Delaware, Georgia, Maryland, Massachusetts, New Hampshire, New Jersey, New York, North Carolina, Pennsylvania, Rhode Island, South Carolina, Virginia
5. The Bill of Rights
6. Speech, religion, assembly, press, to petition the government
7. One hundred
8. The Speaker of the House
9. The Missouri and the Mississippi
10. American Samoa, Guam, Northern Mariana Islands, Puerto Rico, U.S. Virgin Islands
11. Twenty-seven
12. To print money, to declare war, to create an army, to make treaties.

page 244: **A Lot of Bread**

1. Baguette — France
2. Challah — Jewish
3. Pumpernickel — Germany
4. Pita — Arabic/Middle Eastern
5. Tortilla — Mexico
6. Naan — India
7. Crumpet — England
8. Focaccia — Italy

page 246: **Palindromes**

1. Peep
2. Toot
3. Tot
4. Boob
5. Shahs
6. Radar
7. Tenet
8. Deed
9. Civic
10. Level
11. Sagas

page 246: **Trivia—Notable Lasts**

- Mikhail Gorbachev
- Western Union
- Tobacco (cigarettes)
- Apartheid

page 247: **Famous Movie Lines**

1. Sam Spade; Humphrey Bogart; *The Maltese Falcon* (1941) (*Note: Sam Spade was actually referencing—incorrectly—a line from Shakespeare's* The Tempest: *"We are such stuff as dreams are made on."*)
2. Rod Tidwell; Cuba Gooding Jr.; *Jerry Maguire* (1996)
3. Lady Lou; Mae West; *She Done Him Wrong* (1933)
4. "Gold Hat"; Alfonso Bedoya; *The Treasure of the Sierra Madre* (1948)
5. Cole Sear; Haley Joel Osment; *The Sixth Sense* (1999)
6. Osgood Fielding III; Joe E. Brown; *Some Like It Hot* (1959)

7. "Ratso" Rizzo; Dustin Hoffman; *Midnight Cowboy* (1969)
8. Captain Spaulding; Groucho Marx; *Animal Crackers* (1930)
9. Norman Bates; Anthony Perkins; *Psycho* (1960)
10. President Merkin Muffley; Peter Sellers; *Dr. Strangelove* (1964)
11. Joan Crawford; Faye Dunaway; *Mommie Dearest* (1981)
12. Mame Dennis; Rosalind Russell; *Auntie Mame* (1958)
13. John Keating; Robin Williams; *Dead Poets Society* (1989)
14. Loretta Castorini; Cher; *Moonstruck* (1987)
15. George M. Cohan; James Cagney; *Yankee Doodle Dandy* (1942)

page 248: October in History

1400 Geoffrey Chaucer (*Note: Chaucer is credited by some scholars as the first author to demonstrate the artistic legitimacy of the Middle English language. Before that most books were written in French or Latin.*)
1825 The Erie Canal
1867 The Russian flag (*Note: The U.S. bought Alaska from Russia for $57 million—about two cents an acre.*)

1917 Vladimir I. Lenin (He was succeeded in 1922 by Joseph Stalin, who led the country until 1953.)
1923 Turkey
1939 Albert Einstein, Edward Teller, Leo Szilard, and Eugene Wigner
1945 Canada and the United Kingdom
1946 Nuremberg
1947 Chuck Yeager
1961 Roger Maris
1962 Soviet missile bases were discovered on the island.
1975 Dan Aykroyd, John Belushi, Chevy Chase, Garrett Morris, Gilda Radner, Jane Curtin, and Laraine Newman
1980 "Are you better off than you were four years ago?"
1981 Anwar Sadat
1984 A baboon
1984 Indira Gandhi
1985 Rock Hudson
1987 Robert Bork
2004 The Boston Red Sox

page 249: Trivia—Speak Latin

• *Semper Fidelis*
• *Caveat Emptor*
• *Alma Mater*
• *E Pluribus Unum*

CHAPTER SEVEN

page 250: Calculate the Titles

1. 6 (3+3)
2. 34 (12+22)
3. 82 (2+80)
4. 455 (451+4)
5. 20,007 (20,000+7)
6. 107 (101+6)
7. 8 (5+3)
8. 1,004 (1,001+3)
9. 45 (40+5)
10. 19 (3+16)
11. 88 (39+49)

page 251: Endings and Beginnings

1. Back (flashback; backbone)
2. Lock (padlock; locksmith)
3. Day (Sunday; daydream)
4. Note (footnote; noteworthy)
5. Cat (bobcat; catcalls)
6. Proof (weatherproof; proofread)
7. Check (paycheck; checkmate)
8. Stick (drumstick; stickpin)
9. Cake (cupcake; cakewalk)
10. Mail (blackmail; mailbox)
11. Weight (paperweight; weightlifter)

page 251: Classic Riddle— A Bad Movie

The movie was at a drive-in theater. It was a dark night and their car had tinted windows.

page 252: Two-Part Word Game

1. Stone (stole)
2. Eight (light)
3. Dairy (daily)
4. Peace (place)
5. Yeast (least)
6. Shot (slot)
7. Tower (lower, towel)
8. Boots (loots, bolts)
9. Graze (glaze)

10. Purse (pulse)
11. Train (trail)
12. Sick (lick, silk)
13. Save (sale)
14. Prank (plank)
15. Demon (lemon)

page 253: **Think Twice**
1. Tongue Twister
2. Talk Turkey
3. Tall Tale
4. Tea Towel
5. Teeter-Totter
6. Test Tubes
7. Third Trimester
8. Toilet Training
9. Tongue-Tied
10. Tube Top
11. Twist Ties
12. Tourist Trap
13. Think Tank

page 253: **Trivia—Presidents Before and After**
- Before: George H. W. Bush; After: George W. Bush
- Before: Lyndon Johnson; After: Gerald Ford
- Before: Herbert Hoover; After: Harry Truman
- Before: George Washington; After: Thomas Jefferson

page 254: **The Shape of the States**
A. Pennsylvania
B. Tennessee
C. Washington
D. Alabama
E. Utah
F. Wisconsin
G. Kentucky
H. Maryland

I. New Hampshire
J. Nevada
K. Minnesota

page 255: **Replace the ARMADILLO**
1. *The LION, the Witch and the Wardrobe*
2. *The HORSE Whisperer*
3. *Sweet BIRD of Youth*
4. *The Little FOXES*
5. *The Night of the IGUANA*
6. *Island of the Blue DOLPHINS*
7. *All the Pretty HORSES*
8. *The Day of the LOCUST*
9. *The Red PONY*

page 256: **Yo!**
1. Yogurt
2. Yonkers
3. Youngster
4. Yowl
5. Arroyo
6. Yokel
7. Embryo
8. Yonder

9. Yokohama
10. Yom Kippur
11. Yorkshire terrier
12. Yosemite

page 257: **Sobriquets**
1. Mark Felt (Watergate informant)
2. Leona Helmsley
3. Babe Ruth
4. Margaret Thatcher
5. Gene Autry
6. Joe DiMaggio
7. Lon Chaney
8. John Gotti
9. Benny Goodman
10. Helen Hayes
11. Ted Williams
12. The Beatles
13. Leo Durocher
14. Huey P. Long
15. Jake LaMotta
16. William Perry
17. Heidi Fleiss

page 258: **Follow the Rules**
(see below)

---

page 258: **Follow the Rules**
1. F A I T H F U L F R I E N D S
2. F A I *E* T H F U L F R I _ N D S
3. *A* A I E T H A *U* L F R I N D S
4. A A I E _ H A U L *T* F R I N D S
5. A A *R* I E H A *R* U L T F R I N D S
6. A A R I E H A R U L T *O* F R I N D S
7. A A R I E H A R *D* L T O F R I N D S
8. A A R _ E H A R D L T O F R I N D S
9. _ A R E H A R D L T O F R I N D _
10. A R E H A R D _ T O F _ I N D

(FAITHFUL FRIENDS) ARE HARD TO FIND

8. Phone (earphone, headphone, microphone, speakerphone)
9. Foot (tenderfoot, barefoot, clubfoot, hotfoot)
10. Leader (bandleader, cheerleader, ringleader)
11. Shoe (gumshoe, horseshoe, snowshoe)
12. Over (crossover, hangover, pushover, takeover)
13. Craft (spacecraft, witchcraft, hovercraft, needlecraft)
14. Burn (heartburn, sideburn, sunburn, windburn)

page 268: Trimble
1. Carson
2. Wayne
3. Rockefeller
4. McEnroe
5. Kerry
6. Travolta
7. Audubon

Jumble Answer: John Lennon

page 269: Art and Sol
1. Arteries
2. Arthritis
3. Solid
4. Article
5. Solve
6. Articulate
7. Artifacts
8. Solidarity
9. Artificial
10. Artillery
11. Soliloquy
12. Solitude (or solitary confinement)

page 270: November in History
1604 *Othello*
1869 The Suez Canal
1883 The railroad industry, which needed to create uniform time schedules across the country
1918 World War I
1922 Tutankhamen (King Tut)
1938 *Kristallnacht* (Night of Broken Glass)
1942 Boston, Massachusetts
1945 Nuremburg
1959 Charles van Doren
1962 Apartheid
1963 John B. Connolly
1966 Edward Brooke (R) of Massachusetts
1968 George Wallace
1973 Rose Mary Woods
1978 San Francisco. (*Note: The two civic leaders were shot by Dan White, a former City Supervisor whose defense at trial was that his change in diet to Twinkies and other sugary foods was symptomatic of the depression which caused his "diminished capacity." It became known as the "Twinkie defense."*)
1979 Ayatollah Khomeini
1980 Kristin was the one who shot J. R. Ewing in the TV series *Dallas*.
1986 Nicaragua
1991 Earvin "Magic" Johnson
1999 Elian Gonzalez

page 271: Trivia—Going for Gold
- Alpine Skiing
- Figure Skating
- Speed Skating
- Hockey (Brooks was the coach of the 1980 "Miracle on Ice" USA team that beat the USSR and went on to win gold.)

page 272: TV Catch Phrases
1. *The Lawrence Welk Show*
2. *Dragnet*
3. *Family Feud*
4. *Newhart*
5. *Hogan's Heroes*
6. *The Brady Bunch*
7. *See It Now*
8. *Alice*
9. *The Price Is Right*
10. *At the Movies* (Siskel and Ebert)
11. *Get Smart*
12. *Welcome Back, Kotter*
13. *Hill Street Blues*
14. *The A-Team*
15. *Lost in Space*
16. *Monty Python's Flying Circus*

page 273: Stinky Pinky
1. Blue Glue
2. Dumb thumb
3. Swift gift
4. Mango tango
5. Taboo shampoo
6. Bog dog (or boggy doggy)
7. Brown clown
8. Kite fight
9. Racket jacket
10. Perky turkey
11. Loud crowd

page 273: **One-Minute Madness—Border States**

1. Alaska
2. Idaho
3. Maine
4. Michigan
5. Minnesota
6. Montana
7. New Hampshire
8. New York
9. North Dakota
10. Ohio
11. Pennsylvania
12. Vermont
13. Washington

page 274: **Odd Man Out**

1. *Carmen* is the odd man out. The others are famous ballets by Tchaikovsky. *Carmen* is a famous opera by Bizet.
2. Morose is the odd man out. The other words mean "happy." Morose means "sad" or "gloomy."
3. The odd man out is Japan. All the other countries have English as their predominant, if not official, language.
4. Spare is the odd man out. It is the only word in the list that contains a vowel which is not an "i."
5. *Huckleberry Finn* by Mark Twain is the odd man out. It is the only book written by a man. The other three were written by women: *Uncle Tom's Cabin* by

Harriet Beecher Stowe; *To Kill a Mockingbird* by Harper Lee; *The Color Purple* by Alice Walker.
6. Boston is the odd man out. It is the only U.S. city in the list that is also a state capital.
7. Awkward is the odd man out. All of the other words in the list begin and end with a vowel.
8. Mexico is the odd man out. All of the other countries have royal families. (Some are ceremonial; others are rulers.)
9. *Miracle on 34th Street* is the odd man out. It is the only movie set in New York City. All the other movies are set in London.
10. Brass is the odd man out. All of the other words contain a silent "b."
11. Moussaka is the odd man out. It is the only Greek dish. All the others are Spanish dishes.
12. Pocket is the odd man out. It is the only word that does NOT have the name of a body part spelled out within it (ob*eyed*; f*ear*; al*arm*; *hand*some).
13. Anne Bancroft is the odd (wo)man out because she is the only actor in the list who did not star in the movie *Bonnie and Clyde* (1967).

14. London is the odd man out because it is the only capital city in the list that doesn't begin and end with the same letter.

page 275: **Geographical Name Game**

1. Abraham Lincoln
2. Bob Hope
3. Irving Berlin
4. Jack London
5. Michael Jackson
6. Christopher Columbus
7. Joe Montana
8. John Denver
9. Oscar Madison
10. Dick York
11. Grover Cleveland
12. Janet Reno
13. Denzel Washington
14. Montgomery Clift
15. Florence Henderson
16. Tennessee Williams
17. Chelsea Clinton
18. Indiana Jones
19. Georgia O'Keefe
20. Minnesota Fats

page 276: **Kangaroo Words**

1. Stun
2. Cocoa
3. Can
4. Able
5. Amiable
6. Dame
7. Late
8. Allot
9. Art
10. Sad
11. See

12. Urge
13. Vacate
14. City
15. Tutor
16. Tries
17. Part
18. Fiction

page 277: Follow the Rules
(see below)

**page 278: Word Finder—
Beatles Tunes** (see page 390)

**page 279: Replace the
SWAMP**
1. *VALLEY of the Dolls*
2. *Brokeback MOUNTAIN*
3. *A RIVER Runs Through It*
4. "Sitting on the Dock of the
   BAY"
5. "The Lady of the LAKE"
6. *Under the VOLCANO*
7. *The JUNGLE Book*
8. *On the BEACH*
9. *Spoon RIVER Anthology*
10. *ISLANDS in the
    STREAM*

**page 280: What Comes
Next?**
1. Jay Leno (*Tonight Show*
   hosts)
2. Partridge (Birds found
   in "The Twelve Days
   of Christmas" song in
   descending order)
3. August (The months in
   backward order)
4. Michigan (The "M" states in
   alphabetical order)
5. C (Roman numerals: 50, 60,
   70, 80, 90, 100)
6. 96 hours
7. 50 (Values of U.S. coins: 1¢,
   5¢, 10¢, 25¢, 50¢)
8. Antarctica (Continents in
   descending order of size)
9. Jupiter (Planets in order of
   their distance from the sun)
10. Y (First row of letters on a
    standard keyboard)
11. Delta (Greek alphabet)
12. 13 (Prime numbers)
13. # (The last two lines on a
    telephone keypad)
14. Gore (Succession of recent
    vice presidents)

**page 280: Trivia—
Alphabetical World Tour**
- Iceland, Ireland, Italy
- San Marino, Serbia,
  Slovakia, Slovenia, Spain,
  Sweden, Switzerland
- Turkey
- Poland, Portugal

page 281: Rhyme Time
1. Surprise; and disguise
2. Germ; and squirm
3. Disagree; and Tennessee
4. Hello; and Thoreau
5. Squid; and kid
6. Forbid; and Madrid
7. À la carte; and Purple Heart
8. Soufflé; and sorbet
9. Tweed; and knead
10. Pledge; and wedge
11. Throttle; and bottle
12. Vivid; and livid
13. Cantaloupe; and antelope
14. Nut; and putt

**page 282: What's Your
Movie Song IQ?**
1. "The Trolley Song"
   from *Meet Me in St. Louis*
   (1944)
2. "Theme from *Shaft*" from
   Shaft (1971)
3. "You're the One That I
   Want" from *Grease* (1978)
4. "Up Where We Belong"
   from *An Officer and a
   Gentleman* (1982)
5. "9 to 5" from *Nine to Five*
   (1980)
6. "Arthur's Theme (Best
   That You Can Do)"
   from *Arthur* (1981)

page 277: Follow the Rules
1. R A I N D O E S N O T F A L L
2. *N* A I N D O E S *R* O T F A L L
3. *O* N A I *O* N D O E S R O *O* T F A L L
4. O N A I O N D _ E S R O O T F A L *O* L
5. O N A I O N *E* D _ S R O O T F A L O L
6. O N A I O N E D S R O O T F A L O *N* E L
7. O N _ I O N E D S R O O T F A L O N E _
8. O N _ O N E D S R O O _ F A L O N E _
9. O N O N E _ _ R O O F A L O N E

(RAIN DOES NOT FALL) ON ONE ROOF ALONE

7. "(I've Had) The Time of My Life" from *Dirty Dancing* (1987)
8. "Getting to Know You" from *The King and I* (1956)
9. "The Man That Got Away" from *A Star Is Born* (1954)
10. "Cheek to Cheek" from *Top Hat* (1935)
11. "Swinging on a Star" from *Going My Way* (1944)
12. "Born to Be Wild" from *Easy Rider* (1969)

page 283: Par for the Course

1. Parachute
2. Parakeet
3. Parka
4. Paraffin
5. Parasol
6. Partridge
7. Parchment
8. Paregoric
9. Parsnip
10. Parliament
11. Paramedic
12. Parody
13. Parentheses

page 284: Name Merge

1. Valerie Harper Lee
2. Rosalind Russell Crowe
3. Chris Rock Hudson
4. Christopher Lloyd Bridges
5. Arlene Francis Scott Key
6. Allan Sherman Hemsley
7. James Earl Ray Bradbury
8. Jerry Lee Lewis Thomas

page 285: Back to Back

1. Backbone
2. Humpback

3. Backgammon
4. Greenback
5. Backlog
6. Hatchback
7. Backstabber
8. Zwieback
9. Comeback
10. Outback
11. Flashback
12. Kickback

page 278: Word Finder—Beatles Tunes

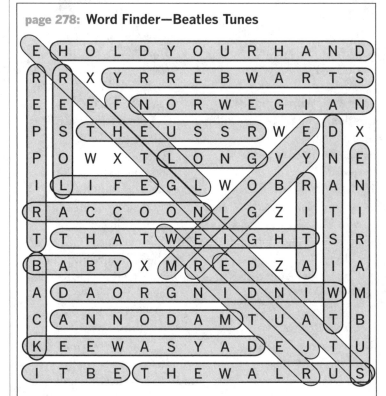

"*Baby*, It's You"
"Back In *the USSR*"
"Can't Buy *Me Love*"
"Carry *That Weight*"
"Day *Tripper*"
"Eight *Days a Week*"
"Eleanor *Rigby*"
"Get *Back*"
"Hey *Jude*"
"I Am *the Walrus*"
"I Saw Her *Standing There*"
"I Want to *Hold Your Hand*"
"I'm a *Loser*"
"If I *Fell*"
"In My *Life*"
"Lady *Madonna*"
"Let *It Be*"
"*Long* Tall Sally"
"Lovely *Rita*"
"*Norwegian* Wood"
"Paperback *Writer*"
"Rocky *Raccoon*"
"*Strawberry* Fields Forever"
"The Long and *Winding* Road"
"*Twist and* Shout"
"Yellow *Submarine*"

page 285: Trivia—Working Women

- Sally Ride
- Louisa May Alcott
- Mary Baker Eddy
- Pearl S. Buck

page 286: Borrowed from Arabic

(*Note: The Arabic origin is in parentheses.*)

1. Coffee (*qahwa*)
2. Zero (*sifr*)
3. Sherbet (*sharba*)
4. Cotton (*qutn*)
5. Assassin (*hashashin*)
6. Guitar (*qiithaar*)
7. Lemon (*laymuun*)
8. Mascara (*maskhara*)
9. Algebra (*al-jabr*)
10. Alcohol (*al-kuhuul*)
11. Checkmate (*shaah maat*)
12. Sugar (*sukkar*)
13. Gauze (*qazz*)
14. Lilac (*laylak*)
15. Almanac (*al-manaakh*)
16. Macramé (*miqrama*)
17. Tambourine (*tunbuur*)
18. Magazine (*makhaazin*)
19. Mohair (*mukhayyar*)
20. Admiral (*al-'amiir*)
21. Alfalfa (*al-fasfasa*)
22. Giraffe (*zaraafa*)
23. Sequins (*sikkas*)
24. Racket (*raaha*)

page 287: One-Minute Madness—Cabinet Members

1. Secretary of Agriculture
2. Secretary of Commerce
3. Secretary of Defense
4. Secretary of Education
5. Secretary of Energy
6. Secretary of Health and Human Services
7. Secretary of Homeland Security
8. Secretary of Housing and Urban Development
9. Secretary of the Interior
10. Secretary of Labor
11. Secretary of State
12. Secretary of Transportation
13. Secretary of the Treasury
14. Secretary of Veterans Affairs
15. Attorney General
16. Vice President

page 288: Sobriquets

1. Philadelphia
2. Canada
3. Hollywood
4. Japan
5. Broadway
6. Paris
7. Ireland (Puerto Rico *is also correct.*)
8. Pittsburgh
9. Rome
10. *The New York Times*
11. Republican
12. The Central Criminal Court in England
13. Milwaukee
14. Australia and New Zealand
15. The British Broadcasting Corporation (BBC)
16. The Press
17. The Bank of England

page 289: Laureates in Literature

1. Rudyard Kipling
2. George Bernard Shaw
3. Sinclair Lewis
4. Eugene O'Neill
5. T. S. Eliot
6. William Faulkner
7. Ernest Hemingway
8. John Steinbeck
9. Samuel Beckett
10. William Golding
11. Toni Morrison

page 290: Where's the Skyline?

A. Beantown (Boston)
B. The Emerald City (Seattle)
C. The City of Angels (Los Angeles)
D. The Windy City (Chicago)
E. The Big Apple (New York City)
F. The Golden Gate City (San Francisco)
G. The Big Pineapple (Honolulu)

page 291: Cheque This Out!

1. Boutique
2. Burlesque
3. Mosque
4. Opaque
5. Pique
6. Plaque
7. Discotheques
8. Risqué
9. Brusque
10. Statuesque
11. Grotesque
12. Appliqué
13. Baroque
14. Basque

page 292: **WHOOZY**
The WHOOZY is Ralph Nader.

CHAPTER EIGHT

page 293: **What Do They Have in Common?**
1. They all have degrees.
2. They all have points.
3. They are all spies.
4. They all have scales.
5. They are all events that occurred in 1969.
6. They all have frames.
7. They are all types of penguins.
8. They all use scoopers.
9. They all have patches.
10. They are all names of U.S. airports. (Ronald Reagan/ Washington, DC; John Wayne/Orange County, CA; Louis Armstrong/ New Orleans; and John F. Kennedy/New York)

page 294: **Double Trouble**
1. Some (awesome, handsome, lonesome, wholesome, irksome)
2. Hold (chokehold, household, withhold, threshold)
3. Ware (cookware, hardware, silverware, software)
4. Board (dartboard, blackboard, washboard, billboard)
5. Time (lunchtime, nighttime, ragtime, lifetime)
6. Down (crackdown, touchdown, countdown, showdown)
7. Where (everywhere, nowhere, elsewhere, somewhere)
8. Right (copyright, forthright, upright, birthright)
9. Well (farewell, inkwell, stairwell)
10. Fire (brushfire, ceasefire, wildfire, campfire)
11. More (furthermore, anymore, nevermore, evermore)
12. Lash (eyelash, backlash, whiplash)
13. Out (blowout, workout, wipeout, strikeout)
14. Plug (earplug, fireplug, sparkplug)
15. Step (footstep, doorstep, lockstep, sidestep)
16. Power (horsepower, willpower, manpower, superpower)
17. Cover (bedcover, hardcover, slipcover, undercover)
18. Over (popover, Passover, leftover, pushover)

page 295: **Run the Alphabet—Four-Syllable Words**
(*Other correct answers are possible.*)
A: Arithmetic, Aluminum
B: Ballerina, Babysitter
C: Conservative, Cauliflower
D: Discovery, Dandelion
E: Economics, Eliminate
F: Feminism, Fascinating
G: Geometry, Generation
H: Hallucinate, Helicopter
I: Information, Identity
J: Jambalaya, Journalism
K: Kaleidoscope, Knowledgeable
L: Leukemia, Librarian
M: Misunderstood, Majority
N: Necessary, Nonconformist
O: Oregano, Oriental
P: Photography, Population
Q: Quantitative, Quintessential
R: Republican, Relaxation
S: Simplicity, Sensational
T: Television, Territory
U: Ubiquitous, Undecided
V: Variety, Ventriloquist
W: Watercolors, Wiretapping
X: Xenophobic, Xylophonist
Y: Yellowhammer
Z: Zoologist, Zirconium

page 296: **It's a Lulu!**
1. Bureau
2. Menu
3. Luau
4. *Adieu*
5. Bayou
6. Tutu
7. Trousseau
8. Guru
9. Impromptu
10. Caribou
11. Ecru
12. Emu
13. Haiku
14. Tofu
15. Jujitsu

page 297: Trimble

1. King
2. Steinbeck
3. Hemingway
4. Mailer
5. Haley
6. Rice
7. Stone

Jumble Answer: John Grisham

page 298: Eponyms

1. Decibel (Alexander Graham Bell)
2. Bloomers (Amelia Bloomer, a women's rights advocate, promoted a change in women's fashion standards that would make their dress less restrictive for regular activities.)
3. Bolivia (Simón Bolívar)
4. Casanova (Giacomo Casanova)
5. Robin, of Batman and Robin (Robin Hood)
6. Sousaphone (John Phillips Sousa)
7. Paparazzi (The character's name was Paparazzo.)
8. Boycott (Captain Charles Cunningham Boycott, 1832–1897)
9. Sideburns (General Ambrose Burnside)
10. Dewey Decimal System (Melvil Dewey)

page 299: Name Merge

1. Les Paul McCartney
2. Mary Stuart Little
3. Mike Wallace Beery
4. Jesse James Earl Jones
5. D. H. Lawrence Welk
6. Lee Marvin Hamlisch
7. Franklin Pierce Brosnan
8. Burgess Meredith Baxter
9. Jesse Jackson Pollock

page 300: Word Finder—Classic Lit

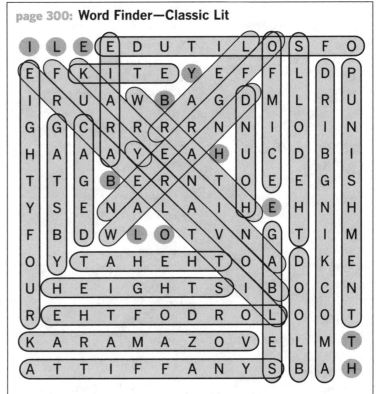

War and *Peace*
Valley of the Dolls
The Grapes of Wrath
God's Little Acre
The Cat in the Hat
The Kite *Runner*
Of Mice *and Men*
King Lear
Wuthering Heights
Madame Bovary
Anna Karenina
In Cold Blood
The Great Gatsby
The Lord of the *Rings*
Crime and Punishment

The Brothers Karamazov
The Sound and the Fury
One Hundred Years of Solitude
Breakfast at Tiffany's
The House of the Seven Gables
The Hound *of the Baskervilles*
Anne of Green *Gables*
To Kill a Mockingbird
Nineteen Eighty-Four
I Know Why the Caged *Bird Sings*

Jumble Answer: The best-selling book of all time is the Holy Bible.

page 300: Word Finder—Classic Lit (see above)

page 301: Word Play
1. The *cross*word puzzle
2. Friday
3. A telephone
4. Edam
5. Lounger
6. Growing older

page 302: All A's
1. Aloha
2. Acrophobia
3. Aroma
4. Alaska
5. Anemia
6. Aurora
7. Austria
8. *Amiga*
9. Ammonia
10. Amnesia
11. Abracadabra
12. Alpaca
13. Amoeba
14. Asphyxia

page 303: T Plus Three
1. Trix
2. Toto
3. Tang
4. Tutu (Desmond Tutu)
5. Tart
6. Team
7. Tofu
8. Teal
9. Toga
10. Tojo
11. Tick
12. Tack
13. Tuba

page 303: Trivia— Geographical Foods
- Baked Alaska
- London Broil
- Philadelphia Cream Cheese
- Yorkshire Pudding

page 304: Compound Word Search
Backfire
Cowboy
Cheesecake
Crowbar
Hatcheck
Jellybean
Keypunch
Nosedive
Toothpick
Rattlesnake
Tailgate
Wallflower

page 306: The Long and the Short of It
1. Shortcut
2. Longhorn (The horns of the Texas Longhorn can extend over seven feet from tip to tip.)
3. Shortening
4. Shortchanged
5. Longitude
6. Shortbread
7. Oblong
8. Shortwave
9. Shortstop
10. Furlong
11. Shortcomings
12. Prolong (Elongate is also an acceptable answer.)
13. Shortsighted
14. Longshoreman

page 307: Famous "Fathers"
1. Alexander Fleming
2. Charles Darwin
3. Mohandas "Mahatma" Gandhi
4. Hippocrates
5. Louis Pasteur
6. Geoffrey Chaucer
7. Martin Luther
8. H. G. Wells (British) and Jules Verne (French)
9. Robert Oppenheimer (A-Bomb) and Edward Teller (H-Bomb)
10. Euclid
11. Joseph Lister

page 308: WHOOZY
The WHOOZY is Chelsea Clinton.

page 309: Answer: WHATZIT
The WHATZIT is the Etch-a-Sketch.

page 309: Trivia—"Z" on the Map
- Nazareth
- Arizona
- Zurich, Switzerland
- Brazil and Venezuela

page 310: Homonyms
1. Through/threw
2. Allowed/aloud
3. Guest/guessed
4. Praise/prays
5. Pour/pore
6. Pi/pie
7. Symbol/cymbal
8. Colonel/kernel
9. Gourd/gored

- Cheddar
- Parmesan (Reggiano)
- Brie (Camembert *is also correct.*)
- Monterey Jack

page 311: Run the Alphabet—Occupations

(*Other correct answers are possible.*)

A: Architect, Attorney
B: Banker, Bookkeeper
C: Carpenter, Chef
D: Dancer, Doctor
E: Economist, Electrician
F: Firefighter, Farmer
G: Geologist, Graphic Designer
H: Hairdresser, Historian
I: Interior Designer, Industrial Engineer
J: Janitor, Judge
K: Kindergarten Teacher, Karate Instructor
L: Librarian, Locksmith
M: Mathematician, Miner
N: Nurse, Nuclear Engineer
O: Optometrist, Orthodontist
P: Plumber, Professor
Q: Quarterback
R: Radiologist, Roofer
S: Secretary, Social Worker
T: Teacher, Tailor
U: Umpire, Upholsterer
V: Veterinarian, Violinist
W: Waiter, Writer
X: X-Ray Technician
Y: Yoga Instructor
Z: Zoologist, Zookeeper

page 312: Put the List in Order

1. France (79.1 million arrivals)
   Spain (58.5 million arrivals)
   United States (51.1 million arrivals)
   China (49.6 million arrivals)
   Italy (41.1 million arrivals)
2. Boston University (63,500)
   Brigham Young University (33,000)
   City College of New York (31,500)
   Princeton University (15,000)
   West Point (4,500)
   (*Note: Population figures are from 2009 and are approximate.*)
3. 32 Tablespoons (equals 2 cups)
   ½ Gallon (equals 8 cups)
   5 Pints (equals 10 cups)
   3 Quarts (equals 12 cups)
4. Kentucky (1792)
   Ohio (1803)
   California (1850)
   West Virginia (1863)
   Arizona (1912)
5. *Elmer Gantry* by Sinclair Lewis (1927)
   Gone with the Wind by Margaret Mitchell (1936)
   The Diary of a Young Girl by Anne Frank (1947)
   The Catcher in the Rye by J. D. Salinger (1951)
   To Kill a Mockingbird by Harper Lee (1960)
6. Hawaii, HI (4,021 sq. miles)
   Kodiak Island, AK (3,588 sq. miles)
   Long Island, NY (1,401 sq. miles)
   Martha's Vineyard, MA (91 sq. miles)
   Manhattan, NY (23 sq. miles)
7. Funeral of Princess Diana, 1997 (2 billion)
   2010 World Cup Final (1.75 billion)
   Funeral of Pope John Paul II, 2005 (1.3 billion)
   Funeral of Michael Jackson, 2009 (1 billion)
   Apollo Moon Landing, 1969 (600 million)
8. *Ben-Hur,* 1959 (11)
   West Side Story, 1961 (10)
   My Fair Lady, 1964 (8)
   Schindler's List, 1993 (7)
9. *The Phantom of the Opera* (In February 2011, it became the first Broadway musical to surpass 10,000 performances!)
   Cats (7,485 performances)
   Oklahoma! (2,212 performances)
   South Pacific (1,925 performances)
   Arsenic and Old Lace (1,444 performances)

page 313: Trivia—Who, What, and Where

- F. Scott Fitzgerald
- Nat "King" Cole
- Roosevelt (Rosey) Grier
- Jesus
- Basketball
- The Atom Bomb

- Ku Klux Klan
- Melanin
- Bethel, New York
- Kansas
- At the base of your spine (It's your tailbone.)
- On the moon (They're craters, not bodies of water.)

page 314: **December in History**
1903 Kitty Hawk
1911 Roald Amundsen
1936 Wallis Warfield Simpson, an American divorcee
1941 Three hundred fifty-three Japanese aircraft attacked the U.S. Pacific Fleet in Pearl Harbor, Hawaii, killing 2,402 military personnel, wounding almost 1,300, and sinking half the fleet of battleships, cruisers, destroyers, submarines and other assets.
1944 Glenn Miller. No trace of the plane, crew, or passengers has ever been found.
1947 The transistor
1954 Senator Joseph McCarthy
1955 Montgomery, Alabama
1957 Presley served in Company D, 32nd Tank Battalion, 3rd Armor Corps in Friedberg, Germany, where he attained the rank of sergeant.
1963 Frank Sinatra

1967 Dr. Christiaan Barnard. The patient lived for eighteen days.
1975 Lynette "Squeaky" Fromme
1980 John Lennon
1981 She was the first American baby conceived via *in vitro* fertilization; she was the first test-tube baby.
1985 The gorilla
1985 Ricky Nelson
1988 Lockerbie
1992 John Major
2000 Al Gore
2001 The bomb was hidden in his shoe.
2006 Saddam Hussein of Iraq

page 315: **Trivia—Ireland**
- "Oh, Danny Boy" ("Londonderry Air")
- Belfast (Northern Ireland) and Dublin (Republic of Ireland)
- Orange is for the Irish Protestants, and green is for the Irish Catholics.
- Snakes

page 316: **What's the Question?**
1. "... who wrote the book of love?"
2. "Where Have All the Flowers Gone?"
3. "Where have you gone, Joe DiMaggio?"
4. "What? Me worry?"
5. *Who's the Boss?*
6. "Who knows what evil lurks in the hearts of men?"
7. Got milk?

8. *Where in the World Is Carmen San Diego?*
9. "Why not?"
10. Romeo

page 317: **Capitonyms**
(*Other correct answers are possible.*)
1. Pearl Bailey
2. Eve Arden
3. John McCain
4. Nick Nolte
5. Brad Pitt
6. Buddy Hackett
7. Dean Martin
8. Faith Hill
9. Ginger Rogers
10. Grace Kelly
11. Lance Armstrong
12. Mike Douglas
13. Ray Romano
14. Robin Williams
15. Iris Murdoch
16. Van Johnson
17. Gene Wilder
18. Victor Mature

page 318: **Wacky Wordies**
1. Crossed eyes
2. Scrambled eggs
3. Second thoughts
4. I'm in seventh heaven
5. Six of one and a half-dozen of the other
6. Be on the right side of the law
7. Long underwear
8. Three-part harmony

page 320: **Rhyme Time**
1. Revenge; and Stonehenge
2. Erase; and embrace
3. Grace; and space

4. Krill; and skill
5. Cookie; and bookie
6. Stainless steel; and steering wheel
7. Train; and skein
8. Sliver; and river
9. Obsolete; and incomplete
10. Sphere; and fear
11. Formal; and normal
12. Congested; and arrested
13. Boast; and ghost
14. Spray; and fray
15. Spackle; and tackle
16. Romaine; and campaign

page 321: Follow the Rules
(see below)

page 322: Find the Words— At the Beach (see pages 398–399)

page 324: Razzmatazz!
1. Klutz
2. Chintz
3. Ersatz
4. Blintz
5. Fizz
6. Hertz
7. Spitz
8. Waltz
9. Spritz
10. Kibbutz
11. Quartz
12. Soyuz

page 324: Trivia—What's the Next Line?
- "Let me count the ways." Elizabeth Barrett Browning, "Sonnet XLIII"
- "…and all the men and women merely players." William Shakespeare, *As You Like It*
- "…but I have promises to keep." Robert Frost, *Stopping by Woods on a Snowy Evening*
- "…while I pondered weak and weary." Edgar Allan Poe, "The Raven"
- "…of the midnight ride of Paul Revere." Henry Wadsworth Longfellow, "Paul Revere's Ride"
- "…the best is yet to be." Robert Browning. "Rabbi Ben Ezra"

page 325: Double Trouble
1. Down (downstairs, downtown, downfall, downsize)
2. Ear (eardrum, earmuff, earphone, earache)
3. Light (lightheaded, lightweight, lighthouse)
4. Man (manhole, manhandle, manpower, manslaughter)
5. Draw (drawback, drawbridge, drawstrings)
6. Over (overcoat, overcast, overboard, overdose)
7. Hard (hardship, hardwood, hardware, hardheaded)
8. In (indoor, infuse, inhale, inmate, install)
9. Air (airbrush, airliner, airport, aircraft)
10. Fore (forearm, forecast, foreclose, forego)
11. Key (keyboard, keyhole, keynote, keystone)
12. Cow (cowboy, cowhide, cowlick, cowpoke)
13. Sand (sandbox, sandbar, sandpaper, sandstorm)
14. Hang (hangover, hangnail, hangout, hangman)
15. War (warfare, warlord, warlock, warship)
16. Sky (skylight, skyscraper, skyline, skydiver)
17. Pea (peacoat, peacock, peashooter, peanut)
18. Court (courtroom, courthouse, courtship, courtyard)

page 321: Follow the Rules
1. C O U N T Y O U R F R I E N D S
2. C O U N T *L* Y O U R F R I E N D S
3. C O U N T L Y O U R F R I E N Y D Y S
4. C O U N T L Y O *N* U R F R I E N Y D Y S
5. C O _ N T L Y O N _ R F R I E N Y D Y S
6. _ O N T L Y O N R _ R I E N Y D Y S
7. O N T L Y O N R R I E N Y D Y S
8. O N T L Y O N R R *A* I E N Y D A Y S
9. O N _ L Y O N _ R A I _ N Y D A Y S

(COUNT YOUR FRIENDS) ONLY ON RAINY DAYS

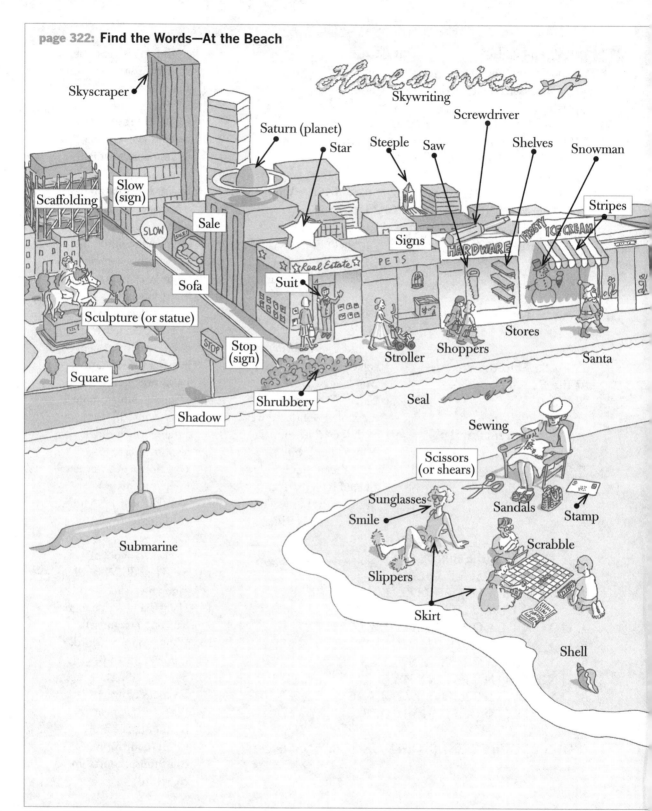

Skyscraper

Skywriting

Screwdriver

Saturn (planet)

Star

Steeple

Saw

Shelves

Snowman

Slow (sign)

Scaffolding

Stripes

Sale

Signs

Sofa

Suit

Sculpture (or statue)

Stop (sign)

PETS

Stores

Square

Stroller

Shoppers

Santa

Shrubbery

Shadow

Seal

Sewing

Scissors (or shears)

Sunglasses

Sandals

Stamp

Smile

Scrabble

Submarine

Slippers

Skirt

Shell

Sky

Smoke

Scarecrow

Seagull

Suspension bridge

Sheep

Saddle (w/stirrups)

Spoon

Shingles

Suspenders

Shirt

Signs

Salt shaker

Stove

Seven

Six

Slingshot

Shoes

Salesperson

Sink

Sailboat

Slot machine

Sheriff

Squirrel

Shorts

Slacks

Sausages

Seesaw

Sneakers

Skates

Slinky

Soldier

Saxophone

Spider

Safe

Shower

Skateboard

Sunglasses
Scarf

Soap

Skunk

St. Bernard (dog)

Stairs (or staircase or steps)

Shampoo

Sled

Spots

Snake

Snowshoes

Seats

Shorts

Shorts

Sword

Shorts

Sandwiches

Snail

Shorts

Seat

Shorts

Sandcastle

Shadow

Shovel

Sheep

page 326: Put the List in Order

1. Hinduism (1500 B.C.)
   Judaism (1400 B.C.)
   Buddhism (460 B.C.)
   Christianity (A.D. 30)
   Islam (A.D. 610).
   (*Note: Dates are approximate.*)
2. Park Place $350 (Royal Blue)
   Marvin Gardens $280 (Yellow)
   Water Works $150 (Utility)
   Connecticut Avenue $120 (Light Blue)
3. Coca-Cola (1886)
   Instant Coffee (1909)
   Kool-Aid (1927)
   Tang (1957)
4. California Gold Rush (1848–1858)
   The Pony Express (1860–1862)
   U.S. Purchases Alaska (1867)
   Ellis Island Opens (1892)
5. Ancient Egypt (3100 B.C. to A.D. 50)
   Ancient Greece (1000 B.C. to A.D. 50)
   The Roman Empire (700 B.C. to A.D. 500)
   Aztec (A.D. 1200 to 1500)
6. Elvis Presley on *The Ed Sullivan Show* (82.6% of households)
   "Lucy Goes to the Hospital" (71.7%)
   O. J. Simpson Verdict (57%) and The Beatles on *The Ed Sullivan Show* (45.1%)
7. Bill Clinton (46)
   Barack Obama (47)
   Franklin Roosevelt (51)
   George W. Bush (54)
8. Fairbanks, AK (64° latitude)
   Stockholm (59° latitude)
   Paris (48° latitude)
   Washington, DC (38° latitude)
   Cairo (30° latitude)
9. Apple Pie, small slice (296)
   Hershey's Milk Chocolate Bar (210)
   Ben & Jerry's Vanilla Ice Cream, half a cup (200)
   Dunkin' Donuts Glazed Donut (180)
   Buttered Popcorn, one cup (85)
10. Wright Brothers; First Flight (1903)
   The *Titanic* Sinks (1912)
   Penicillin Discovered (1929)
   Elvis Presley Born (1935)
   The *Hindenburg* Explodes (1937)

page 327: Classic Riddle—Reward and Punishment

George was a night watchman and should not have been sleeping when he was at work.

page 327: Trivia— The Presidents

• Dwight Eisenhower
• Gerald Ford and Nelson Rockefeller
• Herbert Hoover
• Woodrow Wilson
• Richard Nixon
• John F. Kennedy (1917)
• Jimmy Carter
• William Henry Harrison (1841)

page 328: Trivia—A River Runs Through It

• The Seine
• The Nile
• The Thames
• The Hudson and East Rivers
• The Tigris
• The Danube
• The St. Lawrence
• The Tiber

page 328: Opening Lines

1. *Moby Dick* by Herman Melville (1851)
2. *Pride and Prejudice* by Jane Austen (1813)
3. *1984* by George Orwell (1949)
4. *A Tale of Two Cities* by Charles Dickens (1859)
5. *The Invisible Man* by Ralph Ellison (1952)
6. *The Catcher in the Rye* by J. D. Salinger (1951)
7. *Don Quixote* by Miguel de Cervantes (1605)
8. *The Old Man and the Sea* by Ernest Hemingway (1952)
9. *Fahrenheit 451* by Ray Bradbury (1953)
10. *Robinson Crusoe* by Daniel Defoe (1719)
11. *Animal Farm* by George Orwell (1946)
12. *Gone with the Wind* by Margaret Mitchell (1936)
13. *To Kill a Mockingbird* by Harper Lee (1960)